# D. H. Lawrence

## The Rainbow

## Women in Love

EDITED BY RICHARD BEYNON

Series editor: Richard Beynon

ICON BOOKS

Published in 1997 by Icon Books Ltd.,
Grange Road, Duxford, Cambridge CB2 4QF
e-mail: info@iconbooks.co.uk
www.iconbooks.co.uk

Reprinted 2001

Distributed in the UK, Europe, South Africa and Asia by Faber & Faber Ltd.,
3 Queen Square, London WC1N 3AU or their agents

Distributed in the UK, Europe, South Africa and Asia by Macmillan
Distribution Ltd., Houndmills, Basingstoke RG21 6XS

Published in Australia in 1997 by Allen & Unwin Pty. Ltd.,
PO Box 8500, 83 Alexander Street, Crows Nest, NSW 2065

Distributed in Canada by Penguin Books Canada, 10 Alcorn Avenue,
Suite 300, Toronto, Ontario M4V 3B2

Series editor: Richard Beynon
Managing editor: Duncan Heath
Series devised by: Christopher Cox
Cover design: Christos Kondeatis
Typesetting: Wayzgoose

ISBN 1 874166 69 2

Printed and bound in Great Britain by
Cox & Wyman Ltd., Reading

# Contents

# Introduction

T HE CELEBRATION of Lawrence as a major creative talent is still a comparatively recent phenomenon. During his life, and despite the range and volume of his output, he earned very little money from his work and maintained a precarious existence on the borders of absolute poverty. More significant, though, is the fact that Lawrence's creative genius remained almost entirely unrecognised by critics and the general public, not only while he lived, but for twenty years after his death. It seems astonishing that a writer whose works are now considered as among the finest in the language should have seen two of his books banned, his paintings seized, his plans for travel hindered by the refusal of a passport, and the mass of his work neglected or ridiculed for nearly forty years. The very existence of this volume and its contents, however – which form but a brief snapshot of a vast and ongoing critical activity – offer testament to the fact that Lawrence's reputation *has* undergone a massive revaluation, such that his major works are now given a central place in any account of twentieth-century literature in English. It is the process of that revaluation which forms the core of this book.

Critical guides such as this will be read by students who have grown up with an awareness of certain 'great' English novelists, and amongst the familiar names will be Lawrence's. In the closing years of the 1990s, we naturally accept Lawrence as a major talent who occupies a place amongst the great writers of the century; we are able, now, to appreciate particularly the massive contribution Lawrence has made to the development of what he called 'the highest form of human expression so far attained' – the novel.[1] That this should be the case is, first, a tribute to the enduring qualities of Lawrence's work; second, a result of his determination to realise and articulate an original vision of art and its place in our society; third, the outcome of some meticulous scholarship and tireless campaigning by a number of academics and critics who have persisted in their belief that there were qualities in the work deserving of recognition.

This book attempts to offer its readers an account of some central moments in that slow and uneven process of change to which Lawrence's reputation has been subject during the past eighty years. The extracts and essays reprinted here have been selected (given the usual, but frustrating, constraints of space in a single volume) for their value in marking the progress of the critical debate surrounding Lawrence's work. Some are pieces which speak firmly of the years in which they were written, and act as marking posts on the critical trail, to be taken as representations of the value-systems and attitudes which prevailed in the year of their publication. Others have a more enduring quality and still serve to lead the reader and the critic to new understandings of their subject. Taken together, these writings should be seen as a set of tools to be applied to the novels themselves – for the novels remain always at the heart of the volume.

And, although this book is concerned with only two of his novels – and though they may be said to represent his finest work in fiction – it is not the intention of this book to limit the reader's attention to *The Rainbow* and *Women in Love* alone. To recognise Lawrence's greatness solely as the writer of these two novels is to tell but a small part of a much greater story. It is hoped that the reader will explore the links that are offered to other works and other forms in Lawrence's enormous repertoire – for it was a central part of his vision of art that it had an organic quality, that it afforded a means to define, test, reject and redefine his beliefs across the many forms he attempted. In that respect, there is a satisfying harmony between the many shifts, peaks and troughs in his status and reputation as an artist and the processes at work in his art. In the sentence quoted above from Lawrence's essay 'The Novel', he asserts its ascendancy over all other art forms. He goes on to explain why:

Because it is so incapable of the absolute.

In a novel, everything is relative to everything else, if that novel is art at all. There may be didactic bits, but they aren't the novel.

. . . There you have the greatness of the novel itself. It won't let you tell didactic lies, and put them over.[2]

There was never stillness and certainty in Lawrence's work. Instead, a constant state of warfare existed between the novelist and the novel itself. Which meant, for Lawrence, that his work was never truly finished, never fully defined – and properly so. The novels under scrutiny here should not be seen, then, as existing in any capacity of separateness from the rest of Lawrence's work, for they all form part of his lifelong attempt to test his own beliefs.

By the time his life was ended at forty-four, by the tuberculosis which had plagued him since boyhood, Lawrence had turned his hand to novels, short stories, poetry, full-length works of philosophy, critical essays on a vast range of subjects, translation, plays, painting, travel-books, literary criticism, reviews, thousands of letters – and even a history textbook. According to Anthony Burgess, another prolific and proudly 'professional' writer, 'Lawrence was essentially a man *who wrote*, and the only form which he did not practise was the film scenario'.[3]

It is, in part, because of the sheer range of Lawrence's output that his works are so widely known, so satisfying, and so widely contested upon the critical stage. And by 'range' we should understand not simply the variety of artistic forms he attempted in his life, but the variety of arguments, styles and truths he held up for question. Because he refused to let his own work alone, because he was always ready to come back at his art in another guise, he kept his readers in a more or less constant state of uncertainty – 'everything is relative to itself', he kept reminding them.

We shall be exploring the many critical expressions of puzzlement and, more recently, satisfaction, which Lawrence's artistic method elicited from his critics in this volume, and we shall also begin to see how there is an appropriateness in the diversity of responses to the two novels. The richness and variety of the critical press should stand as something of a tribute to the writer and his work, because he never wanted his art to stand still, to become 'ossiferous', as he felt that much of English fiction had. He rose to new challenges throughout his life, and was never deterred by adverse comments or a hostile critical press.

To refuse categorisation, to insist on the right to contradict and re-invent oneself has always been a risky business for an artist. Today, we hear so much of rock stars', poets', painters' and novelists' attempts to elude categorisation, to refuse to be placed in a movement, trend or 'school'. The artist pulls one way; our demand for order pulls the other. Such individuality is seen as a strength, as the source of original creative energy and as evidence of an innovative drive quite proper to artistry. But we live, now, in a world which embraces postmodern dissonance, in a world of sound-bites, media-snapshots and hype, where more than fifteen minutes of fame is something akin to immortality: it is easier now to be different, for now we lay great store by difference. But such was not the world in which Lawrence lived and wrote. Late Edwardian English society was rooted in tradition and treated difference with scorn. By daring to be different, and by having the temerity to suggest that his readers should be different too, Lawrence risked all. And as we have noted above, his reputation suffered for forty years as a result of the risks he took.

## An Overview

The published writings on Lawrence may be considered as belonging to three broad areas. First, there are those writings, produced during Lawrence's lifetime, which allow for some recognition of early genius, but which point to a gradual falling-off of talent, loss of form and increasing moral waywardness. Second, there is that body of writings which first appeared around the time of Lawrence's death and continued to dominate the critical field throughout the Thirties. These treatments centre chiefly on the personality and psychology of the writer, and may be further divided into two groups: those which offer psychological and psychoanalytical readings of the works, and those which are basically reminiscences and extended personal memoirs about Lawrence. Third, comes that vast body of writings spanning the period from the so-called 'Lawrence Revival' of the early 1950s, to the present. Of this last group, the sub-divisions are practically endless: there are New Critical approaches, moral-formalist approaches, biographical studies, biblio-graphical studies, feminist studies, comparative studies, historical studies, Marxist analyses, post-structuralist readings, and a host of others. What brings these works together, however, is that they are all expressions of serious scholarly activity founded, principally, on the acceptance of Lawrence's status as a great creative talent.

Lawrence first gained recognition for his early poems when, in 1909, he had work published in the *English Review,* edited by the influential critic and novelist Ford Madox Hueffer, later known as Ford Madox Ford (who also discovered Ezra Pound and Wyndham Lewis in the same year). There followed a degree of critical success, and an introduction to literary circles, with the publication of his first two novels, *The White Peacock* (1911) and *The Trespasser* (1912). Lawrence was taken up as a 'talented newcomer', and was highly thought of by a number of promi-nent literary and intellectual figures, including Pound, who told the American poet Harriet Monroe in 1913: 'As a prose writer I grant him first place among the younger men.'[4]

With his third novel, *Sons and Lovers* (1913), Lawrence's popularity and reputation grew. Most reviewers recognised the development that had taken place between the early work and this, his first 'mature' novel. But already there were those who began to express unease at the grow-ing psychological intensity and lyrical richness of Lawrence's writing. A review in *The Standard* complained that his 'weakness is that he is too often the lyrical poet making his creatures speak his thoughts and this is a bad fault for a novelist.'[5]

In *The Westminster Gazette* of the same year we find another early instance of the sort of criticism that would cast a shadow over all of Lawrence's later novels. The anonymous reviewer recognised that '*Sons and Lovers* is a book to haunt and waylay the mind long after it has been laid aside', but seemed uncomfortable with the very aspect of the writing which was to become Lawrence's major artistic preoccupation in his next two novels:

**Nowadays we have done with the hero, and in his place we have the subject. Sensitiveness is the only quality the really modern novelist seeks in the central figure of his tale, and the consequence is that we are in danger of replacing our novels of character by those of character-**

isation. This change, which has come to us from France, is likely enough to work its own revenge on the English novelist, and a warning sign of this danger may be found in . . . *Sons and Lovers*.[6]

For Lawrence, it *was* precisely the desire to approach character in a new way, to turn away from the 'novel of character' which so dominated English fiction, that seemed the way forward to a new form, to a new novel. In the early years of his artistic career he had seemed to work within the boundaries of established and accepted fictional technique. He paid attention to the demands of realism, adhered loosely to the prevailing model of the late-Victorian English novel, and was rewarded with success. When he came to write the two novels with which we are concerned, however, he felt that there was a need for something new, for something beyond that to which the novel was currently attending. In his decision to pursue his instincts, to abandon the safety of the known and acceptable, he moved into a world where his critics could not and would not follow.

After *Sons and Lovers,* and despite the sort of review quoted above, he devoted enormous energy to the search for an expression of a new consciousness which itself would drive and shape the novel. Through the many drafts of the manuscript that Lawrence first called *The Sisters,* later renamed *The Wedding Ring* and eventually divided to form *The Rainbow* and *Women in Love,* he worked at the task of redefining and re-presenting character. In what is now probably one of the most famous and most-quoted of his letters, Lawrence outlined to his friend and early mentor, Edward Garnett, his still hazy, but deeply-felt desire for a new sort of novel. In the first part of the letter, which responds to Garnett's obviously negative comments on a manuscript draft, we see an awareness in Lawrence that his work had changed, and that such a change in the work required a change, too, in the reader:

I don't agree with you about the *Wedding Ring.* You will find that in a while you will like the book as a whole. I don't think the psychology is wrong: it is only that I have a different attitude to my characters, and that necessitates a different attitude in you, which you are not prepared to give.[7]

Further into the letter, Lawrence tries to explain the nature of his 'different attitude' to character:

You mustn't look in my novel for the old stable *ego* of the character. There is another *ego,* according to whose action the individual is unrecognisable, and passes through, as it were, allotropic states which it needs a deeper sense than any we've been used to exercise, to discover are states of the same single radically unchanged element . . . You must not say my novel is shaky – it is not perfect, because I am not expert in what I want to do. But it is the real thing, say what you like. And I shall get my reception, if not now, then before long. Again I say, don't look for the development of the novel to follow the lines of certain characters: the characters fall into the form of some other rhythmic form, as when one draws a fiddle-bow across a fine tray delicately sanded, the sand takes lines unknown.[8]

The review in *The Westminster Gazette*, almost exactly a year before this letter, had recognised then, in *Sons and Lovers*, the earliest signs of the technique which was to be developed fully in *The Rainbow* and *Women in Love*, and which was to distinguish Lawrence from his British contemporaries. That the reviewer had neither understood nor appreciated the value of Lawrence's distinct approach to character is no surprise. The vast majority of Lawrence's reviewers – and even his friends, like Garnett – felt much the same.

In the letter to Garnett, we find a sense of certainty and optimism that readers would, though, 'before long', come to read differently, to accept the truth of the new technique. It was an optimism that Lawrence maintained for only a short time, for as the almost entirely negative reception and swift banning of *The Rainbow* proved, there were few people who could see past the difference in the technique and value the 'real thing'. From the suppression of *The Rainbow* under the Obscene Publications Act in 1915 until he died in 1930, Lawrence wrote not because he thought that public recognition was imminent, but chiefly for the reason that he had to express what he saw as the truth, in a way which itself was truthful. He wrote in spite of his readers, and in spite of the many critics who maligned and misunderstood his aims, ideas and techniques – simply because he believed he was right.

Once *The Rainbow* had been savaged in the public press and banned from sale in his own country, Lawrence ceased to hope for acceptance, for his 'reception', in Britain. Here we find the moment of crisis in his life: from this time, Lawrence's years of isolation really begin. Barely a month after the police action against *The Rainbow*, his changed attitude was evident in a letter written to his literary agent, J. B. Pinker, on 16 December 1915. Responding to criticisms of the structural weaknesses of his novel made by Arnold Bennett, Lawrence delivered the following broadside:

Tell Arnold Bennett that all rules of good construction hold good only for novels which are copies of other novels. A book which is not a copy of other books has its own construction, and what he calls faults, being an old imitator, I call characteristics. I shall repeat till I am grey – when they have as good a work to show, they may make their pronouncements *ex cathedra*. Till then, let them learn respect.[9]

It took 'them' nearly forty years to learn respect. But, as is now a matter of history, Lawrence's assault on the form and style of the English novel did eventually succeed in changing the way we read and receive our sense of the world through fiction, and has had a vital influence on the genre and its place in twentieth-century culture – as much of the remainder of this book will show.

Lawrence was deeply wounded by the response to *The Rainbow*, and in some ways never forgave or forgot the insult perpetrated on his art in 1915. Throughout the remainder of the First World War, he and Frieda simply waited to escape from England. During these years, Lawrence became increasingly obsessed with his long-cherished dream of establishing a utopian community of writers, artists and like-minded folk, to be called 'Rananim' – behaviour symptomatic of his distaste for all he saw around him in Britain. He could no longer conceive of achieving recognition or fulfilment in his own country – so he spent most of the rest of his life engaged in his 'savage pilgrimage', searching for a place where he felt at home, where he felt he could work and live in peace. The search took him, across a period of twenty years, to Italy, Capri, Sicily, Sri Lanka, Australia, the islands of the South Pacific, New Mexico, Mexico, Italy, Switzerland and finally to Vence in the south of France, where he died.

During his life, and despite the difficulties most critics had in understanding his work, Lawrence was generally seen as a gifted writer – even a genius – but one who had somehow failed to live up to the promise of his early work. The fact that he had shown talent early in his career seemed to count increasingly against, rather than for, his reputation.

For a reader of Lawrence's work today, there is little sense of the danger to public morality that was felt to be so acute in his novels during the years of the First World War and the early Twenties. Certain of the essays and reviews which form the earlier sections of this book present views which can hardly be matched with our contemporary sense of Lawrence's worth, but which nevertheless held sway over the critical reception, publication and reprinting of his works for decades. Indeed, to gain any real understanding of the battles which have been fought over Lawrence's reputation we need to consider briefly the staggering rehabilitation that has taken place, which has elevated Lawrence from public menace to cultural institution.

Very few undergraduate students of English literature will now pass through their degree programmes without focusing on some aspect of Lawrence's prose, poetry, philosophy and critical or dramatic writings. Virtually all Women's Studies courses which explore the growth of twentieth-century feminist criticism will have focused on Simone de Beauvoir or Kate Millett's ground-breaking re-evaluations of Lawrence's work.[10] Students of American Literature will, at some time, have turned to Lawrence's *Studies in Classic American Literature* for a refreshing and insightful account of Hawthorne, Melville, Poe or Whitman. For many years, schools and colleges have been teaching A Level syllabuses and Access modules that include *The Rainbow, Women in Love* or short stories by Lawrence, as well as the hugely popular *Sons and Lovers* as part of the GCSE syllabus. In short, it is hard to approach the study of modern literature in English today without encountering Lawrence's work directly, or through its influence on others.

But the extraordinary contemporary interest in Lawrence is not confined to the academic world, for he is one of the few 'serious' artists whose sales have remained at a level more common to a popular novelist. There is scarcely a member of the reading population who has not at some time encountered a novel, story or poem by Lawrence – and huge numbers of cinema-goers and television viewers will have seen one of the many dramatisations of his works on screen. There have been times when even our social values and sense of cultural norms seem to have been bound up with Lawrence's image, ideas or arguments. Since November 1960 and the end of the (in)famous obscenity trial which surrounded the Penguin publication of Lawrence's *Lady Chatterley's Lover,* his name has given our language a new adjective – 'Lawrentian' – which has become firmly established in the general consciousness, with all its (often ill-placed) connotations of full-blooded sexuality, individuality, and earthiness.

In 1967, when Philip Larkin wrote the poem 'Annus Mirabilis', he attempted to sum up something of the magic (and expose something of the myth) of the Sixties by focusing on the sexual liberation the decade was claimed to have ushered in. He selected for the poem two defining moments, two events that seemed to act as markers for the shift in public mood and awareness:

**Sexual intercourse began**
**In nineteen sixty-three**
**(Which was rather late for me) –**
**Between the end of the Chatterley ban**
**And the Beatles' first LP.**[11]

The album did rather well: the novel did even better. Following the enormous publicity of the unsuccessful obscenity actions in America in 1959, and Britain in October–November 1960, the twenty-eight year ban on the novel was finally lifted and *Lady Chatterley's Lover* released in its unexpurgated form in the Autumn of 1960. In the eight months that followed, the novel sold over three million copies in Britain alone.[12]

Lawrence and his work had become a part of the Sixties. The massive sales of *Lady Chatterley's Lover* continued throughout the decade, and led to a huge increase of interest in his other works, so that during the decade as a whole, world-wide sales of Lawrence's books totalled around ten million copies.[13] For many of his readers it seemed that Lawrence had anticipated the mood of the Sixties. From a distance of forty years, he had given voice to much that the well-educated, consumer-rich, but painfully divided society of the Sixties seemed to hanker after. The ideas that were found in the novels, stories, poems and philosophical essays seemed to serve a present need, despite the fact that they were conceived of before universal suffrage, free mass education, civil rights awareness, the Pill, television, the atom bomb and the mini-skirt.

In addition to the explosion in film and television versions of the stories and novels since the Sixties, the visual image of the writer himself has become something of an icon of the modern age. Images of Lawrence have appeared so often on the covers of biographies, critical works and collections of essays (such as this), that he has become one of English literature's most easily recognisable figures. Lawrence's portrait or photograph will be found somewhere on the covers of most editions of his works, and has come to signify an attitude and a style as much as a man.

In the face of the over-used images and neatly coined by-words, and the welter of casual, populist treatments of his writings, academics and students are left with the task of assimilating the ever-developing arguments, approaches and theories surrounding Lawrence's name and literary reputation. Unpicking the innumerable layers of myth to reach something of the original work is a task that has become hugely demanding.

Keeping track of the ever-increasing body of critical writings about Lawrence's work has become a strenuous full-time occupation for academics and research students the world over – though there has never been a shortage of volunteers for the job. For over thirty-five years, reference has been made to a 'Lawrence Industry'[14] suggestive of a hugely prolific grouping of academics, writers, publishers and dramatists who have produced millions of words which serve to advance, adjust and review the currently held images of Lawrence and his work. Though the term is somewhat derisory, it is hard to come upon another workable description which captures the global scale and intense activity of Lawrence scholarship without resorting to some industrial or commercial metaphor. As far back as 1961, when the great critical revival of Lawrence's reputation was still in its youth, Eliseo Vivas offered a wry commentary on the progress made by his fellow scholars:

His life has been thoroughly examined by a large number of biographers, friendly and unfriendly; he has been psychoanalysed, criticised, evaluated, loved in public posthumously; he has been worshipped from a distance as the loveable angel that at times he was, and he has been despised as the demon that he also was. His every move has been charted, his reading scrutinised, his formidable battles with his wife recorded, and his novels have been corrected by checking them against the facts he used as matter for them. We know he cooked, trimmed hats for Frieda, built chicken coops, baked bread in old-fashioned ovens and fell into sadistic tantrums; and we also know that he could be tender after his explosions . . .

Recently his most indefatigable biographer, Harry T. Moore, has added to two very useful books on Lawrence a third; and more recently still, another biographer, Edward H. Nehls, has given us a very valuable composite biography in three volumes. If there is information on his life that has been overlooked, letters that have not yet been printed, surviving relatives and friends not yet interviewed, vital statistics not yet published, it is not likely that they shall alter the picture we have of Lawrence's work and of his character. But if there is such data, it is not the writer of this book who would be interested in finding it.[15]

As Lawrence's reputation has risen, so has the output of material about him or his writing. Also, during the time since Vivas's comments were written, the huge rise of interest in literary theory has provided fresh ground for re-evaluation and re-interpretation of the predominantly New Critical approaches to Lawrence's work. In what is the most thorough of the several bibliographies that have been compiled since the 'Lawrence Revival', James C. Cowan lists more than 4,600 full-length books and articles written across the period 1910–70.[16] For the total of the critical writings produced since 1970, estimates currently run at around 2,300 additional works.[17]

In the face of such an enormous mass of material, students are somehow required to develop a view of Lawrence's writings which is fresh, yet takes account of the critical work which has been undertaken in the past. It is hoped that this volume will be of use in that process.

The freedoms enjoyed by the English novel in the closing years of the twentieth century owe much to Lawrence's artistic honesty and perseverance, to the duty which he felt was owed to the novel, and to the fact that he did not surrender his belief in his art. In 1920, after the seizure and destruction of the first edition of *The Rainbow,* and facing the refusal of British publishers to handle its sequel and sister-work, Lawrence wrote a Foreword to the American edition of *Women in Love.* His vision of the novel's function, and of the novelist's responsibility to that function, remained unshaken, and echoed something of the certainty, if not the optimism, of his 1914 letter to Edward Garnett:

Man struggles with his unborn needs and fulfilment. New unfoldings struggle up in torment in him, as buds struggle forth from the midst of a plant. Any man of real individuality tries to know and to understand what is happening, even in himself, as he goes along. This struggle for verbal consciousness should not be left out in art. It is a very great part of life. It is not super-imposition of a theory. It is the passionate struggle into conscious being.[18]

# CHAPTER ONE

# Contemporary Reviews

IN THE reviews which follow, we find some of the extravagant expressions of moral outrage that greeted *The Rainbow* and *Women in Love* upon their publication – as well as some of the usual, more muted, statements of disappointment at Lawrence's apparently wasting talent in the two novels. To a modern audience, more or less accustomed to Lawrence's techniques, such reviews speak very clearly of the literary conservatism with which he had to deal throughout his life. However, these pieces are not reprinted simply to offer light relief; they are included in this volume for a number of serious reasons.

First, they serve a straightforward and important purpose in reminding readers of the distance between Lawrence and the society in which he lived. Both in terms of moral sensibilities and in their conception of the artist and his place in society, we can see that Lawrence and his reviewers were poles apart. All that the reviewers in popular publications seemed to hold dear, Lawrence found tainted or moribund. All of the conventions upon which Lawrence's society based its expectations for literature, he found false, constricting and dangerous to our future. The sexual frankness of the novels that we now see as derived from Lawrence's attempt to expose and explore the roots of human relationships, the reviewers of the period could only see as filth or sensationalism. In almost every aspect of the writer's purpose, there was a challenge to the outlook and values of his society.

Such contemporary reviews also highlight the ways in which Lawrence was exploring new areas in his fiction, and offer a view of the developments which had taken place in Lawrence's art between the completion of *Sons and Lovers* and the publication of his two great(est) novels. Even a brief study of Lawrence's letters across the period 1914–16 demonstrates that his interest had permanently shifted away from the semi-realist method of *Sons and Lovers*, to a new and (as he admitted) experimental investigation of character psychology and human relations. To draw any comparisons between the earlier novels and *The Rainbow* or *Women in Love* was, for Lawrence, an irrelevance.

A third reason for the presence of the reviews is that they provide us with an invaluable vision of the critical domain into which the novels were released. Students of literature today are conditioned to expect two separate critical responses to novels: the 'popular' reviews in news-papers, magazines and on television, and a second, more specialist set of commentaries emerging from academic journals and collections of scholarly critical essays. Such was not the case in 1915 or 1921. There was no established, serious, academic press in Britain during the period of the First World War and the Twenties – and in general terms, no really serious academic study of literature, even in universities. Thus, to have one's novel reviewed in Britain meant a review in a newspaper, or, if the work was 'literary', some commentary in a magazine like the *Athenaeum*, which catered for a more educated and highbrow audience. Even the *Athenaeum*, which had been one of the country's foremost literary/arts magazines since its foundation in 1828, tended to speak with the voice of the establishment and reflect the more conservative views of the age. There were occasional, subscription-only publications which looked to the more adventurous artistic endeavours of the time, like *Signature*, on which Lawrence, John Middleton Murry and Katherine Mansfield collaborated during 1915, or the *English Review*, edited by Ford Madox Ford during 1908 and 1909, but such ventures were usually aimed at a tiny audience, poorly supported and short of funds. *Signature*, for instance, collapsed after only three editions, whilst *English Review* made losses of £2,800 in its first year, and was subsequently bought by the magnate Sir Alfred Mond, who sacked Ford and installed the less-than-gifted Austin Harrison as editor. The magazine continued publication until 1923, but never recaptured the glory-days of its early editions which had carried contributions by Tolstoy, Hardy, Conrad, H. G. Wells, Ezra Pound, Wyndham Lewis and Lawrence. That Lawrence continued to submit material to *English Review* right up until its closure, despite its obviously declining editorial standards, is suggestive of the dearth of quality literary publications at the time.

To provide us with something of a starting point for the essays and extracts in later sections of this book, then, the following reviews serve as indicators of the critical approaches made to novels during the period 1915–21, and to the ways in which Lawrence's work generally fell foul of those approaches.

## Reviews of *The Rainbow*

The first review, written by James Douglas, appeared in *The Star*, 22 October 1915,[1] a little over three weeks after the publication of *The Rainbow*, by Methuen, and about a month before the publishers were prosecuted for obscenity and forced to destroy all copies of the novel.

Some sections of the review have been cut – generally the more purple passages, which serve only to iterate the central points reproduced here:

There is no doubt that a book of this kind has no right to exist. It is a deliberate denial of the soul that leavens matter. These people are not human beings. They are creatures who are immeasurably lower than the lowest animal in the Zoo. There is no kindness in them, no tenderness, no softness, no sweetness . . . There is no novel in English so utterly lacking in verbal reticence. The subtlety of phrase is enormous, but it is used to express the unspeakable and to hint at the unutterable. The morbidly perverted ingenuity of style is made the vehicle for saying things that ought to be left unthought, let alone unsaid. It is doubtful whether decadence could further go, for the achievement of mastery in the use of words is deliberately set to serve ignoble ends.

Genius is a trust, a sacred trust. Its magical powers are bestowed upon a man to enable him to purify and not to pollute the sanctuary of the soul. Its imaginative grace is not born to serve as a clue to the deepest haunts of hell . . . I suppose it may seem priggish to insist upon the responsibility of the artist, upon the duty of reverence, upon the elementary obligation of restraint and selective conscience. But nevertheless I do insist upon these high, old-fashioned sanctities. Art is not anarchy . . . The artist is not his own law-giver. He must bow before the will of the generations of man.

. . . The wind of war is sweeping over our life, and it is demolishing many of the noisome pestilences of peace. A thing like *The Rainbow* has no right to exist in the wind of war. It is a greater menace to public health than any of the epidemic diseases which we pay our medical officers to fight inch by inch wheresoever they appear. They destroy the body, but it destroys the soul . . . The power to see life as a struggle against putrescence is not a sentimental fad or fancy. Every man and every woman must take sides in that battle, and at their worst they know that they ought to take the side of the angels in their souls against the fiends in their souls. Life can be made very horrible and very hideous, but if literature aids and abets the business of making it horrible and hideous, then literature must perish.

I know it will be said that literature must live at all costs and at any expense of spirit in any waste of shame. Frankly, I do not see the necessity. Life is infinitely more precious than literature. It has got to go on climbing up and up, and if literature strives to drag it down to the nethermost deeps, then literature must be hacked off the limbs of life. It is idle to prate of liberty as a pretext for licence. Where you have unbridled licence you cannot have liberty . . . If Mr. Lawrence were not greater than his offence, his offence would not be so rank. But he possesses the heavenly gift of glamour. He can weave veils of shimmering meretriciousness round unnameable and unthinkable ugliness. He can lift the rainbow out of the sunlight and set its arch over the pit from whose murky brink every healthy foot ought to shrink in fear and abhorrence.

The rainbow is the symbol of strange beauty, of transfigured reality, of dreams that transcend the lower nature. It is the romance of God that springs out of earth into heaven. If Mr. Lawrence desires to save his genius from destruction, let me tell him how to do it. He must discover or rediscover the oldest truth in the world – that man is a moral being with a conscience and an aim, with responsibility to himself and to others . . . The young men who are dying for liberty are moral beings. They are the living repudiation of such impious denials of life as *The Rainbow*. The life they lay down is a lofty thing. It is not the thing that creeps and crawls in this novel.

Douglas's review is useful in that it raises most of the charges made against Lawrence in the various reviews of *The Rainbow*. The language is more heavily charged and hyperbolic here, but essentially the points at issue remain the same.

Running right through the piece, and found in virtually all of the other reviews – even the only two that commented favourably on the novel – is a sense of disappointment that Lawrence should abuse the talent (even 'genius') which had been glimpsed in his earlier work. Such was the view which characterised the critical responses to *The Rainbow*, *Women in Love* and almost all of Lawrence's major works during his lifetime. With the publication of each successive novel, the pattern of criticism would follow a familiar course: the reviewer would offer some more or less disparaging remarks about the particular work at hand, before referring sadly back to *Sons and Lovers* and its unfulfilled promise of better things. Where most other reviewers regretfully pointed to a loss of form, however, Douglas's crusading review finds the betrayal of a holy trust which leads to 'rank' offence.

The second common point of contention in Douglas's review is the distaste he finds for Lawrence's frank treatment of 'sexual matters' – especially women's sexuality. Though Douglas does not refer directly to the offending scenes of the novel which featured so centrally in the subsequent court case, the review is peppered with references to 'unbridled licence', to Lawrence's desire to 'express the unspeakable and to hint at the unutterable', and so on. Virtually all of the other reviews which dealt with *The Rainbow* and *Women in Love* also express some sense of discomfort at the explicitness of the sexual scenes.

Douglas's call for Lawrence to observe the 'responsibility of the artist' is interesting in the way it makes a case not for purity of art itself, but for adherence to a code of public decency as ordained by the traditions of a conservative Christian society – which was presently engaged in a major conflict against another society of similar nature. The review is rich in the language of the Old Testament (with a sprinkling of quotations from *Hamlet* and *Macbeth* to add a tragic flavour), using such phrases as: 'denial of the soul that leavens matter', 'pollute the sanctuary of the soul', 'the artist is not his own law-giver', 'they ought to take the side of the angels in their souls', to develop a canonical authority for its arguments – against a novel which 'creeps and crawls' in its attempt to pollute the Edenic world of English fiction.

Carefully woven through the biblical sermonising is the demand for patriotism in time of war, such that the two injunctions – to Christian purity and arms – become one. According to Douglas, Lawrence is guilty not only of stepping into 'the pit from whose murky brink every healthy foot ought to shrink in fear and abhorrence', but of having done so, it seems, over the bodies of 'the young men who are dying for liberty' in the trenches of the First World War. Although it was never admitted at the time, there is considerable strength in the argument that Lawrence's profound anti-war sentiments, Frieda's German nationality, and the passages in *The Rainbow* where Ursula challenges Skrebensky on his notions of duty and obedience in arms were all significant factors in pro-voking outraged responses from reviewers such as Douglas, and in leading the authorities to take steps for the banning of the novel.[2]

On 13 November 1915, the novel was the subject of an action by the Commissioner of Police under the Obscene Publications Act of 1857, against its publishers, Methuen, at Bow Street Court. Douglas's review, together with another equally virulent review by Clement Shorter, which had appeared in *Sphere*, formed the bulwark of the prosecution case.[3] During the trial, two sections of the novel were specifically held up as examples of the obscenity which would corrupt public morals: the scene in 'The Bitterness of Ecstasy' chapter, in which Ursula and Skrebensky make love, and the 'Shame' chapter, which describes (negatively, as the court failed to recognise) Ursula's affair with Winifred Inger. The presiding magistrate, whose son had been killed in the war just over a month before the hearing, expressed considerable surprise that the publishers had not heeded the warnings sounded in the two reviews and taken the book out of circulation voluntarily. In his judge-ment, he made clear his feelings on the novel, saying that he had 'never read anything more disgusting than this book . . . It was utter filth; nothing else would describe it.'[4]

James Douglas was undoubtedly the most outspoken and hysterical of commentators on the novel. Most reviewers adopted a more moderate, but nonetheless negative stance, as represented here by the following unattributed piece from the *Athenaeum* of November 1915. It is clear from what follows that even the more level-headed reviewers still found

Lawrence's frank treatment of sexuality and psychological turmoil distasteful and difficult to understand:

This book reveals a strong and vivid imagination; a faculty of seeing and describing the countryside that can spring only from a true love of nature combined with poetic insight; and no inconsiderable power of dealing impressively, if not always convincingly, with psychological problems.

*The Rainbow*, like Mr Lawrence's earlier novel, *Sons and Lovers*, is a family piece, but of a far more ambitious character. The first chapter introduces us to the Brangwens, yeomen farmers who had lived for generations on the borderlands of Derbyshire and Nottinghamshire, and sets the stage for the piece with the marriage of Tom Brangwen to Lydia Lensky, the widow of a Polish political incendiary and refugee, and the daughter of a Polish noble by a German wife. Lydia has a four-year-old little girl, Anna. The story is one of three generations, being concerned with the successive loves of Tom Brangwen and Lydia Lensky, of the nephew Will Brangwen and Anna Lensky, and of Ursula Brangwen, daughter of the latter couple, and Anton Skrebensky, a son of another Polish exile by an English wife.

In the story we find no attempt to deal with the possibilities latent in the mating of an aristocratic Polish stock with Midland yeomen. The intermixture appears to be nothing more than the introduction of an unknown factor in order to mask the improbabilities introduced, and the result is an increasing discord between the principal actors and the setting. The minor characters are human beings, and fit better into the scheme.

We must say a word or two concerning the freedom Mr. Lawrence has allowed himself in his treatment of sexual matters. It is often difficult to decide whether such realism is justified or not, but much that is to be found here is, in our opinion, undeniably unhealthy.[5]

Written for the *Athenaeum*,[6] with its educated and literary audience, this piece pays greater attention to the novel's structure and stylistic features than most reviews of the period – but still falls far short of any serious analysis or understanding of Lawrence's purpose or technique. The reviewer does recognise Lawrence's focus on the psychology of his characters, but is forced back onto generalities and the faint praise of the author's 'dealing impressively, if not always convincingly, with psychological problems'. There is comment on the 'strong and vivid imagination', the 'poetic insight', but no sustained or determined attempt to account for the novel's *difference*, and for the extraordinary features of style which separate this work from most of its contemporaries.

Much of the review is taken up with a concern for the possibilities of the novel as a realist work, and with its value as a family chronicle. There is clear regret that Lawrence failed to 'deal with the possibilities latent in the mating of an aristocratic Polish stock with Midland yeomen' in ways that would meet the late nineteenth-century critical expectations of British fiction. And, of course, there is the inevitable reference to *Sons and Lovers*, the novel which was to haunt all of Lawrence's other work until the 1950s. We have already seen in the *Westminster Gazette* review of *Sons and Lovers*, in 1913, the general feeling that Lawrence's future depended upon his ability to produce works in the mould of, say, Arnold Bennett.[7] But, as we know from the 1914 letter to Edward Garnett (see Introduction, pp. 9–10), Lawrence had moved beyond such work, seeing his new novel as meeting a much more urgent and vital need unfulfilled by the 'old' techniques of *Sons and Lovers*.

Far more even-tempered than most commentaries on the novel, and free from the jingoism-as-morality trumpeted by Douglas or Clement Shorter, the *Athenaeum* review at least recognises the 'ambitious' nature of Lawrence's intentions. But such ambition, as expressed through the 'ultra-realism' Lawrence used to explore the psychology and sexual needs of his characters, is treated with a degree of scepticism and distaste. The reference to 'undeniably unhealthy' sexual frankness is echoed through all of the published reviews of *The Rainbow*, and through many of the comments made by Lawrence's friends and literary acquaintances of the time. The banning of the novel (and the later banning of *Lady Chatterley's Lover*) seemed to give the stamp of authority to such views, and came to fix Lawrence in the public's mind as a writer of obscene or pornographic novels. As the remainder of this book demonstrates, the myth of 'Lawrence the pornographer' was hard to dispel.

Just over a week before the suppression of *The Rainbow*, the piece which follows (one of the two reviews that may be considered sympathetic to Lawrence's aims in the novel[8]) was printed in *The Glasgow Herald*. The reviewer is Catherine Carswell, a friend of the Lawrences and literary editor of *The Glasgow Herald* from 1908 until the publication of this review, for which she was sacked.

This is a book so very rich both in emotional beauty and in the distilled essence of profoundly passionate and individual thinking about human life, that one longs to lavish on it one's wholehearted praise. It betrays, moreover, the hand of a master writer. There are passages here – the accounts of Anna Brangwen's childhood, the narration of Tom Brangwen's wooing, the descriptions of Will Brangwen's home life, and of Ursula Brangwen's bitter baptism as an uncertificated teacher in Ilkeston School – which must take rank with the best work done by great novelists in any age. But for himself Mr. Lawrence is aiming at something quite different and distinct from mere good fiction, and it is this aim of his which principally claims the serious reader's respect and his consideration. The difficulty is to define even to one's self what Mr. Lawrence's aim exactly is, and whether it is in any way constructive. What he certainly does in this finely processional but mostly painful history of the loves of successive generations of the Brangwen family is to make clear his conviction that the modern heart is in a disastrous muddle where love between the sexes is concerned. If *The Rainbow* tells us anything it tells that love in our modern life, instead of being a blessed, joyous, and fruitful thing, is sterile, cruel, poisonous, and accursed . . . The modern world, according to Mr. Lawrence, is mad and sick and sad because it knows not how to love. Further, in this book at any rate, he does not go. There is no cure offered, nothing but a merciless, almost gloating description of the disease which will be strongly offensive to most readers. It is a pity too that the impassioned declaration is marred by the increasingly mannered idiom which Mr. Lawrence has acquired since the writing of *Sons and Lovers*. The worst manifestations of this at present are a distressing tendency to the repetition of certain words and a curiously vicious rhythm into which he constantly falls in the more emotional passages.[9]

Carswell's brave attempts at praise begin well enough, but she soon runs into the problem which haunts all of the reviewers of *The Rainbow* (and, to an extent, those who wrote on *Women in Love*): she is, quite simply, unable to come to terms with the techniques at work in the novel. Neither her friendship with Lawrence nor her general recognition of his abilities as 'a master writer' assist her in grasping his central intentions in the work – so, as a direct result, she is distracted away from an objective assessment of the novel's innovative features to comment chiefly upon those aspects which seem to betoken slips of judgement by an admired friend.

It is frustrating that Carswell sometimes seems so close to grasping the central points that Lawrence tries to make in the novel yet, finally, she fails to make the connection between the radically new style and form to arrive at a comprehensive account of what takes place within its pages. She muddles around the novel's treatment of 'the modern world', but fails to note the clash of industrial and human activities that form a background to all of its action; she remarks on the descriptions of Anna's childhood, Tom's romance, Ursula's early working life, yet seems to value these sections for their realist depictions of a family's passage through six decades, rather than for the ways they are used by Lawrence to explore changes in the very nature of human relationships. Standing right at the centre of Carswell's review is the admission that her 'difficulty is to define . . . what Mr. Lawrence's aim exactly is, and whether it is in any way constructive'. To point this out is not to offer any particular criticism of Carswell's reading or attitude towards Lawrence; it is worth noting simply because it is symptomatic of the response from critics who thought there *was* promise in Lawrence's work, but were not sure exactly how or where such promise was made manifest. As we shall see in the next chapter of this book, the well-intentioned, but fundamentally simplistic commentaries of friends and admirers of Lawrence's errant genius tended to dominate the critical debate over his work in the Twenties and early Thirties – and, against the best of their intentions, tended to restrict the development of any serious critical study of his work.

## Reviews of *Women in Love*

The publication of *Women in Love* was a problem for Lawrence. After the scandal which surrounded the release of *The Rainbow*, he could not easily find a publisher courageous enough to face possible prosecution or risk association with the sequel to an obscene novel. Thus, *Women in Love*, though completed in 1916, was not published commercially until 1921.

Any hopes of recognition for *The Rainbow* and *Women in Love* in his own country had long since faded for Lawrence. He had escaped from Britain and its repressive culture as soon as he and Frieda could obtain passports at the end of the First World War, and such was his disillusionment with his native land that throughout the remaining years of his life he was to make only four brief visits to Britain, spending a little less than five months in the country. Increasingly, Lawrence looked to America for recognition and some sort of reliable income from his work. (During the most bleak period of his life, while he completed *Women in Love* through 1915–16, he had also considered Florida as a possible location for his 'liberated' colony, Rananim.) It was fitting, then, that the first publication of *Women in Love* was undertaken in America – though even there, the work had to be privately printed in the first instance.

The private publication of *Women in Love* saw 1,250 copies printed in November 1920, of which some fifty were carefully distributed in Britain. The small number of copies released, and the fact that the publication had been undertaken privately in New York, meant that there were comparatively few reviews of the novel written in Britain during 1920 and the early part of 1921. When it was finally published in a commercial edition in Britain (though still in a very small print-run of 1,500 copies), the novel did attract some critical notice.[10]

Lawrence had no illusions about the likelihood of a negative response to the novel. He knew that his work was going to attract the same accusations of indecency, opacity, tub-thumping and theorising that had dogged *The Rainbow*. To forestall such criticism, he wrote a Foreword to the American edition of the novel which attempted to address a new audience, one that he hoped would respond to the novel with a more accepting and appreciative mind:

The book has been offered to various London publishers. Their almost inevitable reply has been "We should like very much to publish, but feel we cannot risk a prosecution." They remember the fate of *The Rainbow*, and are cautious. This book is a potential sequel to *The Rainbow*.

In England, I would never try to justify myself against any accusation. But to the Americans, perhaps I may speak for myself. I am accused, in England, of uncleanness and pornography. I deny the charge, and take no further notice.

In America the chief accusation seems to be one of "Eroticism". This is odd, rather puzzling to my mind. Which Eros? Eros of the jaunty "amours", or Eros of the sacred mysteries? And if the latter, why accuse, why not respect, even venerate?

Let us hesitate no longer to announce that the sensual passions and mysteries are equally sacred with the spiritual mysteries and passions. Who would deny it any more? The only thing unbearable is the degradation, the prostitution of the living mysteries in us. Let man only approach his own self with a deep respect, even reverence for all the creative soul, the God-mystery within us, puts forth. Then we shall all be sound and free. Lewdness is hateful because it impairs our integrity and our proud being.

The creative, spontaneous soul sends forth its promptings of desire and aspiration in us. These promptings are our true fate, which is our business to fulfil. A fate dictated from outside, from theory or from circumstance, is a false fate.

This novel pretends only to be a record of the writer's own desires, aspirations, struggles; in a word, a record of the profoundest experiences in the self. Nothing that comes from the deep, passional soul is bad, or can be bad. So there is no apology to tender, unless to the soul itself, if it should have been belied.

Man struggles with his unborn needs and fulfilment. New unfoldings struggle up in torment in him, as buds struggle forth from the midst of a plant. Any man of real individuality tries to know and to understand what is happening, even in himself, as he goes along. This struggle for verbal consciousness should not be left out in art. It is a very great part of life. It is not superimposition of a theory. It is the passionate struggle into conscious being.

We are now in a period of crisis. Every man who is acutely alive is acutely wrestling with his own soul. The people that can bring forth the new passion, the new idea, this people will endure. Those others that fix themselves in the old idea, will perish with the new life strangled unborn within them. Men must speak out to one another.

In point of style, fault is often found with the continual, slightly modified repetition. The only answer is that it is natural to the author: and that every natural crisis in emotion or passion or understanding comes from this pulsing, frictional to-and-fro, which works up to culmination.

The Foreword was not printed, as Lawrence had planned, with either the first American edition of the novel or the British edition of 1921, and did not actually appear in print until 1936. Instead, the novel was released and reviewed with only Lawrence's other works – and his tarnished reputation – to guide the reviewers and public. The two extracts that follow are indicative of British reviewers' reactions to the novel: both are hostile and both, albeit in vastly different ways, express profound dismay that the possessor of a great literary gift should be brought so low. The first, unattributed, review comes from the *Saturday Westminster Gazette*:

Mr. D. H. Lawrence's new and very long novel *Women in Love* is not unlike a serious elaboration of the well-known advertisements 'Mr. and Mrs. Smith, having cast off clothing of all descriptions, invite inspection. Distance no object.' Not only do all the heroes and all the heroines of this crowded tale cast off clothing whenever there is any excuse . . . but they do it unexpectedly – at garden parties (Gudrun and Ursula) – after dinner, over their cigarettes (Birkin and Crich), while talking round the fire on a winter morning (ever so many people), for no revealed purpose so far as their consequent actions are recorded, but possibly to give greater case and intimacy to their interminable conversations, and to provide Mr. Lawrence with repeated opportunities for vivid pictorial records of chiaroscuro, plein-air, genre, and figure-painting in words. This he does to adoration as always, though the fastidious may complain that he chooses the vocabulary of the butcher's shop in preference to that of the anatomy class. It is possible to justify this choice by the effect it produces, but Mr. Lawrence has already in his own characteristic repetitive style a medium for producing certain effects. The particular atmosphere of physiological reaction to psychological experience which Mr. Lawrence aims at creating is rather destroyed than increased by a violent vocabulary in reiteration . . .

Then, to return to the illustration with which this notice began, even as Mr. and Mrs. Smith baited their offer with the enigmatical phrase, 'Distance no object', so does Mr. Lawrence adorn his tale with unpremeditated incident. In the midst of a perfectly peaceful wedding party, for instance, while Gerald is talking to Birkin as wedding-guest to wedding-guest, Mr. Lawrence suddenly observes, 'Gerald as a boy had accidentally killed his brother. What then!' It is shocking: but then, some shocks make you giggle.

Not that Mr. Lawrence makes you giggle much. He falls too often into long and shallow pseudo-philosophical discussion, sometimes in the form of terribly boring dinner-table talk and sometimes in direct reflection . . .

All the characters talk and think like this except when they are feeling, and they feel a great deal. There is in particular Hermione Roddice, who didn't quite kill Birkin. She 'writhed in her soul knowing what she couldn't know' on hardly any provocation at all, and when she had a successful house-party 'she seemed in a swoon of gratification convulsed with pleasure, and yet sick like a *revenant*' because her guests wore bright-coloured dinner gowns. Clothes play parts of their own in the tale. 'Enter a purple gown, green stockings, and amber necklace' would do for a stage direction if *Women in Love* could ever be dramatised. The two heroines, Ursula and Gudrun, are almost as indistinguishable in character and conversation as they are in their amours and their clothing. They have innumerable pairs of stockings, which they change several times in a chapter. But no diversification of pink hat, blue stocking, orange jumper really distinguishes one from the other, and when towards the end of the feverish tale they both go abroad even the young men who accompany them – Birkin and Crich – lose their identities and become one and the same young man. It is, perhaps, in a last effort to reintegrate their personalities that Mr. Lawrence makes one of them die of a conversation in the high Alps: '"I couldn't love *you*" she said, with stark cold truth. A blinding flash went over his brain, his body jolted, his heart had burst into flame'. So he throws himself over the precipice. It certainly is a new and original end, and, in a novel when all the characters suffer the pangs of dissolution several times a week, possibly the only fitting one. Still . . . [11]

Witty though it is, this piece makes serious charges against Lawrence and finds severe fault with the novel. The reviewer attacks Lawrence on four basic counts: first, that he uses the 'vocabulary of the butcher's shop' in preference to more dignified expression; second, that the novel is tiresomely weighted with iteration and reiteration of ideas and phrases; third, that there is an unnecessary obsession with clothing and colour when describing, mostly, female characters; fourth, presumably a concomitant to the clothing issue, that the central characters are barely distinguishable from one another.

Such criticisms are not wholly new and do not rest in this reviewer's mind alone. We have already seen the first two accusations levelled, in much the same tone, against *The Rainbow* by its three quoted reviewers, and we shall see comment made on the third by Philippa Tristram in her essay in Chapter 5 of this book – fifty-seven years after this piece was written, and in an altogether different context. With regard to the fourth criticism, the reviewer seems to express a view peculiar to the period, as several other commentators (including John Middleton Murry, below) also seem to find equal difficulty distinguishing Gudrun, Ursula, Gerald and Birkin from one another. The difficulty for these reviewers seems to spring from their expectations that Lawrence should make use of 'the old stable ego of character' in the novel. As we have seen in the letter to Edward Garnett (quoted in the Introduction, pp. 9–10), which Lawrence used to outline some of his ideas for the form and style of *The Wedding Ring*, as far back as 1914, he had abandoned the approach to character demanded by his reviewers. He was certain, though, that the essential quality of his characters, what he described as their 'element', could be discovered if the novel was read correctly: 'There is another *ego*, according to whose action the individual is unrecognisable, and passes through, as it were, allotropic states which it needs a deeper sense than any we've been used to exercise to discover are states of the same single radically unchanged element . . .'[12] It should also be said that plenty of people were able to distinguish between the various characters of the novel. Ottoline Morrell, for example, was so appalled at Lawrence's depiction of her through the character Hermione Roddice, that she cut all communication with him, until an eventual reconciliation was effected by letter in 1928.

That the novel is weighted with repetition and iteration is a complaint with which modern readers – including the most sympathetic to Lawrence – will agree. There is no question that Lawrence's novels are demanding and, at times, appear flawed in their style. Even F. R. Leavis, the greatest defender and rehabilitator of Lawrence's reputation,[13] admitted in *D. H. Lawrence: Novelist* (1955) that 'at each re-reading in the course of thirty years, I still do not question that the book has faults.'[14] To explore the nature of those faults, he quotes the passage from the 'Excurse' chapter that describes Birkin as 'an Egyptian Pharaoh', and arrives at the following assessment:

**It seems to me that in these places Lawrence betrays by an insistent and over-emphatic explicitness, running at times to something one can only call jargon, that he is uncertain – uncertain of the value of what he offers; uncertain whether he really holds it – whether a valid communication has really been defined and conveyed in terms of his creative art . . .** [15]

Most students of Lawrence's novels in the Nineties have an awareness of Leavis's part in the great re-assessment of Lawrence's work, and have hence developed a more sophisticated understanding of the ways in which Lawrence's fiction is used to explore the more urgent aspects of the human psyche than was open to his critics in the Twenties. The repetition of phrasing and the 'jargon' used to capture and relay heightened states of emotion now seem minor flaws in an enterprise of sufficient scale and newness that we are drawn to agree with Leavis's view that such passages are 'marginal in their unsatisfactoriness', rather than damaging to the work as a whole. To the reviewers encountering such techniques for the first time, not only in Lawrence's work but in *any* work, the uses of language and, indeed, the aims of such usages seemed perplexing and even repellent. Where we can accept the value of Lawrence's entire undertaking in the novel, and thus place in context the occasional weaknesses of style, the reviewers who read *Women in Love* in 1921 saw simply the bending of language to an aim which itself was unsavoury and antithetical to the moral standards of literature as they understood it.

In the piece which follows, John Middleton Murry reviews *Women in Love* for the *Athenaeum*, which he edited between 1919 and 1921. Murry and his lover Katherine Mansfield had been involved in a heated and often stormy friendship with the Lawrences since their first meeting in June 1913. Murry and Mansfield had been the only witnesses to Lawrence and Frieda's marriage in July 1914, had maintained a voluminous correspondence on matters literary and personal, and had moved to be their close neighbours in Buckinghamshire between October 1914 and January 1915. The intensity of the friendship proved too suffocating, and eventually the two couples moved away from each other, but still communicated by letter. Such was the power of Lawrence's personality, however, that he was again able to persuade Murry and Mansfield to share a house (in Cornwall) with himself and Frieda between April and mid-June 1916.

The rekindling of the friendship and the second attempt at communal living took place during the crucial period of work on the earlier parts of the *Wedding Ring* manuscript which became *Women in Love*. There is no doubt that the events of these months had some bearing on the portrayal of the Rupert Birkin/Gerald Crich relationship of the novel, which draws heavily on Lawrence's perception of his own friendship with Murry. To deal satisfactorily with the connections between the relationship of the two characters and the two writers would take far more space than is available here, but it is sufficient to note that Murry was disturbed by Lawrence's insistent projection of a loving, non-physical, blood-bond (*Blutbrüderschaft*) between them – or their fictional counterparts. Although it is generally accepted that Lawrence had no thoughts of a homosexual relationship, claiming on many occasions to be appalled by what he saw as the sterile nature of such relations, the sheer intensity of his proposal still unsettled Murry. We see much of his discomfort in his review of the novel:

Mr. Lawrence is set apart from the novelists who are his contemporaries by the vehemence of his passion. In the time before the war we should have distinguished him by other qualities – a sensitive and impassioned apprehension of natural beauty, for example, or an understanding of the strange blood bonds that unite human beings, or an exquisite discrimination in the use of language, based on a power of natural vision. All these things Mr. Lawrence once had, in the time when he thrilled us with the expectation of genius: now they are dissolved in the acid of a burning and vehement passion. These qualities are individual no longer; they no longer delight us; they have been pressed into the service of another power, they walk in bondage and in livery . . .

Mr. Lawrence is what he is: a natural force over which we have no power of command or persuasion. He has no power of command or persuasion over himself. It was not his deliberate choice that he sacrificed his gifts, his vision, his delicacy, and his eloquence. If ever a writer was driven, it is he.

Not that we absolve him from responsibility for his own disaster. It is part of our creed that he must be responsible; but it is part of his creed that he is not. We stand by the consciousness and the civilisation of which the literature we know is the finest flower; Mr. Lawrence is in rebellion against both. If we try him before our court, he contemptuously rejects the jurisdiction. The things we prize are the things he would destroy; what is triumph to him is catastrophe to us. He is the outlaw of modern English literature; and he is the most interesting figure in it. But he must be shown no mercy.

*Women in Love* is five hundred pages of passionate vehemence, wave after wave of turgid, exasperated writing impelled towards some distant and invisible end; the persistent underground beating of some dark and inaccessible sea in an underworld whose inhabitants are known by this alone, that they writhe continually, like the damned, in a frenzy of sexual awareness of one another . . . they emerge from dark hatred to darker beatitudes; they grope in their own slime to some final consummation, in which they are utterly 'negated' or utterly 'fulfilled'. We remain utterly indifferent to their destinies, we are weary to death of them.

At the end we know one thing and one thing alone: that Mr. Lawrence believes, with all his heart and soul, that he is revealing to us the profound and naked reality of life, that it is a matter of life and death to him that he should persuade us that it is a matter of life and death to ourselves to know that these things are so . . . He would, if he could, put us all on the rack to make us confess his protozoic god; he is deliberately, incessantly, and passionately obscene in the exact sense of the word. He will uncover our nakedness. It is of no avail for us to protest that the things he finds are not there; a fanatical shriek arises from his pages that they are there, but we deny them.

If they are there, then it is all-important that we should not deny them. Whether we ought to expose them is another matter. The fact that European civilisation has up to the advent of Mr. Lawrence ignored them can prove nothing, though it may indicate many things. It may indicate that they do not exist at all; or it may indicate that they do exist, but that it is bound up with the very nature of civilisation that they should not be exposed. Mr. Lawrence vehemently believes the latter . . . He claims that his characters attain whatever they do attain by their power of going back and re-living the vital process of pre-European civilisation . . .

Is Mr. Lawrence a fanatic or a prophet? That he is an artist no longer is certain, as certain as it is that he has no desire to be one; for whatever may be this 'deep physical mind' that expresses its satisfaction in 'a subtle mindless smile', whether it have a real existence or not, it is perfectly clear that it does not admit of individuality as we understand it. No doubt Mr. Lawrence intends to bring us to a new conception of individuality also; but in the interim we must use the conceptions and the senses that we have . . . We should have thought that we should be able to distinguish between male and female, at least. But no! Remove the names, remove the sedulous catalogues of unnecessary clothing – a new element and a significant one, this, in our author's work – and man and woman are indistinguishable as octopods in an aquarium tank.

We have given, in spite of our repulsion and our weariness, our undivided attention to Mr. Lawrence's book for the space of three days; we have striven with all our power to understand what he means by the experience $x$ (enjoyed by Birkin and Ursula) . . . we have compared it with the experience $y$, which takes place between the other pair of lovers, Gudrun and Gerald; we can see no difference between them . . . We are sure that not one person in a thousand would decide that they were anything but the crudest kind of sexuality, wrapped up in what Mr. S. K. Ratcliffe has aptly called the language of Higher Thought. We feel that the solitary person may be right; but even he, we are convinced, would be quite unable to distinguish between experience $x$ and experience $y$. Yet $x$ leads one pair to undreamed-of happiness, and $y$ conducts the other to attempted murder and suicide.

We believe Mr. Lawrence's book is an attempt to take us through the process. Unless we pass through this we shall never see the light. If the experiences which he presents to us as a part of this process mean nothing, the book means nothing; if they mean something, the book means something; and the value of the book is precisely the value of those experiences. Whatever they are, they are of ultimate and

fundamental importance to Mr. Lawrence. He has sacrificed everything to achieve them; he has murdered his gifts for an acceptable
offering to them. Those gifts were great; they were valuable to the
civilisation which he believes he has transcended. It may be that we
are benighted in the old world, and that he belongs to the new; it may
be that he is, like his Rupert, a 'son of God'; we certainly are the sons
of men, and we must be loyal to the light we have. By that light Mr.
Lawrence's consummation is a degradation, his passing beyond a
passing beneath, his triumph a catastrophe. It may be superhuman,
we do not know; by the knowledge that we have we can only pronounce it sub-human and bestial, a thing that our forefathers had
rejected when they began to rise from the slime.[16]

Many comments made by the other reviewers of *The Rainbow* and *Women
in Love* are echoed here by Murry. We find the usual anger that Lawrence
has 'murdered his gifts', that he has turned away from fiction which
betokened a 'sensitive and impassioned apprehension of natural beauty'
and 'an exquisite discrimination in the use of language, based on a
power of natural vision' to pursue a set of experiences the value of
which Murry clearly cannot comprehend. The outrage and disgust
Murry feels at Lawrence's attempt to 'uncover our nakedness' and thus
thrust English literature and culture back into a pre-civilised state is not
so far removed from that expressed by James Douglas in his early review
of *The Rainbow* – indeed, in its closing paragraph, this piece even slips
into the same sort of Biblical language and imagery used by Douglas to
condemn Lawrence.

One notable feature of the review is the apparent ease with which
Murry all but ignores the style and structure of the novel. He makes
several indirect references to its surface features, and raises the complaint about the indistinguishability of its characters, but never really
subjects the prose to any detailed commentary. The chief concern seems
to be with Lawrence as an agent of literary anarchy, rather than with the
work itself. Such an approach was not at all unusual in its time; much of
the study of literary works was concerned with biographical detail in
texts, and most were read as being symptomatic of their author's moral
outlook, state of mind and relation to society. As the comparatively new
study of psychology came to gain a stronger place in the public consciousness across the first three decades of the century, so more reviews
tended towards a reading of novels as psychological maps of their
author's condition. In the next section of this book, for example, we shall
see the more pronounced manifestation of the 'psychological approach'
in another of Murry's works, *Son of Woman*, which dominated the critical
view of Lawrence's novels in the 1930s, both in its own right and
because of the defensive reaction it prompted from those who sought to

record their own, more favourable, image of Lawrence.

At the centre of this review, then, lies a confusion about the precise nature of the experience that Lawrence sought to uncover in his novels. Murry's inability to see what Lawrence was aiming to achieve reminds us very strongly of Catherine Carswell's difficulty in defining 'even to one's self what Mr. Lawrence's aim exactly is, and whether it is in any way constructive' when reviewing *The Rainbow*. The same confusion is expressed by various means through all of the reviews in this chapter – only the vehemence of the reviewers' denunciations vary.

That there should be so little ground for disagreement between so many reviewers, and so much shared confusion about Lawrence's ideas, is clear evidence of the general response to the novels across the period 1915–21. Perhaps we can understand something of the startled reaction to *The Rainbow*, given the fervent jingoism of the war years, and the fact that Britain was burdened with an Edwardian, or even Victorian, view of art and culture. But that there should have been practically no broadening of critical outlook or understanding in the five years which separated the publication of the two novels is remarkable, and it speaks very forcefully of the distance between Lawrence and his contemporaries. That Murry could not understand what lies at the heart of *Women in Love* should not be seen as a particular failing on his part. Likewise, we should not think of the other reviewers quoted here as particularly insensitive or reactionary – they simply spoke from their time and applied the critical methods available to the novels Lawrence published.

It has been the purpose of this chapter to provide something of a step back from our current understanding of Lawrence and his work, so that we may view the progress of his critical reputation from its beginnings. By offering an account of the hostile critical arena into which *The Rainbow* and *Women in Love* were released, it is hoped that the reader will recognise and remember the almost universal resistance to Lawrence's ideas and techniques at the time these novels were written. In the chapters which follow, we shall be examining the continued decline of Lawrence's reputation through the 1930s, before turning to the struggle that faced those who sought to promote a new account of his art, and to shift the prevailing critical practices which had governed the public and academic response to his work.

# CHAPTER TWO

# The Thirties and Forties: Psychobabble, Total Recall and Obscurity

L AWRENCE'S DEATH in March 1930 occasioned a massive surge
in publication on his life, his ideas, and his position as an artist.
James C. Cowan's bibliography of works about Lawrence numbers
at 220 the total publications for 1930–31 – an enormous increase in the
number for 1926–27 (74), and 1928–29 (83).[1] Given the difficulties
Lawrence encountered with critics during his life, one would expect his
obituary press to be almost wholly negative. Indeed, until the publication of Dennis Jackson's study of press reactions to Lawrence's death in
the *D. H. Lawrence Review*,[2] it was generally assumed that Lawrence's reputation only suffered at the hands of the obituarists. But as Jackson's
work proved, in the English-language press world-wide, there were
many favourable commentaries, and many predictions that his work
would one day be valued more highly than it had been during his life.

Paul Rosenfield, for instance, declared that Lawrence's work, though
not satisfactorily accomplished as a single body, nevertheless centred
upon a vision more truthful than that offered by his contemporaries –
naming, amongst others, Joyce and Proust.[3] E. M. Forster conducted a
vigorous campaign on Lawrence's behalf during 1930, publishing four
articles in the *Nation and Athenaeum*, and one in *The Listener*, in which he
asserted that the thing Lawrence chiefly lacked was a public capable of
reading his work – a truth which Lawrence himself had recognised in his
letter to Edward Garnett about *The Wedding Ring* as long ago as 1914.[4]
Forster apparently had no doubts about Lawrence's talent or about the
enduring quality of his work, and was ready to argue his view – against
negative commentaries from T. S. Eliot and Clive Bell – across the pages
of the *Nation and Athenaeum* for several months. In one piece, Forster
summed up his forward-looking appraisal of Lawrence's major fiction,
by recognising that 'he was the greatest imaginative novelist of our
generation'.[5]

In a pair of studies which demonstrate the early stirrings of a twenty-five-year critical battle to establish Lawrence's reputation and place in the canon, Cambridge academic F. R. Leavis sought to demonstrate through his reading of the novels the 'sincerity in the record of emotional life such as is possible only to genius'.[6] In the second of the two pieces, Leavis made particular reference to *The Rainbow* and the 'sensuous richness' which elevated it beyond the other novels. He felt, however, that Lawrence's later work was dominated by prophetic aims and that the over-emphatic style of those novels could often result in writing that was tedious. Lionel Trilling, who also would champion Lawrence's cause for many years, wrote of the central 'thread of social interest' that unified Lawrence's work, but recognised that the novels were generally misunderstood.[7]

All of the serious commentaries written in the year following Lawrence's death suggest that there was room for a re-appraisal of his reputation, for a serious attempt to examine the qualities of the writing away from the accusations of obscenity and immorality that so clouded any discussion of the novels in the popular press. But there were powerful factors which restricted the level of debate on Lawrence's work: circulation of most academic or serious literary journals was tiny; the discussions of literary matters that such journals engaged in hardly took in the mass of the population (the total number of students in higher education in Britain, for instance, ran at something under three percent of the population during the Thirties); two of the major novels – *The Rainbow* and *Lady Chatterley's Lover* – were still banned in Britain, and, possibly most significant, Lawrence's novels were difficult to read and understand. It was, for most people, easier to follow the colourful, popular reports of Lawrence's life and bizarre theories, so that the few thoughtful and dispassionate accounts of Lawrence's work that were published had little influence on the image of Lawrence that persisted throughout the decade.

As is still the case today, the death of a 'celebrity artist' like Lawrence acts as a commercial prompt to the many people who knew him during his lifetime, drawing them to the lucrative 'fame industry' that has become a feature of modern publishing. During the Thirties, around a dozen of Lawrence's friends (Mabel Dodge Luhan, Dorothy Brett), former lovers and girlfriends (Jessie Chambers, Helen Corke), family (Ada Lawrence), fellow writers and artists (John Middleton Murry, Catherine Carswell), and travelling-companions (Earl and Achsah Brewer), felt compelled to write books about him. For many, the aim was altruistic, born of an honest desire to set the record straight on their friend. For others, the driving force was a desire to share in fame or simply make money at the expense of truth. Thus, despite the efforts of a small number of critics who tried to take a fresh view of the novels, the vast majority of published works in the ten years that followed

Lawrence's death were concerned with strongly personalised and partial memories of the man, not the writing.

Of the more influential book-length works published during the Thirties, two stand out as influencing the course of Lawrence's critical reputation and status: *Son of Woman* (1931) by John Middleton Murry, and Aldous Huxley's edition of *The Letters of D. H. Lawrence* (1932). Both are much concerned with the personality of their subject, but both take as their core-material Lawrence's writing and his outlook as an artist.

Murry's work makes strenuous use of psychological theorising and quasi-Freudian analysis to arrive at the conclusion that virtually all of Lawrence's works are fatally flawed by his failure to reach a satisfactory statement of his sexual self. Lawrence's unusually close relationship with his mother and his sparring relationship with Frieda are brought into the equation as factors that led to a fruitless search for *Blutbrüderschaft* and dominance over his female characters by means of various closely-identified hero-selves in the novels.

Despite its often vicious attacks on Lawrence's personality and art, Murry's study did come to occupy a significant place in the course of Lawrence criticism, and certainly dominated the popular critical vision of him throughout the Thirties. As Colin Clarke has suggested:

**Significant commentary on *The Rainbow* and *Women in Love* may be said to begin with Middleton Murry's *Son of Woman*, published in 1931, a year after Lawrence's death. Though he has little belief in the importance of either of the novels as achieved art . . . Murry has a sharp if partial and distorted comprehension of the tensions which are at work within them and which, in demanding to be ordered and controlled, help to determine their form.**[8]

Murry's book deals with most of Lawrence's major works, employing an approach which draws heavily upon biographical detail and personal reminiscence to provide a framework for critical commentary. *Son of Woman*, then, is a study of both writer and works, wherein Murry himself, his partner Katherine Mansfield, friends and contemporaries such as Catherine Carswell, Lady Ottoline Morrell, Cynthia Asquith and others regularly appear as participating figures in this quasi-psychoanalytic reading of Lawrence's texts.

A central feature of Murry's general argument lies in his assertion that the poetry collected in the volume *Look, we have come through!* (1917) has close associations with the ideas and tensions evident within the two novels, and that both are reflective of conditions prevailing in Lawrence's life and psyche during the period 1912–17. Certainly, the poetry derives from the same period as the novels and draws upon the same set of experiences which shaped Lawrence's attitudes during the writing of the prose works. Lawrence's own Preface to his *Collected Poems*, written in

1928, makes the case for an initial linkage between the poems and the writer's experience. Referring to *Look, we have come through!*, he says:

It seems to me that no poetry, not even the best, should be judged as if it existed in the absolute, in the vacuum of the absolute. Even the best poetry, when it is all personal, needs the penumbras of its own time and place and circumstance to make it full and whole . . . What was uttered in the cruel spring of 1917 should not be dislocated and heard as if sounding out of the void.[9]

Of the poems, we can accept as much. Even when dealing with the major novels, Murry's reading of the relationships between the works and the life of this period has some interest, if only in the fact that his account is largely first-hand and can furnish us with some insight into Lawrence's activities and feelings during such an important period. There is, however, the tremendous weakness in Murry's argument – that he fails to recognise Lawrence's fundamental belief that the novel has a particular character, an organic power which re-works and transfigures details drawn from life or philosophy of life. Though there are many incidents and characters in *The Rainbow* and *Women in Love* derived from the events of Lawrence's life during the period of composition, they always, to use the phrasing of *Study of Thomas Hardy*, 'subserve the artistic purpose'. This point Lawrence clearly makes in his essay 'The Novel':

The novel is the highest form of human expression so far attained. Why? Because it is so incapable of the absolute.

In a novel, everything is relative to everything else, if that novel is art at all. There may be didactic bits, but they aren't the novel.[10]

There are a few occasions when Lawrence did thrust the life so carelessly into the art that the whole lacks that internal energy and creative flux which marks the best of his work: in *Kangaroo* we find many such awkward passages, and in the 're-discovered' novel *Mr Noon* there is a distinct failing of artistic vision resulting from an insistent autobiographical agenda.[11] (In the extracts from Frank Kermode's *Lawrence*, later in this book, we find a consideration of Lawrence's blending of metaphysic and tale.)

Murry starts each of his chapters on the novels with a confirmation of the links between the life, the poems and the prose. Opening the discussion of the earlier novel, Murry transfers his thesis of the 'inconceivable' woman, sought by the Lawrence of the poems, to the characters of *The Rainbow*:

In *The Rainbow* is a still more intimate record of the experience confessed in *Look, we have come through!* The correspondence is exact and unmistakable. The story of Anna Lensky and Will Brangwen is, in its essentials, the same story as the story of the poems; but the story is told more richly, and more fearfully.[12]

The 'story' to which Murry refers is one almost entirely derived from what the critic saw as Lawrence's disastrous personal relationships and sexual inadequacies. The earlier novel, *Sons and Lovers*, was, by Murry's account, a treatment of the repressive and ultimately paralysing mother–son relationship from which Lawrence struggled to free himself. *The Rainbow* is seen as a protracted account of Lawrence and Frieda's failed sexual and marital relationship: 'radically, the history of Lawrence's final sexual failure'.[13] Dealing with *Women in Love*, Murry finds that the sexual hunger and frustration expressed in *The Rainbow* and the poems now comes to its destructive climax in Birkin's attempts to subdue and master Ursula:

[The] endeavour to force upon the woman a sexual or sensual homage to the man is the chief clue to Lawrence's . . . novel *Women in Love*. In that novel Ursula Brangwen becomes, quite recognisably, the woman; and Lawrence himself also appears, quite recognisably, as Rupert Birkin. The culmination of their relation is described in the chapter 'Excurse'. To anyone who reads the novel in isolation, and without the necessary clue, it is an obscure and difficult chapter; but it strikes even the unadvised reader as invented and untrue. He scents in it a fundamental falsity, as of a forced conclusion. Perhaps Lawrence himself half acknowledged this by giving the chapter its strange title 'Excurse'.[14]

Quoting at length from the section of the chapter where Birkin and Ursula conduct their violent argument about Birkin's relationship with Hermione, Murry proceeds to express some confusion as to the chapter's purpose and direction. He also depicts Lawrence as engaging in a degree of wish-fulfilment through his male character's actions and aspirations:

It was, within the limits of the story, quite impossible for Ursula to know anything about 'the foulness of the sexlife' of Birkin and Hermione Roddice. Their liaison is over before Ursula ever meets Birkin; and he tells Ursula nothing about it. We must say, if we keep to the rules of the game, that Ursula's knowledge was due to a flash of imaginative intuition. But, with Lawrence, it is impossible to keep to the rules of the game; with him, there is no 'game'. He did not conceal himself, and we cannot conceal him. Rupert Birkin is Lawrence, and what Lawrence knew about Birkin, he knew about himself. Birkin, indeed, makes no attempt to deny the truth of Ursula's knowledge. On the contrary,

'He knew she was in the main right. He knew he was perverse, so spiritual on the one hand, and in some strange way, degraded on the other. But was she herself any better? Was anybody any better?'

Wherein did this depravity, of which Lawrence was conscious, consist? It consisted in this demand that the woman 'should take him as he had taken her,' with a sense of 'the contiguous, concrete, terrifying *other flesh*.' It is a demand for sexual contact, without the oblivion of passion, without the ecstasy of union – cold, conscious, calculating sensuality. And the woman instinctively repels it; probably, she is completely incapable of it. Probably, the majority of ordinary men and women are completely incapable of it; probably, it is only practicable in a man of physical and spiritual constitution resembling that of Lawrence.

The point, and the falsity of 'Excurse', is that it represents Ursula as giving way to Birkin's demand. In Lawrence's quasi-mystical language, 'she had thought there was no source deeper than the phallic source'; now, at his demand, she discovers it. 'She had had lovers, she had known passion. But this was neither love nor passion.' That was true enough. But what is completely false is that Ursula, or her original, acknowledged its supremacy. The evidence of this is Lawrence's work. This ultra-phallic consummation, in which Birkin and Ursula are represented as finding complete fulfilment, disappears almost completely from Lawrence's subsequent books. If it really had been the consummation which he represented it to be, this disappearance would be inconceivable. The true fulfilment between man and woman is not discovered simply in order to be forgotten: for it is, for Lawrence, and for many men, the Holy Grail itself. One does not throw the Holy Grail into the kitchen-midden. That alone is evidence enough that this consummation was not what Lawrence represented it to be.

Having questioned the validity of Lawrence's 'representation', Murry is clear as to the purpose of the conflict and resolution between the characters: it is, again, a hopeless and degrading search for release through masculine dominance and self-assertion, at the expense of the novel's 'truth'.

As a matter of fact, Lawrence is so immersed in his personal experience that he forgets his story. Birkin had not taken this knowledge of Ursula in the novel. Lawrence had taken it of the woman in life, and the record is in 'Manifesto'. There it only remained for him to be known even as he knows, without which he cannot be free. Now, in the novel, where he is master, he gives himself this 'liberation'. Ursula Brangwen is made to desire what the poet of 'Manifesto' desired that his woman should desire.

. . . So the dream is made to come true. Ursula has 'the full mystic knowledge of his suave loins of darkness'; she has discovered that 'there were strange fountains of his body, more mysterious and potent than any she had imagined or known, more satisfying, ah, finally, mystically-physically satisfying. She had thought that there was no source deeper than the phallic source.' Now, she knew better. The something that remained, the something which prevented Lawrence from satisfying the ultimate hunger of his 'ache for being,' is achieved. And we see what this 'ache for being' really is; it is the ache to establish his own masculinity. It cannot be done in sexual possession, in which he is always the dependent, the victim; but it can be done in this new mode of sexuality, which consists in touch, in which there is none of the 'abhorred mingling.' In the sexuality of touch, of complete separateness, he may be lord and master – a very Pharaoh.

When we grasp this, we grasp the meaning of the strange chapter, 'Moony,' where Birkin throws stone after stone, in an unintelligible frenzy, at the reflection of the moon in a pool, while Ursula watches him in agony. It seems quite meaningless, until we realise that Birkin is destroying Aphrodite, the divinity under whose cold light Ursula annihilated the core of intrinsic male in Lawrence's last incarnation as Anton Skrebensky. To annihilate the female insatiably demanding physical satisfaction from the man who cannot give it her – the female who has thus annihilated him – this is Lawrence's desire. To make her subject again, to re-establish his own manhood – this is the secret purpose of *Women in Love*. In imagination, he has his desire. He creates a sexual mystery beyond the phallic, wherein he is the lord; and he makes the woman acknowledge the existence of this ultra-phallic realm, and his own lordship in it. He triumphs over her in imagination, but not in life. Aphrodite can only be appeased within the phallic realm, and Lawrence is no master there . . . [15]

In the closing pages of his chapter on *Women in Love*, Murry moves to a consideration of the relationship between Birkin and Gerald. He argues that Lawrence's motivation in developing Birkin's peculiar desire 'to love a man purely and fully' derives from the failure of his relationships with women – as worked out in either fiction or life. The search for blood-brotherhood (*Blutbrüderschaft*), for an intimate relationship between men, has been the source of some confusion and contention for critics since the novel's appearance. That Birkin's desire for 'the additional perfect relationship between man and man – additional to marriage' is a search for homoerotic satisfaction has been generally rejected, though as late as 1969, there have been attempts to read the novel in such a fashion.[16] (See Mark Spilka's essay later in this volume for further discussion of the concept.)

Murry rightly treats Birkin's quest for *Blutbrüderschaft* as secondary to the Birkin–Ursula relationship. As we may see from the phrasing of Birkin's statements, Lawrence clearly saw the search for a fulfilling male–male relationship as 'additional' to the marriage and consummation sought with Ursula, but also as essential to the true realisation and working of that union. Murry's account fails to realise such a central point; the longing for brotherhood is seen simply as an 'issue' (in the meaning of a 'way-out' or 'escape') from his difficulties with women in life and art:

. . . The hunger for a woman has proved disastrous, in spite of the assertions of actual, and the reports of imaginary fulfilment; it was inevitable that Lawrence should turn towards the possibility of a rela- tion with a man. There is the same confusion between spirituality and sensuality. The love between Rupert Birkin and Gerald Crich is, on Birkin's side, half-spiritual, half-sensual. 'We are mentally, spiritually intimate,' says Birkin to Crich, 'therefore we ought to be more or less physically intimate.' Accordingly, the two men wrestle naked together, and Birkin swoons away. But the main interest of their relation is the indecision which Birkin reveals. He says to Crich:

'You've got to take down the love-and-marriage ideal from its pedestal. We want something broader. I believe in the *additional* perfect relationship between man and man – additional to marriage.'

That, indubitably, was in Lawrence's own mind at this moment; he expressed his thought, even more strongly, in his letters. But, since we know what underlay the 'perfect' marriage-relation between Ursula and Birkin, and that its 'perfection' consisted precisely in the substitution of 'the mystery beyond the phallic' for the phallic mys- tery, we know that it is not the addition of one perfection to another that he is seeking, but rather to escape to a man from the misery of his own failure with a woman. This had always appeared to Lawrence a way out. In *The White Peacock* his love for a man is more perfect than his love for a woman; and, truly, in actual fact I believe it was a happier and less tortured relation for him. But always it was brief and fugitive. Lawrence was always, and inevitably, disappointed.

'We ought to swear to love each other, you and I,' says Rupert to Gerald, 'implicitly and perfectly, finally, without any possibility of going back.' Again he pleads: 'We will swear to stand by each other – be true to each other intimately – infallibly – given to each other, organically, without possibility of going back.' Gerald withdraws from the proffered alliance, puts it gently aside, and the novel pur- ports to show us how, in consequence of this refusal, he is destroyed. He chooses Ursula's sister, Gudrun. This, Birkin says (and Lawrence makes it so), is a disaster . . .

The other way was to accept Rupert's offer of alliance, to enter into the bond of pure trust and love with the other man, and then subsequently with the woman. If he pledged himself with the man he would later be able to pledge himself with the woman: not merely in legal marriage, but in absolute, mystic marriage.

Such 'absolute, mystic marriage', namely, as Rupert and Ursula achieve: their imaginary ultra-phallic consummation. Since the desire for this consummation, and the hunger for the man also, is the effect of Lawrence's phallic failure, Rupert's demand of Gerald is the last extremity of self-deception. It means nothing, or if it means anything, it means that his man-friend must be the repetition of himself, just such another phallic failure, just such another sex-crucified man.

Lawrence's hunger for a man could never have been satisfied. He came to know, and in part to confess it later. But at this time he did not know it, he was only vaguely aware of the depth upon depth of self-deception in which he was involved. He was gratifying himself with a dream. Gerald, because he refuses Rupert's offer of alliance, is delivered over to the destructive Aphrodite and to death . . . In a sensual ecstasy, Gerald seeks to murder Gudrun, and dies in a final ecstasy of dissolution in the snow, in the light of a painful brilliant-shining moon, 'from which there was no escape.'

The book comes to a close with a conversation between Rupert and Ursula about the dead man [in which Birkin argues for the validity of his vision of 'eternal union with a man'] . . . Was he or Ursula right? Surely, Ursula. Not that love of a woman and love of a man are incompatible. That is not the question at all. The question is entirely personal: whether Lawrence can find an issue, by way of a relation with a man, from the strange and terrible situation in which he is now caught. Lawrence is bewildered and lost. He feels that he is disintegrating; his inward division is become terrible to himself; his life a nightmare.[17]

Given its now-obvious failings and considering its often vicious personal attacks on Lawrence, it seems curious that *Son of Woman* should have exerted such influence on the critical treatment of his work, as it did, during the Thirties and even into the Forties. The answer lies in the combination of prevailing national attitudes, Murry's personal reputation and the timing of *Son of Woman*'s publication.

During the period 1914–30, Murry had achieved something of the status of a 'national voice', with a reputation as a leading (if not *the* leading) popular British critic of the post-war period. During the war, he had been the Chief Censor at the War Office (for which he was awarded the O.B.E. in 1920), and had been a staunch advocate for moral responsibility in art in the post-war decade. As editor of the *Athenaeum*, and later founding-editor of *Adelphi* and *New Adelphi*, he had been able to exercise considerable influence on literary attitudes for fifteen years.

Murry was also in the happy position of being the first well-known and influential British critic to produce a full-length study of Lawrence's work. Although there had been three book-length studies and one bibliography of Lawrence's writings published in the period to 1930, all but one of these had been written by Americans, had been released in America and were not widely available in Europe.[18] The only British critical volume to precede Murry's, *D. H. Lawrence: A First Study*, by Stephen Potter, had been largely ignored by the British literary and popular press, with the exception of the *Times Literary Supplement*, which had carried a very negative review (30 April 1930).

Regrettably, it was probably one of the bigger commercial attractions of the book, that Murry had been a close friend and confidant of Lawrence, that made *Son of Woman* such a success and so damaging a work for serious Lawrence criticism. During the period 1926–31, Murry had established himself as the authoritative voice on Lawrence, publishing sixteen essays of reminiscence and criticism, including an eight-part monthly series, 'Reminiscences of D. H. Lawrence', in the *New Adelphi*, following the writer's death in March 1930. Amongst the flurry of obituaries, reviews and commentaries which appeared in 1930, Murry's own *New Adelphi* 110-page 'Special Edition' stood out as providing both first-hand knowledge of the subject and critical seriousness, with contributions by Rebecca West, Waldo Frank, James Young and Richard Rees. When *Son of Woman* did appear, then, it faced a virtually clear field and was assured of a healthy level of public interest – such interest having been nurtured not least by Murry's own *New Adelphi*.

To return to Colin Clarke's comments, above, there is no doubt that *Son of Woman*, whatever its shortcomings, did mark the starting point for serious study of Lawrence's work. Many of the assertions made in the book and many of the accusations levelled at Lawrence have formed the basis for later critical debates, as we shall see in many of the essays in this volume. In the short-term, however, its focus on the man as much as, and often more than, the writings, meant that *Son of Woman* only served to thicken the atmosphere of scandal and sensationalism which surrounded Lawrence in Europe.

As Aldous Huxley assembled and edited Lawrence's letters for publication, during the year following the publication of *Son of Woman*, it was absolutely apparent to him that a clear and less partisan approach to his subject was needed to revive some critical sanity about Lawrence. As a firm friend of both the Lawrences, but possessing sufficient self-awareness to respect Lawrence's talent without becoming a disciple of his views, Huxley was better placed than most to edit and introduce the first edition of the letters.

Huxley had first met Lawrence in 1913 as part of the literary circle who gathered (or were collected) regularly at Ottoline Morrell's country home, Garsington. They remained close throughout the rest of Lawrence's life, such that Huxley and his wife Maria helped Frieda nurse

Lawrence through his last days, and formed two of the group of ten people who attended his silent funeral at Vence cemetery. As a successful novelist and essayist, Huxley had no need or desire to seek fame from his association with Lawrence, and, as his introduction to the *Letters* makes clear, he understood more about the creative and artistic aspects of Lawrence's personality than anyone who wrote about him during the Thirties.

The extract that follows is taken from Huxley's long introduction to the *Letters* – an essay which both acts as a rejoinder to Murry's attacks in *Son of Woman*, and as a starting point for a new consideration of Lawrence as a committed and selfless artist who obeyed the 'gift' he had been given to render 'the immediately experienced otherness in terms of literary art.' In the midst of the publishing frenzy that marked the years after Lawrence's death, Huxley's essay offers a powerful antidote to the heated outpourings of the numerous memoirists who claimed Lawrence as their own – for Huxley, Lawrence had no belonging but to his art.

It is impossible to write about Lawrence except as an artist. He was an artist first of all, and the fact of his being an artist explains a life which seems, if you forget it, inexplicably strange. In *Son of Woman*, Mr. Middleton Murry has written at great length about Lawrence – but about a Lawrence whom you would never suspect, from reading that curious essay in destructive hagiography, of being an artist. For Mr. Murry almost completely ignores the fact that his subject – his victim, I had almost said – was one whom "the fates had stigmatised 'writer.'" His book is *Hamlet* without the Prince of Denmark – for all its metaphysical subtleties and its Freudian ingenuities, very largely irrelevant. The absurdity of his critical method becomes the more manifest when we reflect that nobody would ever have heard of a Lawrence who was not an artist.

An artist is the sort of artist he is, because he happens to possess certain gifts. And he leads the sort of life he does in fact lead, because he is an artist, and an artist with a particular kind of mental endowment. Now there are general abilities and there are special talents. A man who is born with a great share of some special talent is probably less deeply affected by nurture than one whose ability is generalised. His gift is his fate, and he follows a predestined course, from which no ordinary power can deflect him.

. . . Lawrence's biography does not account for Lawrence's achievement. On the contrary, his achievement, or rather the gift that made the achievement possible, accounts for a great deal of his biography. He lived as he lived, because he was, intrinsically and from birth, what he was. If we would write intelligibly of Lawrence, we must answer, with all their implications, two questions: first, what sort of gifts did he have? and secondly, how did the possession of these gifts affect the way he responded to experience?

Lawrence's special, and characteristic, gift was an extraordinary sensitiveness to what Wordsworth called "unknown modes of being." He was always intensely aware of the mystery of the world, and the mystery was always for him a *numen*, divine. Lawrence could never forget, as most of us almost continuously forget, the dark presence of the otherness that lies beyond the boundaries of man's conscious mind. This special sensibility was accompanied by a prodigious power of rendering the immediately experienced otherness in terms of literary art. Such was Lawrence's peculiar gift. His possession of it accounts for many things. It accounts, to begin with, for his attitude towards sex. His particular experiences as a son and as a lover may have intensified his preoccupation with the subject; but they certainly did not make it. Whatever his experiences, Lawrence *must* have been preoccupied with sex; his gift made it inevitable. For Lawrence, the significance of the sexual experience was this: that, in it, the immediate, nonmental knowledge of divine otherness is brought, so to speak, to a focus – a focus of darkness. Parodying Matthew Arnold's famous formula, we may say that sex is something not ourselves that makes for – not righteousness, for the essence of religion is not righteousness; there is a spiritual world, as Kierkegaard insists, beyond the ethical – rather, that makes for life, for divineness, for union with the mystery. Paradoxically, this something not ourselves is yet a something lodged within us; this quintessence of otherness is yet the quintessence of our proper being. "And God the Father, the Inscrutable, the Unknowable, we know in the flesh, in Woman. She is the door for our in-going and our out-coming. In her we go back to the Father; but like the witnesses of the transfiguration, blind and unconscious." Yes, blind and unconscious; otherwise it is a revelation, not of divine otherness, but of very human evil. "The embrace of love, which should bring darkness and oblivion, would with these lovers (the hero and heroine of one of Poe's tales) be a daytime thing, bringing more heightened consciousness, visions, spectrum-visions, prismatic. The evil thing that daytime love-making is, and all sex-palaver!" How Lawrence hated Eleonora and Ligeia and Roderick Usher and all such soulful Mrs. Shandies, male as well as female! What a horror, too, he had of all Don Juans, all knowing sensualists and conscious libertines! (About the time he was writing *Lady Chatterley's Lover* he read the memoirs of Casanova and was profoundly shocked.) And how bitterly he loathed the Wilhelm-Meisterish view of love as an education, as a means to culture, a Sandow-exerciser for the soul! To *use* love in this way, consciously and deliberately, seemed to Lawrence wrong, almost a blasphemy. "It seems to me queer," he says to a fellow writer, "that you prefer to present men chiefly – as if you cared for women not so much for what they were in themselves as for what the men saw in them. So that after all in your work women seem not to have an existence, save they are the projections of the men . . . It's the *positivity* of women you seem to deny – make them sort of instrumental." The instrumentality of Wilhelm Meister's women shocked Lawrence profoundly.

(Here, in a parenthesis, let me remark on the fact that Lawrence's doctrine is constantly invoked by people, of whom Lawrence himself would passionately have disapproved, in defence of a behaviour, which he would have found deplorable or even revolting. That this should have happened is by no means, of course, a condemnation of the doctrine. The same philosophy of life may be good or bad according as the person who accepts it and lives by it is intrinsically fine or base. Tartuffe's doctrine was the same, after all, as Pascal's. There have been refined fetish-worshippers, and unspeakably swinish Christians. To the preacher of a new way of life the most depressing thing that can happen is, surely, success. For success permits him to see how those he has converted distort and debase and make ignoble parodies of his teaching. If Francis of Assisi had lived to be a hundred, what bitterness he would have tasted! Happily for the saint, he died at forty-five, still relatively undisillusioned, because still on the threshold of the great success of his order. Writers influence their readers, preachers their auditors – but always, at bottom, to be more themselves. If the reader's self happens to be intrinsically similar to the writer's, then the influence is what the writer would wish it to be. If he is intrinsically unlike the writer, then he will probably twist the writer's doctrine into a rationalisation of beliefs, an excuse for behaviour, wholly alien to the beliefs and behaviour approved by the writer. Lawrence has suffered the fate of every man whose works have exercised an influence upon his fellows. It was inevitable and in the nature of things.)

. . . It was the same in the sphere of ethics as in that of art. "They want me to have form: that means, they want me to have their pernicious, ossiferous, skin-and-grief form, and I won't." This was written about his novels; but it is just as applicable to his life. Every man, Lawrence insisted, must be an artist in life, must create his own moral form. The art of living is harder than the art of writing. "It is a much more delicate thing, to make love and win love than to declare love." All the more reason, therefore, for practising this art with the most refined and subtle sensibility; all the more reason for not accepting that "pernicious skin-and-grief form" of morality, which *they* are always trying to impose on one. It is the business of the sensitive artist in life to accept his own nature as it is, not to try to force it into another shape. He must take the material given him – the weaknesses and irrationalities, as well as the sense and the virtues; the mysterious darkness and otherness no less than the light of reason and the conscious ego – must take them all and weave them together into a satisfactory pattern; *his* pattern, not somebody else's pattern. "Once I said to myself: 'How can I blame – why be angry?' . . . Now I say: 'When anger comes with bright eyes, he may do his will. In me he will hardly shake off the hand of God. He is one of the archangels, with a fiery sword. God sent him – it is beyond my knowing.'" This was written in 1910. Even at the very beginning of his career Lawrence was envisaging man as simply the locus of a polytheism. Given his particular gifts of sensitiveness and of expression it was inevitable. Just as it was inevitable that a man of Blake's peculiar genius should formulate the very similar doctrine of the independence of states of being. All the generally accepted systems of philosophy and of ethics aim at policing man's polytheism in the name of some Jehovah of intellectual and moral consistency. For Lawrence this was an indefensible proceeding. One god had as much right to exist as another, and the dark ones were as genuinely divine as the bright. Perhaps (since Lawrence was so specially sensitive to the quality of dark godhead and so specially gifted to express it in art), perhaps even more divine. Anyhow, the polytheism was a democracy. This conception of human nature resulted in the formulation of two rather surprising doctrines, one ontological and the other ethical. The first is what I may call the Doctrine of Cosmic Pointlessness. "There is no point. Life and Love are life and love, a bunch of violets is a bunch of violets, and to drag in the idea of a point is to ruin everything. Live and let live, love and let love, flower and fade, and follow the natural curve, which flows on, pointless."

Ontological pointlessness has its ethical counterpart in the doctrine of insouciance. "They simply are eaten up with caring. They are so busy caring about Fascism or Leagues of Nations or whether France is right or whether Marriage is threatened, that they never know where they are. They certainly never live on the spot where they are. They inhabit abstract space, the desert void of politics, principles, right and wrong, and so forth. They are doomed to be abstract. Talking to them is like trying to have a human relationship with the letter x in algebra." As early as 1911 his advice to his sister was: "Don't meddle with religion. I would leave all that alone, if I were you, and try to occupy myself fully in the present."

. . . Lawrence's dislike of abstract knowledge and pure spirituality made him a kind of mystical materialist. Thus, the moon affects him strongly; therefore it cannot be a "stony cold world, like a world of our own gone cold. Nonsense. It is a globe of dynamic substance, like radium or phosphorus, coagulated upon a vivid pole of energy."

Matter must be intrinsically as lively as the mind which perceives it and is moved by the perception. Vivid and violent spiritual effects must have correspondingly vivid and violent material causes. And, conversely, any violent feeling or desire in the mind must be capable of producing violent effects upon external matter. Lawrence could not bring himself to believe that the spirit can be moved, moved if need be, to madness, without imparting the smallest corresponding movement to the external world. He was a subjectivist as well as a materialist; in other words, he believed in the possibility, in some form or another, of magic. Lawrence's mystical materialism found characteristic expression in the curious cosmology and physiology of his speculative essays, and in his restatement of the strange Christian doctrine of the resurrection of the body. To his mind, the survival of the spirit was not enough; for the spirit is a man's conscious identity, and Lawrence did not want to be always identical to himself, he wanted to know otherness – to know it by being it, know it in the living flesh, which is always essentially *other*. Therefore there must be a resurrection of the body.

Loyalty to his genius left him no choice; Lawrence had to insist on those mysterious forces of otherness which are scattered without, and darkly concentrated within, the body and mind of man. He had to, even though, by doing so, he imposed upon himself, as a writer of novels, a very serious handicap. For according to his view of things most men's activities were more or less criminal distractions from the proper business of human living. He refused to write of such distractions; that is to say, he refused to write of the main activities of the contemporary world. But as though this drastic limitation of his subject were not sufficient, he went still further and, in some of his novels, refused even to write of human personalities in the accepted sense of the term. *The Rainbow* and *Women in Love* (and indeed to a lesser extent all his novels) are the practical applications of a theory, which is set forth in a very interesting and important letter to Edward Garnett, dated June 5th, 1914. "Somehow, that which is physic – nonhuman in humanity, is more interesting to me than the old-fashioned human element, which causes one to conceive a character in a certain moral scheme and make him consistent. The certain moral scheme is what I object to. In Turgenev, and in Tolstoi, and in Dostoievsky, the moral scheme into which all the characters fit – and it is nearly the same scheme – is, whatever the extraordinariness of the characters themselves, dull, old, dead. When Marinetti writes: 'It is the solidity of a blade of steel that is interesting by itself, that is, the incomprehending and inhuman alliance of its molecules in resistance to, let us say, a bullet. The heat of a piece of wood or iron is in fact more passionate, for us, than the laughter or tears of a woman' – then I know what he means. He is stupid, as an artist, for contrasting the heat of the iron and the laugh of the woman. Because what is interesting in the laugh of the woman is the same as the binding of the molecules of steel or their action in heat: it is the inhuman will, call it physiology, or like Marinetti, physiology of matter, that fascinates me. I don't so much care about what the woman *feels* – in the ordinary usage of the word. That presumes an *ego* to feel with. I only care about what the woman is – what she is – inhumanly physiologically, materially – according to the use of the word . . . You mustn't look in my novel for the old stable ego of the character. There is another ego, according to whose action the individual is unrecognisable, and passes through, as it were, allotropic states which it needs a deeper sense than any we've been used to exercise, to discover are states of the same single radically unchanged element. (Like as diamond and coal are the same pure single element of carbon. The ordinary novel would trace the history of the diamond – but I say, 'Diamond, what! This is carbon.' And my diamond might be coal or soot, and my theme is carbon.)"

. . . Psychological reality, like physical reality, is determined by our mental and bodily make-up. Common sense, working on the evidence supplied by our unaided senses, postulates a world in which physical reality consists of such things as solid tables and chairs, bits of coal, water, air. Carrying its investigations further, science discovers that these samples of physical reality are "really" composed of atoms of different elements, and these atoms, in their turn, are "really" composed of more or less numerous electrons and protons arranged in a variety of patterns. Similarly, there is a common-sense, pragmatic conception of psychological reality; and also an un-common-sense conception. For ordinary practical purposes we conceive human beings as creatures with characters. But analysis of their behaviour can be carried so far, that they cease to have characters and reveal themselves as collections of psychological atoms. Lawrence (as might have been expected of a man who could always perceive the otherness behind the most reassuringly familiar phenomenon) took the un-commonsense view of psychology. Hence the strangeness of his novels; and hence also, it must be admitted, certain qualities of violent monotony and intense indistinctness, qualities which make some of them, for all their richness and their unexpected beauty, so curiously difficult to get through. Most of us are more interested in diamonds and coal than in undifferentiated carbon, however vividly described. I have known readers whose reaction to Lawrence's books was very much the same as Lawrence's own reaction to the theory of evolution. What he wrote meant nothing to them because they "did not feel it here" – in the solar plexus. (That Lawrence, the hater of scientific knowing, should have applied to psychology methods which he himself compared to those of chemical analysis, may seem strange. But we must remember that his analysis was done, not intellectually, but by an immediate process of intuition; that he was able, as it were, to *feel* the carbon in diamonds and coal, to *taste* the hydrogen and oxygen in his glass of water.)

Lawrence, then, possessed, or, if you care to put it the other way round, was possessed by, a gift – a gift to which he was unshakeably loyal. I have tried to show how the possession and the loyalty influenced his thinking and writing. How did they affect his life? The answer shall be, as far as possible, in Lawrence's own words. To Catherine Carswell Lawrence once wrote . . . "I think you are the only woman I have met who is so intrinsically detached, so essentially separate and isolated, as to be a real writer or artist or recorder. Your relations with other people are only excursions from yourself. And to want children, and common human fulfilments, is rather a falsity for you, I think. You were never made to 'meet and mingle,' but to remain intact, *essentially*, whatever your experiences may be."[19]

Such identification of artistry in others can come only, as Huxley suggests, from an artist who himself remained 'intact, *essentially* . . .'

The essay speaks clearly of the energy and determination of the Lawrence who wrote *The Rainbow* and *Women in Love*, in place of the crippled genius suggested by Murry's work. Huxley also manages to avoid the wilder flights of fancy or hero-worship that characterise the efforts of Lawrence's other more protective memoirists during the early Thirties, so that we are left with a more balanced image of Lawrence than was provided by any other commentator on his life until the early 1950s. There is in Huxley's account (a little over half of which is extracted here) clear recognition of Lawrence's greatness as a writer – but equal recognition that he could be a difficult and contradictory person.

Despite the quality of Huxley's prose, and the honesty with which he treats Lawrence, we are still left with a stronger impression of the artist than the art itself. Whilst such an outcome was entirely fitting for an introduction to a collection of letters, and clearly served Huxley's purpose in dismissing the more ill-judged and venomous memoirs of Murry and others, it does little to shed light on the works themselves. We are left with a much more rounded picture of the writer, but still the nature of Lawrence's 'gift' remains something of a mystery.

Huxley's essay did help to address the more scurrilous and inaccurate judgements made of Lawrence by his contemporaries, but the general public impression of him as a haunted and somehow dangerous artist was nonetheless established and shaped by Murry's *Son of Woman*, despite Huxley's efforts. When, in 1933, T. S. Eliot published *After Strange Gods: A Primer in Modern Heresy*, which examined the works from an orthodox Christian standpoint, Lawrence's reputation as a 'heretic' and as a threat to literary tradition and Christian values seemed to be confirmed in both artist and art.[20] The attack on Lawrence was one of several made by Eliot during the Thirties, but by far the most sustained and damaging to Lawrence's reputation in Britain and America.

Eliot found in Lawrence's writing 'exceptionally acute perception, or profound insight, of some part of the truth' – but a tendency to identify the ills and sicknesses of modern society without offering any hopes of salvation or regeneration. For Eliot, Lawrence seemed to turn away from orthodoxy and from the strength of tradition which helped establish coherence and spiritual order in society, offering instead a call to those who would work towards the collapse of moral values: 'a man like Lawrence – with his acute sensibility, violent prejudices and passions – lack of intellectual and social training – and a soul destitute of humility and filled with self-righteousness is a blind servant and a fatal leader.'

During the course of his argument against Lawrence, Eliot calls for support on Wyndham Lewis's essay of 1927, 'Paleface; or, "Love? What ho! Smelling Strangeness"',[21] which accuses Lawrence of offering 'an invitation to suicide addressed to the White Man'. Lewis's contention was that Lawrence had been sufficiently influenced by the philosophies of Bergson and Spengler to advocate the limitation of intellect and rational thought in favour of the instinctive, 'soulless' ways of 'Primitive Man'. He accuses Lawrence of indulging in a 'romantic primitivism', of glorifying the 'backward cults' which are to be found in the societies and ways of 'the primitive Indian or the Black' – at the expense of the 'superior' beliefs and structures erected in the name of (white) civilisation and intellectual classicism.

Both Lewis and Eliot seemed unaware that their racial and cultural arrogance, and their blind advocacy of a value-system in danger of rapid disintegration under the strains of modernity actually posed powerful arguments *in favour* of Lawrence's call for a re-valuation of human society and relations. That their assumptions and arguments should have been so little challenged in either the popular or intellectual press of the day, however, speaks clearly of the threat that Lawrence's work was still thought to pose to the traditions and cultural norms of Western society during the early Thirties.[22]

The economic hardships of the early-Thirties Depression and the ominous events unfolding in Europe during the second part of the decade tended to draw interest away from Lawrence's work and ideas. Where he was discussed, he tended increasingly to be 'claimed' by those supporting particular political movements, or castigated by those (usually on the Left) who felt he had failed to develop a workable political philosophy.

With the rise of fascism in Germany, Spain and Italy, Lawrence's negative views on democracy and his belief in the need for strong leadership in any successful society led to some debate about his relationship to, or support of, the ideas underpinning fascism. In 1934 John Strachey had written *Literature and Dialectical Materialism*, in which he attacked Lawrence for abandoning his working class roots and joining the bourgeoisie. Though not actually claiming Lawrence had espoused fascist views, Strachey did argue that his language and ideology were examples of a drift into 'the school of "the fascist unconscious."' During the years 1936 and 1937, the arguments over Lawrence's fascist tendencies occupied a more prominent place amongst the articles and books written: of the sixteen published works on Lawrence, five were concerned with his alignment to fascist thinking. Increasingly, also, the press on Lawrence and his work was taking a more European flavour. Jacques Debu-Bridel reviewed *Aaron's Rod* for *Nouvelle Revue Française*, and found strong links between the politics of the novel and the ideas found in Hitler's *Mein Kampf*.[23] Ernest Seillière argued in *David Herbert Lawrence et les Récentes Idéologies Allemandes* that Lawrence's work was heavily influenced by the writings of a number of German Romanticists, particularly Ludwig Klages, whose ideas had assumed a powerful position in the Nazi ideology. Seillière further argued that Lawrence's interest in *Blutbrüderschaft* was threatening to relations between men and women, and that the whole philosophical base of Lawrence's ideas tended towards the negative aspects of humanity rather than the positive.[24]

The publication of *Phoenix: The Posthumous Papers of D. H. Lawrence*[25] in 1936 was a significant event in itself, for it showed that there was still interest in Lawrence and his ideas. But, after the initial reviews of the collection (which commented mostly on the book's ability to tell readers about Lawrence himself, rather than his work) the most thoroughly developed debate amongst critics centred on whether or not *Phoenix* demonstrated Lawrence's alignment to fascist ideas. In a series of letters and essays that was carried by the journal *New Republic* through 1936 and into 1937, Granville Hicks, Arvin Newton and T. K. Whipple argued that there were fascist sentiments which acted as a base to Lawrence's work, while Harry T. Wells argued (twice) that there was no evidence for such argument, and that, in fact, Lawrence could be seen as a proletarian writer.[26]

The outbreak of war in Europe in 1939 meant that the level of publication on all subjects declined sharply, and in the case of critical writing on Lawrence, almost to nothing. The pre-war debate on Lawrence's political stance was never fully resolved because publication about him practically ceased during the war years. In 1942, the lowest point of his critical history, there were only six published articles or essays on Lawrence.

With peace in 1945, the level of interest in Lawrence's work began to revive. The publication of the *Viking Portable D. H. Lawrence* in 1947 marked a renewal of interest in his work amongst readers in America, and later, in Britain, when the volume was re-issued as *The Indispensable D. H. Lawrence* in 1950.[27] The increasing availability of the novels themselves towards the end of the Forties and into the early Fifties helped pave the way for the 'Lawrence revival' – which forms the substance of the next chapter of this book.

# CHAPTER THREE

# The 'Lawrence Revival'

I T IS always hard to account for the major change in critical status and reputation of the sort that affected Lawrence. Usually the factors involved in such a re-appraisal and revival are many, involving a shift in societal attitudes, a change in publication practice, and a change in attitude amongst critics and academics. Where these overlap, and where they are dependent upon one another is difficult to decide, even in hindsight. Usually it is a case of several factors occurring coincidentally, each giving force and encouragement to the other.

In their introduction to *Critical Essays on D. H. Lawrence*, Dennis and Fleda Brown Jackson offer some linked reasons for the comparatively sudden interest in Lawrence's work after such a long period of neglect:

Several things help to explain why the climate of opinion regarding Lawrence's status changed so markedly during the 1950s. Enough time had passed to allow the battle smoke to clear from most of the violent controversies that his life and art had sparked decades earlier. Moreover, as [William York] Tindall has observed [in his book *Forces in Modern British Literature, 1885–1946* (1947)], Lawrence's ideas seemed more serious and acceptable to readers at mid-century. Also, western society by that time had developed more permissive standards regarding sexual behaviour so Lawrence's writings about sex no longer seemed as shockingly "licentious" as they had to earlier readers. Thus the way was cleared for readers to make a more discerning estimate of his life and work, and by mid-century a critical and biographical "revival" of his reputation was under way. Concurrent with and more important than all the writings about Lawrence then was the large-scale reprinting of his own works in England and America. During the decade Heinemann published in its hardbound "Phoenix" series ten of his novels and a good deal of the rest of his canon, and Penguin Books issued many of his works in cheap paperback editions, thus making his literature available to a much wider audience.[1]

Running alongside the public's and publishers' revival of interest in the works themselves was a new, more reasoned and scholarly interest in Lawrence's life and ideas. The personalised memoirs and quasi-psychological analyses of the Thirties (as discussed in Chapter 2) now gave way to biographies and critical biographies which examined the works through the various stages and reference-points of Lawrence's life. Two of the most memorable and durable of the new breed of biographies came from the American academic Harry T. Moore, who published in 1951 *The Life and Works of D. H. Lawrence*, and, in 1954, *The Intelligent Heart* (which was later reprinted, enlarged and revised, as *The Priest of Love* in 1974).[2]

Moore's earlier book takes as a framework for the analysis of Lawrence's life and work four major stages in his artistic development, within each of which he examines the works completed. In the section of the book which deals with the phase of Lawrence's life when he wrote *The Rainbow* and *Women in Love*, 1913–19, the novels are judged to possess an integration of style and form not matched in earlier or later works. In Moore's discussion of the two novels also, we find an early expression of their primacy in the Lawrence canon – a point which F. R. Leavis was later to champion.

*The Intelligent Heart*, though 'essentially a biography' as Moore intended, did rely on 'critical values' to underpin its discussion of Lawrence's life. The book brought much new material to light and gave readers access to hitherto unknown aspects of Lawrence's early life, beliefs and experiences, which would contribute to the new reading of his works. Moore's dispassionate and meticulously researched account of the artist's life played a significant part in laying to rest many of the assumptions and prejudices that had dogged public (mis)understanding of the writer and his creative influences – and the book, in its revised form, is still regarded as one of the finest biographies of Lawrence.

In 1955, a year after the publication of *The Intelligent Heart*, a book was published which contributed more than any other to the revival of Lawrence's critical reputation. F. R. Leavis's *D. H. Lawrence: Novelist* made a full assault on 'the grosser stupidities of our intellectual élite', who had failed or denied the 'profound originality' of Lawrence's work. For Leavis, there was absolutely no doubt that 'the failure of criticism and of the cultivated in respect of Lawrence, the long unchecked prevalence of misrepresentation and malice, is a disgraceful chapter of English literary history.'[3]

Leavis (1895–1978) was a major force in English criticism from the early Thirties until the early Sixties, and it is hard to overstate his contribution to the restoration of Lawrence's reputation as a great creative writer and literary influence. He began teaching at Cambridge in the Twenties and found the methods of criticism there, and in most academic institutions, to be impressionistic and largely driven by concern with the life and psychology of the author. (Some of the earlier works dealt with in this volume – notably Middleton Murry's *Son of Woman* – offer clear examples of this approach.)

Leavis, along with many other critics (including T. S. Eliot), began to push English criticism towards a 'close reading' of text, maintaining a view of the written work as an independent and self-sufficient object whose complex and inter-related components are founded and held in the specifically literary language of the work at hand. Though never strictly a New Critic, Leavis's methods and approaches have much in common with the American school of New Criticism, which dominated the critical scene until the late 1950s. (The New Critical method originated chiefly in I. A. Richards's work *Principles of Literary Criticism* in 1924, and finally inherited its popular title after the publication of John Crowe Ransom's *The New Criticism* in 1941.) It was Leavis who effected the move away from the 'pure' and 'contextual' practices of early New Criticism, to a broader critical method which, though it retained the close reading of the New Criticism, gave more attention to moral values and spiritual imperatives in literary works. To many of the early New Critics, Lawrence had been (to quote T. S. Eliot) a 'heretic', standing outside accepted boundaries of belief and creed. With Leavis's broader definitions of the 'moral' and 'spiritual', Lawrence could be accommodated in the fold.

It was Leavis's primary aim to refute the errors of critical judgement that had led to Lawrence's works being maligned, underestimated or ignored during the previous decades, by means of a close analysis and evaluation of the major texts and a discussion of their relation to what he called The Great Tradition of the English novel – existing in the work of Jane Austen, George Eliot, Henry James and Joseph Conrad. It was Leavis who succeeded in establishing *The Rainbow* and *Women in Love* as Lawrence's greatest works, who brought to critical notice the tales and novellas, and who finally quashed the more outrageous misconceptions about Lawrence and his ideas.

In his examination of the novels, Leavis took pains to address the most common complaints made about Lawrence's style and philosophy since the publication of *The Rainbow*. Through his discussion of the individual works Leavis dismisses the widely-held view that Lawrence was 'a genius, but . . .' by arguing that he possessed a fine intelligence and sharp intellectual judgement grounded on wide reading and a solid education. Also, Leavis refuted the claim that Lawrence was sex-obsessed – or in T. S. Eliot's phrase, possessed of 'sexual morbidity' – by pointing to the great human concerns of the novels, and the ways in which Lawrence only regarded sex and sexual relations as a means to proper moral and spiritual fulfilment for men and women. The charge that Lawrence consistently failed to achieve a satisfactory unity in his novels is countered by a treatment of *The Rainbow* and *Women in Love* as 'dramatic poems' in which each image, scene, action or character interaction serves only to develop and bring to fruition the major themes of the novels.

There is insufficient room in this volume to do anything but provide the reader with a general sense of Leavis's concerns and arguments: to realise the full force of those arguments, *D. H Lawrence: Novelist* must be read in its entirety. The readings of *The Rainbow* and *Women in Love* are, even at a distance of more than forty years, fresh, persuasive and frequently surprising. To encounter Leavis for the first time is to encounter the beginnings and foundations of modern Lawrence criticism – for there exists little today in discussions of Lawrence's work which does not have its origins in, or take its point of departure from, Leavis's analysis.

The extract that follows is taken from the book's first chapter, 'Lawrence and Art', in which Leavis outlines and refutes many of the complaints made against Lawrence by so many of his critics:

*What*, above all, is Lawrence? As what shall we primarily think of him? There has always been a readiness to think of him as a genius; but as what, above all, has he established his indisputable existence and his permanence?

The answer that T. S. Eliot made a point of disputing at the time when Lawrence, having died, was being dismissed to a long relegation from among living subjects would, I think, be pretty generally accepted: Lawrence is a great artist, a creative writer. It is an answer I like, and, in fact, had myself proposed at that now distant time; but it is not delimiting enough. It does not exclude with sufficient finality the view, expressed by Desmond MacCarthy – expressed, then, not for the first or the last time . . . that Lawrence has close affinities with Carlyle. Nor does it exclude the view that his genius is above all 'lyrical', and that in the novels it is to be found pre-eminently in the 'descriptive writing' and in the poetic evocation of scenes, environments, and atmospheres.

What needs to be said is this: Lawrence is before all else a great novelist, one of the very greatest, and it is as one of the major novelists of the English tradition that he will above all live. To give the proposition its due force I have to refer to a conception of the history of prose fiction in English that I have proposed elsewhere. It involves the view that, if depth, range, and subtlety in the presentment of human experience are the criteria, then in the work of the great novelists from Jane Austen to Lawrence – I think Hawthorne, Dickens, George Eliot, Henry James, Melville, Mark Twain, Conrad – we have a creative achievement that is unsurpassed; unsurpassed by any of the famous phases or chapters of literary history. In these great novelists . . . we have the successors of Shakespeare; for in the nineteenth century and later the strength – the poetic and creative strength – of the English language goes into prose fiction. In comparison, the formal poetry is a marginal affair. And the achievement of T. S. Eliot, remarkable as it was, did not reverse the relation. This is a truth that adds an irony to the insistent leading part played by Eliot in retarding the recognition of Lawrence . . . The point I am making is that Lawrence is incomparably the greatest creative writer in English of our time – if I say, of Eliot's time, I make plain the phase of our civilisation that is in question; he is one of the greatest English writers of any time; and, in the nature of his greatness, has his significant relation with what is most vital in the century before him.

His genius is distinctively that of a novelist, and as such he is as remarkable a technical innovator as there has ever been. It is *The Rainbow* and *Women in Love* that most demand attention. The need is to get recognition for the kind of major achievement they are. Together they constitute his greatest work, or perhaps it is better to say that, in their curious close relation and their separateness, they are his two greatest works. They represent the enormous labour, the defining of interests and methods, the exploration, the technical innovation, on which the case of the later work is based. This is not to dismiss *Sons and Lovers*, which is certainly a work of striking original genius. But *Sons and Lovers* has not lacked attention; it has been widely appreciated, and the nature of its originality recognised. And for my purpose, which demands a close insistence on the essential, there would be little point in giving the book a fresh examination here. Remarkable as it is, its qualities and its achievement, on the one hand, are obvious enough, and, on the other, they are not, I think, such as to suggest that the author was going to be a great novelist.

. . . With *Sons and Lovers* Lawrence put something behind him. Not for nothing did he warn Edward Garnett not to expect anything else of that kind: 'I shan't write in the same manner as *Sons and Lovers* again.'[4] Lawrence, of course, has more than one subsequent 'manner', but what he is recognising here is that he has put something behind him for good. The acute emotional problem or disorder which queered his personal relations and the play of his intelligence has been placed – has been conquered by intelligence, manifesting and vindicating itself in creative art. He is now freed for the work of the greatest kind of artist.

It is *The Rainbow* and *Women in Love*, written during the next few years – from early 1913 on – that prove him to be that. I should have said that they prove it triumphantly and incontestably if the depressing fact of history had not been what it is: they have had essentially no recognition at all. Not only has the supreme creative achievement they represent been ignored; the grossest untruths about Lawrence's attitudes – untruths running clean counter to the spirit and actuality of that achievement, as of his work everywhere – have been freely current, and accepted generally for the unquestioned truth about him. In fact, the record in respect of him stands out even in the annals of the treatment of great original writers. It is the more notable in that from the beginning Lawrence has been recognised to have 'genius' – 'genius' was the accepted word, and yet not only was his genius abusively denatured and its greatness denied while he lived; even after his death, which might have been expected to be followed by the irony of decisive recognition and a rapidly spreading enlightenment, the misrepresentation held the field for two decades.

This is partly to be explained by the fact that his death coincided with the opening of a particularly bad phase of English literary history – or of the English literary world. It coincided with the arrival of Auden. In the period in which Auden was so rapidly established as a major poet and remained one for so long, and Spender became overnight the modern Shelley, it was not to be expected that the portrayer of Rico would receive the sympathetic attention denied him in the emancipated twenties. The period of the Poetical Renaissance was as little favourable to intelligence about Lawrence as that dominated by the ethos of the old Bloomsbury had been . . .

For the grosser stupidities of our intellectual *élite* at Lawrence's expense the explanation must be discreditable to the English literary world of the last decades; but of course *The Rainbow* and *Women in Love* – to come back to these works in particular – can hardly have been altogether understood by anyone at first reading. They present a difficulty that is a measure of their profound originality. Lawrence's art in them is so original in its methods and procedures that at first we again and again fail to recognise what it is doing or what it is offering – we miss the point. And this technical originality was entailed by the originality of what Lawrence had to convey. The important truths about human experience are not necessarily at once obvious. The importance of some is to be measured by the difficulty with which we recognise them. They have no place in our habits of conscious thought, and what we say and what we believe with our conscious minds ignores or denies them.[5] Lawrence's insight was penetrating and clear, and he was marvellously intelligent, and the worst difficulty we have in coming to terms with his art is that there is resistance in us to what it has to communicate – if only the kind of resistance represented by habit; habit that will not let us see what is there for what it is, or believe that the door is open. And learning to recognise the success and the greatness of *Women in Love* – I speak for myself – was not merely a matter of applying one's mind in repeated re-readings and so mastering the methods of the art and the nature of the organisation; it was a matter, too, of growing – growing into understanding.

Yet it remains true that the failure of criticism and of the cultivated in respect of Lawrence, the long unchecked prevalence of misrepresentation and malice, is a disgraceful chapter of English literary history.

. . . He was certainly unfortunate in the phases of English literary culture and of the English literary world that have marked those decades. It has to be recorded, as among the adverse conditions, that he had against him the major personal influence of the time (and it was a peculiarly powerful and pervasive one for a good many years) – the major personal influence in the climate of literary opinion: that of T. S. Eliot. It was not merely that the literary and intellectual fashions promoted by Eliot were inimical to the appreciation of Lawrence's genius. The sad and undeniable fact is that Eliot did all that his immense prestige and authority *could* do to make the current stupidities about Lawrence look respectable. He talked of Lawrence's 'sexual morbidity' as of a *donnée* that needed no arguing. He made a point of denying that Lawrence could properly be called an artist.[6] It is in keeping with this denial that he should have been able to pronounce Lawrence incapable of 'what we ordinarily call thinking',[7] subscribing thus to the general view that, wherever Lawrence's strength might lie, it was not, emphatically not, in intelligence. Of Lawrence's novels he spoke (addressing the public of *La Nouvelle Revue Française*) as '*extrêmement mal écrits*'.[8] A quarter of a century later, having perhaps noted that this compact and memorable judgement had been challenged, he emended it to: 'To me, also, he seems often to write very badly: but to be a writer who had to write often badly in order to write sometimes well.'[9]

One wouldn't, it is true, call Lawrence, any more than one would call Shakespeare, a 'stylist'; but he seems to me to be plainly one of the greatest masters of what is certainly one of the greatest of languages; and I have already stated my conviction that as a creative writer he is of the greatest kind . . . But it is, I think, worth inquiring at this point how, if I am right in sum about Lawrence's genius and achievement, a mind capable of Eliot's best criticism can have been so wrong in matters so important. It is worth inquiring because the challenge leads us to certain useful formulations regarding the nature of Lawrence's greatness and the significance of his work.

The answer, I think, is to be found in some things that Lawrence says about Flaubert and the conception of art Flaubert represents. He speaks, in a review of Thomas Mann,[10] of 'that will of the writer to be greater than the undisputed lord over the stuff he writes which is figured to the world in Gustav Flaubert'. It seems to him, he says, that 'this craving for form is the outcome, not of artistic conscience, but of a certain attitude to life'.

> Thomas Mann seems to me the last sick sufferer from the complaint of Flaubert. The latter stood away from life as from a leprosy. And Thomas Mann, like Flaubert, feels vaguely that he has in him something finer than ever physical life revealed. Physical life is a disordered corruption, against which he can fight with only one weapon, his fine aestheticism, his feeling for beauty, for perfection, for a certain fitness which soothes him, and gives him an inner pleasure, however corrupt the stuff of life may be.

One may not have thought of comparing Eliot's creative work to Flaubert's, but Eliot's attitude to life is, not less than Flaubert's, one of distaste and disgust. His art, consequently, is involved in the contradiction of which Flaubert is the great example. For it is, surely, a contradiction that Flaubert's case presents classically – all that would-be creative intensity, that intensity of 'doing', devoted to expressing attitudes in which distaste, disgust, and boredom have so decisive a part; a cult of art that amounts to a religion, and the directing spirit of it a rejection of life.

. . . It is the significance of that lamentable record at Lawrence's expense, that persisting and grievous default of intelligence in a gifted writer, that I have in mind in these observations. And it is plain, I think, that the significance is what I pointed to in Lawrence's diagnostic placing of Flaubert's and Mann's kind of addiction to art. Eliot's 'standing-off' from life – it can manifest itself when he is off guard in that *'afin de rendre l'amour supportable'*[11] – is certainly not a less intense or a less radical sickness of the spirit than Flaubert's.[12]

. . . The un-Flaubertian spirit of Lawrence's work, while producing its characteristic vital perfections, has of course its own tendencies to imperfection.

> 'Nothing outside the definite line of the book', is a maxim. But can the human mind fix absolutely the definite line of a book, any more than it can fix absolutely any definite line for a living being?[13]

Lawrence had not planned, or foreseen, the separating-out of *The Sisters* into *The Rainbow* and *Women in Love*. They represent, none the less, these novels, an immense labour of art, an untiring solicitude to get things right. His methods of work were characteristically un-Flaubertian (and un-Joycean). It is plain from the letters and other sources that he went forward rapidly once he had started on an enterprise, writing long stretches in remarkably little time as the creative flow carried him on. The first draft written, he revised, not by correcting locally or re-working parts, but by re-writing the whole with the same kind of creative *élan* as had gone to the earlier version (and this he habitually did yet again). His concern clearly was that the whole of himself should be engaged; that the book in its completeness should come from the living being. But, as he remarks in the passage I have just quoted, for a 'living being' it is not possible to fix 'any definite line'. Rapidly as he worked at *The Sisters*, he developed more rapidly and had to recognise that he had changed. It was that which determined the separating-off of *The Rainbow* as something complete and left behind. The conclusion with which, so to speak, he cut it loose is written in a momentarily recaptured spirit; a spirit that *The Rainbow* itself in its later part has outgrown, so that these closing pages come with a certain incongruity.[14]

In *Women in Love* there is no such embarrassing development; but it might be said in criticism of that novel that the normative aspiration it clearly represents is not as fully realised as Lawrence (one guesses) had, in the first conception, hoped: the diagnosis represented by Gerald and Gudrun is convincing – terribly so; but Birkin and Ursula as a norm, contemplated in the situation they are left in at the close of the book, leave us wondering (and, it must in fairness be added, leave Lawrence wondering too). That is, if a certain symmetry of negative and positive was aimed at in *Women in Love*, Lawrence has been defeated by the difficulty of life: he hasn't solved the problems of civilisation that he analyses. This criticism, if it is a criticism, is different in kind from that called for by the close of *The Rainbow*. And in any case, whatever criticisms may be urged against them, both books are, in sum, magnificently achieved great novels, major creations.

Lawrence never again worked at a novel in that way. He had embarked on the immense undertaking, the conception that was at first *The Sisters*, in the conviction that it challenged him with an inclusive significance the defining of which demanded, not only an originality of art locally and daring inventions of methods in the part, but resources of organisation in the whole as remarkable as any that had ever gone to a creative work. He doesn't seem to have been possessed again with a conviction of that kind – a conviction impelling him to a work of anything like that order. It might be said that the unsettled life foreshadowed in the close of *Women in Love* didn't favour such works. But the taking to such a mode of life is itself, of course, a significant fact.

To have had *The Rainbow* banned and to have been unable to publish *Women in Love* – this was a bad enough blow for Lawrence, isolated and without a public and unfriended among the powers of the contemporary literary world, and yet conscious of what he had achieved. But the major seismic experience was the war. The life dealt with in *The Rainbow* and *Women in Love* and the momentum carrying those works through belong to before the war. The spirit of *Women in Love* belongs to a phase when the Bottomley horror, the nightmare hopelessness of the later years through which the war dragged on, had not yet closed down on Lawrence. But already, before the war had made its decisive impact on him, he had had, in order to bring *The Rainbow* to a close, to recapture wilfully a buoyant note that, in his rapid development since beginning *The Sisters*, he had outgrown. The mood of *Women in Love* is not buoyant or sanguine. And to this inevitable growth – inevitable, with experience and advancing maturity, in a Lawrence – into something remote at any rate from easy hopefulness about modern civilisation the years from the Somme to the Armistice brought calamitous fostering.

But it was not in Lawrence's nature to rest in negation. He was acquainted with horror and foreboding and a state bordering on despair, but it was not possible for him to be defeatist. The affirmation of life was always strong in him, and he had always that profound sense of responsibility which, whatever one may conclude about some of its manifestations, is of his strength and his genius. ('But in the novel', he says in 'Why the Novel Matters', 'you can see, plainly, when the man goes dead, the woman goes inert. You can develop an instinct for life, if you will, instead of a theory of right and wrong, good and bad.') The novels that succeed *Women in Love* are exploratory and experimental. In them Lawrence lives his problems in a tentative and immediately personal way that gives these books a different status as works of art from that of *Women in Love* and *The Rainbow*.

Published in the same year as *D. H. Lawrence: Novelist* was American academic Mark Spilka's *The Love Ethic of D. H. Lawrence*.[15] Spilka stood amongst the younger generation of New Critics, and shared many of Leavis's views and definitions of literary worth. In *The Love Ethic of D. H. Lawrence*, Spilka sought to address the long-standing critical 'custom to divide D. H. Lawrence into aesthetic and prophetic halves, one of which wrote the good portions of his novels, the other the bad.' The solution to the problem of balancing the two parts of Lawrence's achievement was, according to Spilka, to see 'Lawrence as a religious artist, and [to accept] that all his work was governed by religious ends.' The novels were written in 'a kind of fourth-dimensional prose, so as to give the reader the effect of religious depth,' and were prophetic and didactic because Lawrence wanted to lead people to understand his vision. Thus, if the novels do read like sermons, it was because 'the art of the novel was the religious art for Lawrence.'[16]

In his book, Spilka discusses four of Lawrence's novels (*Sons and Lovers, The Rainbow, Women in Love, Lady Chatterley's Lover*), and the novella *The Man who Died*, attempting throughout to demonstrate 'that

Lawrence wrote about man in the universe, and that he tried to connect cosmology with psychology, or the "life-force" with a well-developed psychology of life.' The chapter on *The Rainbow* deals with the differences between Lawrence's and the Christian view of morality and meta-physics, and is followed by two chapters which examine the 'mystic marriage' between men and women, and the brotherhood-bond (*Blutbrüderschaft*) between men as explored in *Women in Love*.

One of the notable features of Spilka's analysis is the early recognition that Lawrence developed and discarded ideas throughout his fiction. The search is thus not for a fixed set of beliefs or principles in Lawrence's work, but for a series of 'testings' whereby the philosophies and concepts are thrown open to exploration and, if necessary, abandoned. In the extract reproduced here, taken from Spilka's chapter on blood-brotherhood and male-relations in *Women in Love*, we find a clear example of the process of testing to which Lawrence subjects his beliefs. The search for *Blutbrüderschaft* which occupies Birkin throughout the novel is explored by Spilka and set in the context of Lawrence's ongoing search for a meaningful addition to relations between men and women.

In the novel, Spilka argues, Lawrence finds the problems raised by a search for a non-sexual physical relationship to be insoluble: the ending of *Women in Love* clearly shows that there is no resolution and no fulfil-ment offered by *Blutbrüderschaft*. The search for a broader definition of relations between individuals is tested and explored further in the 'lord-ship theme' of the 'leadership' novels (specifically *Kangaroo* and *The Plumed Serpent*), and eventually settled in the 'tenderness theme' of *Lady Chatterley's Lover*.

The extract which follows also allows for a look back at earlier assess-ments of Lawrence's techniques and ideas, in particular, to Middleton Murry's *Son of Woman*. Spilka's discussion of the organic and spiritual elements of Lawrence's work offers a far more satisfactory explanation for what takes place within *Women in Love* than Murry's aggressively psychologising account. The comparison gives us, also, a startling example of the developments in Lawrence criticism across a quarter-century.

**Lawrence belongs to that school of writers whose work is often more explorative, more interrogative, than affirmative.[17] His function is to ask new questions, to confront us with new values and inescapable contradictions – or in his own words, to "lead into new places the flow of our sympathetic consciousness, and [to] lead our sympathy away in recoil from things gone dead." Thus he shows us Paul Morel, at the end of *Sons and Lovers*, stepping out quickly in a new direction, away from his three discarded loves; or Ursula Brangwen, in *The Rainbow*, facing that radiant arch expectantly, her soul newborn, her old selves shed behind her like so many wrinkled skins; and now, in *Women in***

*Love*, he gives us Rupert Birkin, lopped and bound in a marriage which gives him peace but already pulls too tightly on his freedom to develop. Birkin is no sooner married, for example, than he begins to expound to Gerald Crich on the repulsive nature of marriage in the old sense. "It's a sort of tacit hunting in couples: the world all in couples, each couple in its own little house, watching its own little interests and stewing in its own little privacy – it's the most repulsive thing on earth." Gerald promptly agrees, and the two men search for a more expansive way of life:

> "You've got to take down the love-and-marriage ideal from its pedestal. We want something broader. I believe in the *additional* perfect relationship between man and man – additional to marriage."

> "I can never see how they can be the same," said Gerald.

> "Not the same – but equally important, equally creative, equally sacred, if you like."

> Gerald moved uneasily. "You know, I can't feel that," said he. "Surely there can never be anything as strong between man and man as sex love is between man and woman. Nature doesn't provide the basis."

> "Well, of course, I think she does. And I don't think we shall ever be happy till we establish ourselves on this basis. You've got to get rid of the *exclusiveness* of married love. And you've got to admit the unadmitted love of man for man. It makes for a greater freedom for everybody, a greater power of individuality both in men and women."

> "I know," said Gerald, "you believe something like that. Only I can't feel it, you see." He put his hand on Birkin's arm, with a sort of deprecating affection. And he smiled as if triumphantly. (p. 403)

Gerald's triumphant smile coincides, I think, with our own. We find no place, in our society, for that "unadmitted love of man for man" which Lawrence tried to project throughout his writings. And so we tend to explain the male-love theme in his works on personal or psychological grounds: hence Harry Moore examines the possibility of homosexuality, and then discards it; or he describes the wrestling bout in *Women in Love* as a form of athletic mysticism, and then suggests – "Only as a possibility" – that Lawrence was merely trying to identify his personal frailness, in such chapters, with the hero's physical strength (*Life and Works*, pp. 165–66). Perhaps he was. But with one or two exceptions, the friendship scenes in other books do not involve athletics, so that argument falls through on the simple grounds of logic. As for homosexuality (which Moore discounts), the plain fact is that Lawrence was aware of it, and that he rejected it himself as mechanistic and destructive.[18]

Actually, it is a question here of values, and of emotional possibilities, rather than personal failings: we cannot "psychologise" the problem away; we have to face it in terms of the gaps and failures in modern thought itself. For if other cultures than our own have struggled with the friendship problem (the Greeks, the Elizabethans, the old Germanic tribes, the medieval knights), today we largely deny that such a problem exists. Apparently, we see a kind of no man's land between the casual and the homosexual liaison – and if Lawrence has been foolish enough to inhabit it, that is largely his affair. But let us see, at the least, how much of the forbidden ground he has explored, and with what success, if any.

The major expression of the brotherhood theme occurs in *Women in Love* but a later story, "The Blind Man," may serve here as a short and simple introduction to Lawrence's position. As you may remember, the "blind man," Maurice Pervin, is caught and held within a state of blood-prescience as the story opens. He has enjoyed the rich sensual consummation with his wife, but somehow the experience has proved inadequate. Occasionally, a terrible weariness, a sense of being closed in and swamped with darkness, overwhelms them both. Isabel nearly screams with the strain; she seeks out friends for comfort, but finds them shallow and impertinent in the face of the rich, dark world she shares with her husband. Maurice too is seized with fits of depression, for at times his sensual flow is checked and thrown back, so that a kind of "shattered chaos" occurs within his blood. In the end, however, his energies are aligned and utilised through the friendship rite with Isabel's cousin, the intellectual neuter, Bertie Reid. To repeat only the crucial passage: the two men are talking together in the barn, when Pervin suddenly asks the bachelor lawyer if he may touch him; Bertie complies, and Maurice covers his face, shoulder, and arm with his sensitive fingers, and then asks him to touch his own blind eyes; again Bertie complies –

> He lifted his hand, and laid the fingers on the scar, on the scarred eyes. Maurice suddenly covered them with his own hand, pressed the fingers of the other man upon his disfigured eye-sockets, trembling in every fibre, and rocking slightly, slowly, from side to side. He remained thus for a minute or more, whilst Bertie stood as if in a swoon, unconscious, imprisoned.

> Then suddenly Maurice removed the hand of the other man from his brow, and stood holding it in his own.

> "Oh, my God," he said, "we shall know each other now, shan't we?

We shall know each other now." (*The Portable D. H. Lawrence*, p. 103)

Yet as Maurice overflows "with hot, poignant love," Bertie shrinks back, afraid for his life. And when both return to Isabel: "He could not bear it that he had been touched by the blind man, his insane reserve broken in. He was like a mollusc whose shell is broken." On the other hand, Maurice now stands before his wife, feet apart, "like a strange colossus": "We've become friends," he shouts, and though Isabel's gaze turns, painfully, on the haggard, broken lawyer, she replies, "You'll be happier now, dear." A path, a way out of the darkness has just been opened up for them, then quickly and ironically shut off by Bertie's fear of close, passionate friendship. Yet the human possibility is also clearly there: before this experience, Maurice had seemed strong-blooded and healthy to Isabel, but at the same time, cancelled out; now a new world has been revealed to him, beyond the binding intimacy of marriage and the obvious limitations of a single form of consciousness.

Clearly this is the primary function of male friendship in Lawrence's world: the step beyond marriage which makes marriage possible, the break-through to a fuller life which Lawrence tried to project, in a dozen different ways, in all his novels. This is the first important thing to remember, at any rate, when considering the friendship theme in *Women in Love*.

In the second chapter of that novel, there is a sharp quarrel between Rupert Birkin and his friend, Gerald Crich. Then the two men part with casual unconcern, and each of them suppresses his strange, burning attraction towards the other. Their friendship takes a sharp upswing, however, when Gerald's sister Diana drowns, and Birkin tries (unsuccessfully) to draw him away from the dreadful scene. In the stress of the moment, Gerald confesses that he would rather chat with Birkin than do anything else: "You mean a lot to me, Rupert, more than you know." Later, when Birkin becomes ill, Gerald does visit him, and sits indulgently by his bed, musing, as they talk, that the quick, slim man beside him seems too detached for any depth of friendship. Birkin's thoughts run on opposite lines: he suddenly sees his lifelong need "to love a man purely and fully," and so he tosses forth a first crude version of *Blutbrüderschaft*:

"You know how the old German knights used to swear a Blutbruderschaft," he said to Gerald, with quite a new happy activity in his eyes.

"Make a little wound in their arms, and rub each other's blood into the cut?" said Gerald.

"Yes – and swear to be true to each other, of one blood, all their lives. That is what we ought to do. No wounds, that is obsolete. But we ought to swear to love each other, you and I, implicitly and perfectly, finally, without any possibility of going back on it.". . .

Birkin sought hard to express himself. But Gerald hardly listened. His face shone with a certain luminous pleasure. He was pleased. But he kept his reserve. He held himself back.

"Shall we swear to each other, one day?" said Birkin, putting out his hand towards Gerald.

Gerald just touched the extended fine, living hand, as if withheld and afraid.

"We'll leave it till I understand it better," he said, in a voice of excuse.

Birkin watched him. A little sharp disappointment, perhaps a touch of contempt came into his heart.

"Yes," he said. "You must tell me what you think, later. You know what I mean? No sloppy emotionalism. An impersonal union that leaves one free." (p. 235)

After this conversation, the problem drops to the background and the two men go their separate ways. Crich plunges back into business and devotes his energies to the great industrial system he wants to establish; he also makes his first advances toward Ursula Brangwen's sister, Gudrun. Birkin leaves for the south of France, returns, and finally comes to closer terms with Ursula herself. But when his hasty proposal ends in fiasco, he walks furiously away from the Brangwen home, straight towards Gerald Crich at Shortlands. He finds Crich restless and irritable with his own emptiness, and therefore glad enough to see him, and, as an antidote to boredom, equally glad to learn the rudiments of jiu-jitsu. The famous wrestling scene follows, Gerald pitting his powerful mechanical strength against Birkin's more elusive and organic energies:

So the two men entwined and wrestled with each other, working nearer and nearer. Both were white and clear, but Gerald flushed smart red where he was touched, and Birkin remained white and tense. He seemed to penetrate into Gerald's more solid, more diffuse bulk, to interfuse his body through the body of the other, as if to bring it subtly into subjection, always seizing with some rapid necromantic foreknowledge every motion of the other flesh, converting and counter-acting it, playing upon the limbs and trunk of Gerald like some hard wind. It was as if Birkin's whole physical intelligence interpenetrated into Gerald's body, as if his fine sublimated energy entered into the flesh of the fuller man, like some potency, casting a fine net, a prison, through the muscles into the very depths of Gerald's physical being.

So they wrestled swiftly, rapturously, intent and mindless at last, two essential white figures working into a tighter closer oneness of struggle, with a strange, octopus-like knotting and flashing of limbs in the subdued light of the room; a tense white knot of flesh gripped in silence between the walls of old brown books. Now and again came a sharp gasp of breath, or a sound like a sigh, then the rapid thudding of movement on the thickly-carpeted floor, then the strange sound of flesh escaping under flesh. Often, in the white interlaced knot of violent living being that swayed silently, there was no head to be seen, only the swift, tight limbs, the solid white backs, the physical junction of two bodies clinched into oneness. Then would appear the gleaming, ruffled head of Gerald, as the struggle changed, then for a moment the dun-coloured, shadow-like head of the other man would lift up from the conflict, the eyes wide and dreadful and sightless. (pp. 307–08)

As the two fall back exhausted, Birkin slips off toward unconsciousness, then rouses to the terrible hammer-stroke of his heart. Gerald too is dimly unconscious, but when Birkin attempts to steady himself their hands accidentally touch: "And Gerald's hand closed warm and sudden over Birkin's, they remained exhausted and breathless, the one hand clasped closely over the other." Then the two slip back to normal consciousness, and Birkin marks out the significance of their experience: "We are mentally, spiritually intimate, therefore we should be more or less physically intimate too – it is more whole"; "I think also that you are beautiful . . . and that is enjoyable too. One should enjoy what is given"; "At any rate, one feels freer and more open now – and that is what we want." This is the *Blutbrüderschaft*, then, which Birkin has been seeking, for the aim here is not sexual gratification (most critics agree on this) but the consummation of friendship.[19] The question remains, of course: just what significance does Lawrence attach to such consummation? My own interpretation follows.

First of all, we have just witnessed a spontaneous rite or ceremony between Birkin and Crich. If the terms "spontaneous" and "rite" seem contradictory, please remember that the essence of any religious rite is communion, contact, or rapport between the performers and their god or gods. And for Lawrence the life-flow itself is sacred, so that the flow between Birkin and Gerald becomes a religious pledge or vow, a unique and binding experience which stems quite naturally from their separate emotional predicaments and their mutual love. This same pattern recurs, incidentally, through all the rest of Lawrence's writings on the brotherhood problem, though the rites involved are never quite the same. In "The Blind Man," for example, the clasp of Reid's hands over Pervin's eyes becomes a pledge to Pervin: "We're all right together now, aren't we? . . . It's all right now, as long as we live, so far as we're concerned?" In *Sons and Lovers* the violent fight between Paul Morel and Baxter Dawes becomes a pledge or bond of friendship between them. And in *Aaron's Rod* the writer Lilly pulls the sick flutist, Aaron Sisson, off the street, cares for him in his rooms, and (when Aaron falters in his will to live) saves him with a motherly rubdown:

> Quickly he uncovered the blond lower body of his patient, and began to rub the abdomen with oil, using a slow, rhythmic, circulating motion, a sort of massage. For a long time he rubbed finely and steadily, then went over the whole of the lower body, mindless, as if in a sort of incantation. He rubbed every speck of the man's lower body – the abdomen, the buttocks, the thighs and knees, down to the feet, rubbed it all warm and glowing with camphorated oil, every bit of it, chafing the toes swiftly, till he was almost exhausted. Then Aaron was covered up again, and Lilly sat down in fatigue to look at his patient. He saw a change. The spark had come back into the sick eyes, and the faint trace of a smile, faintly luminous, into the face. Aaron was regaining himself. But Lilly said nothing. He watched his patient fall into a proper sleep.
> (p. 112)

Aaron recovers, of course, and the two men grope and waver toward leader-follower unison for the rest of the novel.

A similar friendship ceremony occurs in *Kangaroo*, when the writer Somers soothes the aching throat of fatherly Ben Cooley, the would-be dictator of Australia; but Somers is looking for something beyond blood brotherhood, so the friendship fails to take. That "something beyond" – the holy leader-follower compact – is firmly established between Cipriano and Ramon, the two religious leaders in *The Plumed Serpent*: for the strange sensual rite between them is not a friendship pact but an initiation into the pantheon of living gods. Let me insist, however, that each of these incidents involves a sudden radical pledge to some more than casual relationship between two men. These men do not hold wrestling bouts, or rub each other down, or ease each other's eyes and throats at periodical intervals. Instead they pledge or fail to pledge themselves in unique, significant rites, either to "life-submission" or fuller love: mental, spiritual, physical.

By physical love Lawrence means something other than homosexuality. Indeed, he makes the point, in *Fantasia of the Unconscious*, that male relations involve the upper, spiritual poles of consciousness, instead of the lower sexual poles:

Is this new polarity, this new circuit of passion between comrades and co-workers, is this also sexual? It is a vivid circuit of polarized passion. Is it hence sex?

It is not. Because what are the poles of positive connection? – the upper, busy poles. What is the dynamic contact? – a unison in spirit, in understanding, and a pure commingling in one great *work*. A mingling of the individual passion into one great *purpose* . . . Knowing what sex is, can we call this other also sex? We cannot . . . It is a great motion in the opposite direction. (p. 151)

This tends to explain, I think, why Pervin is attracted to an intellectual in "The Blind Man," or why Birkin likes an industrialist in *Women in Love*: for Laurentian brotherhood seems aimed, from the first, at "a unison in spirit, in understanding, and a pure commingling in one great *work*."

Yet the sensual element is also present from the first. To explain it, we must turn to the Laurentian concepts of "touch" and "warmth" in human relationships, for the two concepts are closely connected. Thus touch is an emotional, not merely a sensual experience for Lawrence; and even as a sensual experience, *per se*, touch is not necessarily sexual. Think back, in both respects, to the episode in *Sons and Lovers*, when Paul Morel falls sick and his mother sleeps with him at night: at the height of his fever she clasps him to her breast, and the sensual contact helps to cure him.[20] The scene here is based upon a sensual expression of love (Paul "realises" his mother), but not a sexual one. And the same holds true for the sensual contacts which we have just examined, between man and man. As Mellors puts it in *Lady Chatterley's Lover*, "I stand for the touch of bodily awareness between human beings . . . and the touch of tenderness"; as for sex, it is only "the closest of all touch." What Mellors constructs here, in effect, is a scale of sensuality, with physical contact between human beings as the basic experience, and with heterosexual love at the farthest range of the sensual scale: thus other forms of contact, between man and man, woman and woman, or parent and child, can also give valid expression to other, less intimate forms of love.[21]

As we draw these various strands of thought together, the wrestling bout in *Women in Love* begins to take on proper meaning: first of all, it functions as part of a general step beyond marriage to some further living relationship; second, it functions as the spontaneous pledge to keep that relationship alive; and third, it involves an actual physical communion, between self and self, or soul and soul, and therefore functions as a mutual realisation of the beloved. One can legitimately protest, of course, that the scene at hand goes far beyond these functions, and that Lawrence has blown it up out of all proportion to man's actual experience – that he has overstressed, in other words, man's capacity for physical, nonsexual communion with his fellow man, and has therefore left himself exposed to honest (and dishonest) criticism. But he has only done so as part of a more general attempt to place *Blutbrüderschaft* itself upon an ideal pedestal – and even here he has incorporated his fault into the very body of his work, and has made it part of a *problem posed*, rather than a problem solved. Birkin himself, for example, is scarcely convinced of the final validity of *Blutbrüderschaft*: "I *know* I want a perfect and complete relationship with you," he tells his wife. "But beyond that. Do I want a real, ultimate relationship with Gerald? . . . or don't I?" This question is partially answered, I think, by the total failure of the *Blutbrüderschaft* to take hold, and by Ursula's final pointed criticism:

> "Why aren't I enough?" she said. "You are enough for me. I don't want anybody else but you. Why isn't it the same with you?"

> "Having you, I can live all my life without anybody else, any other sheer intimacy. But to make it complete, really happy, I wanted eternal union with a man too: another kind of love," he said.

> "I don't believe it," she said. "It's an obstinacy, a theory, a perversity ... You can't have two kinds of love. Why should you?"

> "It seems as if I can't," he said. "Yet I wanted it."

> "You can't have it, because it's false, impossible," she said.

> "I don't believe that," he answered.

The book ends on this stubborn note, with Birkin's brotherhood scheme exploded in fact and theory: the concept of twin loves proves ephemeral, that is, within the fictional testing vat, and Ursula's pointed question – "Why should you?" – remains unanswered. But a decided residue of truth is left over, and Birkin echoes this in his final words. If the love of man for man can never function as a perfect parallel to married love, the question still remains, how does it function? For Birkin's insistence that Gerald should have loved him – that it would have made some difference if he did – is borne out "dramatically" in the book. As Lawrence tells us, marriage would have been a hoax for Gerald, until he achieved some pure relationship with another human being: "If he pledged himself with the man he would later be able to pledge himself with the woman: not merely in legal marriage, but in absolute mystic marriage" – or star-equilibrium. And indeed, the only point in the book at which Gerald is set free, in perfect balance with another human being, occurs just after the wrestling bout with Birkin. Had the pledge between them held, Crich might have received some badly needed nurturing of the soul. Then too, his warm, vivid chats with Birkin, taken seriously, might well have cleared away that basic mental confusion which thwarted his will to live. But Gerald had no respect for Birkin's notions: his mind was bound by convention, his will was bent toward self-annihilation, and so, as the omen of "Northern ice-destruction," he chose to break himself in the struggle with Gudrun Brangwen.

So the first sortie outward from the narrow circle of marriage ends in failure for Birkin – and death for Gerald Crich. But at the same time, the possibility of some kind of brotherhood is established. In the novels that follow, Lawrence reworks this possibility along wholly different lines, scrapping brotherhood *per se* for the lordship principle, and moving much more clearly into the realm of purposive (and spiritual) endeavour.[22]

By the final year of the Fifties the vast majority of critics accepted the basis of the Leavisian claim for Lawrence's greatness, and the 'Lawrence Revival' was assured of permanence. The acceptance of Lawrence as a major literary figure meant that public and critical interest in discussions of the works began to rise dramatically: in 1959 there were over 140 articles, books and essays written about Lawrence and his work, compared with just nineteen a decade earlier.

Most critics of the decade tended to focus on the ideas and themes that were seen to run through the novels, and there was considerable debate (as we have just seen in Mark Spilka's work) on the mystical and religious aspects of Lawrence's thinking, and on the form of the novels. In the following essay, which completes the selection of extracts taken from the Fifties, we find something of a departure from the general critical approach to date, and something of a look forward to works of the Sixties and even the feminist-inspired criticism of the Seventies.

Marvin Mudrick's essay, which originally appeared in the journal *Spectrum* in 1959, makes two major statements about *The Rainbow*: 'it is the first English novel to record the normality and significance of physical passion; and it is the only English novel to record, with a prophetic awareness of the consequences, the social revolution whereby Western man lost his sense of community and whereby men – and more especially women – learned, if they could, that there is no help any longer except in the individual and in his capacity for a passional life.'

In the first of the essay's points, Mudrick looks towards the more liberated commentaries of the Sixties – and the more liberated reading habits and experiences of the population of that decade. His writing seems to anticipate the results of the unsuccessful obscenity actions against *Lady Chatterley's Lover*, and the huge changes in literary and social attitudes of the coming decade. In relation to the essay's second major point, we can see here an early form of the class-conscious and ideologically-concerned criticisms of the late Sixties, Seventies and even early Eighties. Many of the concerns raised in Graham Holderness's *D. H. Lawrence: History, Ideology and Fiction* (1982), for instance (see pages 134–46), are raised here by Mudrick. Additionally, we can see the emergence of a firm response to the position and presentation of Lawrence's female characters in Mudrick's discussion of Ursula and Lydia Brangwen. Many of these ideas were to be echoed and given full consideration in essays by Kate Millett and Philippa Tristram (see pages 115–28).

The essay is a long piece, reprinted here at almost its full length, but rewards the reader and remains one of the finest of critical commentaries on *The Rainbow* to date.

Manners and morals: they are, critics agree, what novels properly concern themselves with; and the specialist in the English novel can readily demonstrate the English novelist's expert attention to both from *Moll Flanders* to the latest thriller by Graham Greene. Certainly, fiction is of all literary genres the most intractable to description or definition, and we are grateful for any indices to its nature. We are also proud of our language and literature; and the novel in English has an illustrious history, no doubt about it. So the manners and morals, and the fiction, we are specially interested in are English and American. It may not, then, seem chauvinistic to us when Caroline Gordon [In *How to Read a Novel* (New York: The Viking Press, 1957)] discovers the world history of the novel to be a triumphant progress toward apotheosis in the work of the Anglo-American, Henry James, who was obliging enough to scrutinize, with the tact of an exquisite sensibility, Anglo-Saxon manners and morals – of only a few social groups, to be sure – on both sides of the Atlantic. Even Dr. Leavis, who demotes or dismisses Richardson, Fielding, Sterne, Smollett, Dickens, Thackeray, Hardy, and Joyce, expresses much admiration for Hawthorne, and finds a great tradition in Jane Austen, George Eliot, James, Conrad, and Lawrence, in whose work, as it seems to him, manners are so chosen and placed as to reflect on their particular surfaces the image of that sober absolute morality, essentially secular and embattled, which for two centuries has been the strength of England if not of the entire civilized world.

It is just here, regarding the rest of the world, that a doubt arises. Compare, for instance, George Eliot and Tolstoy, or Conrad and Dostoevsky – comparisons that Dr. Leavis, at any rate, ought to accept as fair, since one great tradition ought to be able to stand up against another, and since George Eliot and Tolstoy share a preoccupation with the social and ordinary as Conrad and Dostoevsky share a preoccupation with the psychological and extraordinary. Or compare

Stendhal and Jane Austen, or Turgenev and James, or almost any nineteenth century French or Russian novelist and Hawthorne.

Fiction, and a tradition of fiction, may be genuine without being great. Greatness is, after all, relative, and when we compare George Eliot and Tolstoy we are aware of such differences in magnitude that to describe the two of them by the same honorific epithet is to do no service to either. Nor is George Eliot a feeble representative of the tradition Dr. Leavis singles out: *Middlemarch*, at least, is a very impressive novel; with a breadth of intelligent sympathy it fixes for all time the manners and morals of its own place and time, and it is perhaps the only English novel that sensitively registers something like a whole society. Yet it is, as the author notes, "A Study of Provincial Life." There is, in fact, no English novel that registers a whole society; and, in the balance with Continental fiction, there is almost no English novel that cannot fairly be described as provincial.

. . . We must come to it at last, the bourgeois imperative which has defended the materialist order against its gravest threat, and which Anglo-Saxon fiction had perforce to accept for two centuries: the imperative against human normality. You may, the imperative declares, transcend sex by the rhetoric of a grand passion, you may cheapen it as by Fielding's characteristic resort to comic-strip prurience, you may ignore it or jeer at it, you may even in extremity be clinical about it, but you may not regard it as a serious, normal, central preoccupation of mankind, and you may not attempt to understand it.

The first literary effect of such a proscription was to deprive English fiction of normal women. The sphere of decision for women, in Western civilization at least, has always been love and marriage; and if the woman is not permitted to take into account the most serious impulse of her private existence, she may surrender to domesticity or the vapors and become one of Dickens' brave Biddys or dumb Doras, or she may be encouraged to transcend sex before going to the trouble of learning what it is, like George Eliot's Dorothea or Emily Brontë's Cathy or any other Gothic or Romantic heroine. There are even relatively few *interesting* women in English fiction, and most of these are interesting because their authors understand and document the pathology of their reduction: Jane Austen's Emma, Dickens' Estella (his only powerful insight into a woman's sensibility). And there are a very few whose normality has the protective coloration of intelligence and so passes undetected: Jane Austen's Elizabeth Bennet and Anne Elliot, for example. Generally speaking, however, the heroine of English fiction is likely to be a dead loss – think of all the unrememberable Amelias hung like decorative albatrosses round the necks of the heroes of Victorian novels. And then think of Tolstoy's Natasha and Anna, Dostoevsky's women supreme in their passionate abnormality, the whole range of unapologetic women in Stendhal and Balzac and Flaubert, the gallery of unhurried female sensuality in Colette: not only a definable *sex* in contrast to the poor sticks of English heroines, but almost a different species. The English hero, true, has always been allowed some scope of heroic action in adventure (often commercial), in working his way up, in "becoming a success." Still, to eradicate half the human race, and to confine the energies of the other half mainly within the bounds of materialistic aspiration – this is not to survey, through morals and manners, the limits of human possibility. It was this order of things that D. H. Lawrence confronted when he began writing the novel the first part of which eventually became *The Rainbow*.

Literary revolutions are as various and frequent as political elections: some are important, most are not. When what has been called the Flaubertian tradition (a French import which, though it deeply influenced two representatives of his own "native" tradition, Dr. Leavis regards with a somewhat xenophobic distaste) was introduced into English fiction, and such novelists as James, Conrad, Ford, and Joyce adopted and developed the techniques available to a conscious craftsmanship in fiction, one important and irreversible revolution had occurred – the most important, some critics believe, in the history of English fiction. Certainly, it produced important and original work, even though it has inflicted upon us, unavoidably, all the gimmickry of craft-consciousness and myth-mongering and symbolifying criticism, as well as some of the doleful justification for such criticism in those pointless manipulations of technique into which the tradition may tempt the novelist: Conrad, for example, somberly picking his way through the underbrush of half a dozen intervening points of view, in that disastrous virtuoso exercise, *Chance*, to report on a man's tying a shoelace.

To this tradition, and to the revolution it achieved, Lawrence does not belong. Joyce belonged to them, but he participated in another literary revolution, the revolution against the Anglo-Saxon (and Irish) censor; and here he and Lawrence may be said to have stood in a common cause. Joyce's publishing and distributing difficulties with *Dubliners* and *Ulysses* strikingly resemble Lawrence's with *The Rainbow* and *Lady Chatterley's Lover*. Nevertheless, there is censorship and censorship. When Judge Woolsey issued his celebrated decision admitting *Ulysses* into the United States, he remarked, in denying that it came within the legal definition of obscenity, that its effect on the reader was more likely to be "emetic" than "aphrodisiac." The interesting judicial principle was thus established that, for the Anglo-Saxon commonwealth, to vomit is, if not positively healthier, at least less baneful than to engage in sexual intercourse. The judge rightly inferred that Joyce's sexual imagery and naughty language were no vital threat at all to Anglo-Saxon mores, but only the signs by which a whole culture manifested its nausea and self-disgust. The Joycean Revolution of the Word has brought freedom, it is novel, obvious, mainly for cynical clinicians and cautious pornographers, the freedom to spit and hiss (and leads directly to such a May-fly oddity of literary entomology as the San Francisco Renaissance). Today, a quarter-century after the canonization of Molly Bloom, the Woolseyan principle has been challenged: *Lady Chatterley's Lover*, which audaciously attempted to rehabilitate sexual imagery and the old Anglo-Saxon words as signs of health and tenderness (and which, by the way, succeeded), has at last been legally published in both the United States and the United Kingdom.

Still, *Lady Chatterley's Lover* is, by the pressures of its subject and of the lateness of its hour, as close to being hortatory as a work of art can afford to be; even without its four famous words (all of them used more frequently, of course, in *Ulysses* and in almost any current popular novel), its radical extraliterary intent is clear. *The Rainbow* – which marked the outbreak of the Lawrencean revolution – is in fact a more dangerous work because it is less open to philistine retaliation, because it bases itself confidently on no exhortation at all, only on the assumption that sex is a serious, normal, central preoccupation of mankind. After its early skirmish with suppression (which showed, not how acutely prescient, but how very silly, English censors could be in 1915), *The Rainbow* has been widely accessible in print, and is even becoming generally accepted – at least the first half of it – as a brilliant record of English manners and morals over three generations, a really great English family-chronicle novel, not less respectable and beyond comparison better than anything in this line by Arnold Bennett.

True enough, there is, beside it, no family-chronicle novel in English that deserves mention; and anything that will certify the respectability of *The Rainbow* is to be prized, just as we ought to prize Lawrence's subliterary reputation as a sensational novelist for making more of his fiction accessible in cheap paperback American reprints than that of any other major English author. *The Rainbow* is not, after all, so respectable as Galsworthy: there are reasons for Lawrence's notoriety, as well as for his boring and disappointing the common reader, to whom he is notorious; and the reasons are all in *The Rainbow*. Nothing promises to be more, and proves on inspection to be less, sensational than this family-chronicle novel which assumes not only that generations are generated, but that the relationship between husband and wife is the central fact of human existence, that the living nucleus of this relationship is the act of sexual union, that the act of sexual union is infinitely serious, complex, and difficult, and that an act of such radiant significance must be fairly treated by the honest novelist.

Graham Hough, however, disapproves of Lawrence's candor: "As for physical passion . . . no one should try to present it as . . . [Lawrence] does, and traditional literary good sense has always known it." [*The Dark Sun* (London: Gerald Duckworth, 1956) p. 63.] This appeal to timeless good taste would be plausible if it were not for the very special conditions against which Lawrence had to contend. Most authors of the past, and of other cultures, who have dealt with physical passion have not, indeed, presented it directly. Chaucer did not, nor did Colette; but the reason is that neither needs to: for Chaucer, the sacramental nature of passion, and for Colette, the various joys of an indulged sensuality are self-evident and unchallenged; medieval Catholic humanism and modern French hedonism meet in their conviction of the power of sexual gratification, which can bring to peace and stillness men and women alike. Lawrence, very much on the other hand, has a unique problem: he must reassert this life-renewing power against two centuries of a culture and literature that have muffled and denied its very existence, and he can reassert it only by presenting its actuality as a reminder to the deaf and blind. Lawrence's terrible candor is necessary only because there has been so mendacious and destructive a silence; and yet, because it is so peremptorily called for, it not only reclaims old truths but rushes on to make discoveries. The long reign of English philistinism – in both life and letters – is Lawrence's provocation and his unexampled opportunity.

Of course Lawrence has the advantage of springing from the country community of English workingmen-farmers, a community not bound or even much influenced by the shopkeeper code, and he comes to maturity at a time when the whole structure of class and community is about to encounter the disintegrating shock of World War I. In his historic moment, Lawrence has before him the life of the last English community: not the manners of the province (which are in any case the manners of the provincial petty bourgeoisie and minor gentry), but a life rich in productive labor and in continuity with the passing seasons, rooted in the earthly and physical, inarticulate without grossness or stupidity, a life seemingly permanent yet fated to pass away in the general breakdown of codes and communities and to be replaced or transcended – if by anything – by individual aspiration. It is this process, over three generations, which is the subject and theme of *The Rainbow*; the process is the most momentous human fact of the past century; and it is a process which, in *The Rainbow*, discloses itself poignantly and most crucially in the sexual histories of individuals. The revolutionary nature of *The Rainbow* is, then, twofold: it is the first English novel to record the normality and significance of physical passion; and it is the only English novel to record, with a prophetic awareness of consequences, the social revolution whereby Western man lost his sense of community and men – more especially, women – learned, if they could, that there is no help any longer except in the individual and in his capacity for a passional life.

As soon as the critic of Lawrence begins to favor such terms as community and *passion*, he risks being suspected of imagining, obsequiously on cue from his author, a unanimity of social feeling that never was and a potency of personal feeling that never could be, under idyllic and perpetually recurring circumstances in the rural districts of the English Midlands up to, say, the turn of our century. But Lawrence presents no idylls. The community in *The Rainbow*, like every other, is an abstraction from its individuals, who are its only embodiment; and it lives as more than a mere term of discourse only so long as it provides forms and sanctions for the abiding impulses of their separate natures. These impulses are, besides, not all of them communal and sympathetic: Lawrence's individuals are just that, different and distinct from one another except when a strength of sympathy draws them together for moments out of the reciprocal alienations of individuality; and every relationship in *The Rainbow* testifies, not how easy and renewable, but how hard to come by, how precarious, and how irrecoverably unique each instance of passion is, even in a nature as faithful to itself and as sensitively patient as Tom Brangwen's.

. . . Tom Brangwen's apprehensions are not, after all, merely the customary timeless ones of husbands, but unprecedented seismic shocks: *The Rainbow* is recording a community in its last flare of vitality and gradual dying away, and all relationships and feelings are shaken by the great change. The foreignness of Tom's wife represents, disturbingly enough, the essential distance between all men and especially between the sexes; but it is already a terrifying difference beyond natural difference. Tom is no simple farmer: his aspiration toward the irreducibly alien woman is an inarticulate but not unconscious aspiration toward the experience of a life beyond the receding satisfactions of a community in process of dissolution. Until he meets Lydia he refuses, in drink and solitude, the only life his community offers him. Now, his dissatisfactions are new, and the brave chances he takes are new.

It was the coming of the colliery, years before, bringing canal and railway through the Brangwen land, which cut across the past and offered a promise of the future:

> As they drove home from town, the farmers of the land met the
> blackened colliers trooping from the pit-mouth. As they gathered
> the harvest, the west wind brought a faint, sulphurous smell of
> pit-refuse burning. As they pulled the turnips in November, the
> sharp clink-clink-clink-clink-clink of empty trucks shunting on

the line, vibrated in their hearts with the fact of other activity going on beyond them.

Tom, the young farmer awakened to a troubled sense of the restrictions of the Brangwen life, comes eventually into his own vision of a life beyond, once he has had his encounter with the complaisant pretty girl and his little talk with her Frenchman escort, the "ageless" and "monkey-like" gracious and imperial gentleman from elsewhere. When Tom sees the foreign lady walking toward him on the road, he knows that she is the awful chance he must take, and the best he can do. Yet the impulse outward moves, necessarily, more rapidly than the possibility of comprehending and fulfilling it: the break-up of the community is too sudden and unanticipated as railways and canals cut across the enclosed spaces of the mind, and the individual is freed from traditional unquestioned preoccupations in order to think and do – what? Tom Brangwen seeks out and lives with strangeness; but his satisfaction and his anguish remain equally resistant to statement or analysis, shy of words, still therefore plausibly connected with the old inarticulate traditional world. His steadiness, halfway between two worlds, is constantly in danger from the incompleteness of its commitment to either; it can be shaken, as by his stepdaughter, Anna, whom he desperately loves but who has come too far from the past to rest in mute suspensions of judgement:

> . . . She tried to discuss people, she wanted to know what was meant. But her father became uneasy. He did not want to have things dragged into consciousness. Only out of consideration for her he listened. And there was a kind of bristling rousedness in the room. The cat got up and, stretching itself, went uneasily to the door. Mrs. Brangwen was silent, she seemed ominous. Anna could not go on with her fault-finding, her criticism, her expression of dissatisfactions. She felt even her father against her.

Individual aspiration, once it is released, has no certain or obvious goal; and how can it be held in check somewhere, how can one keep it from making all action or repose seem premature and insufficient, how can the skeptical analytic mind be quieted? In fact, even for Tom these questions have force; the speechless remoteness of his marriage – for all of its passion – is finally not enough, his pathetic paternal jealousy of his stepdaughter's choice of a husband poisons even as it recalls to him his sense of his own life:

> What was missing in his life, that, in his ravening soul, he was not satisfied? He had had that friend at school, his mother, his wife, and Anna? What had he done? He had failed with his friend, he had been a poor son; but he had known satisfaction with his wife,

let it be enough; he loathed himself for the state he was in over Anna. Yet he was not satisfied. It was agony to know it. Was his life nothing? Had he nothing to show, no work? He did not count his work, anybody could have done it. What had he known, but the long, marital embrace with his wife! Curious, that this was what his life amounted to! At any rate, it was something, it was eternal. He would say so to anybody, and be proud of it. He lay with his wife in his arms, and she was still his fulfilment, just the same as ever. And that was the be-all and the end-all. Yes, and he was proud of it.

But the bitterness, underneath, that there still remained an unsatisfied Tom Brangwen, who suffered agony because a girl cared nothing for him. He loved his sons – he had them also. But it was the further, the creative life with the girl, he wanted as well. Oh, and he was ashamed. He trampled himself to extinguish himself.

So Tom Brangwen dies, drunk as Noah to forget the wearying puzzles of his middle age, drowned in the flood of rain, and his women mourn him:

They cleared and washed the body, and laid it on the bed.

There, it looked still and grand. He was perfectly calm in death, and, now he was laid in line, inviolable, unapproachable. To Anna, he was the majesty of the inaccessible male, the majesty of death. It made her still and awe-stricken, almost glad.

Lydia Brangwen, the mother, also came and saw the impressive, inviolable body of the dead man. She went pale, seeing death. He was beyond change or knowledge, absolute, laid in line with the infinite. What had she to do with him? He was a majestic Abstraction, made visible now for a moment, inviolate, absolute. And who could lay claim to him, who could speak of him, of the him who was revealed in the stripped moment of transit from life into death? Neither the living nor the dead could claim him, he was both the one and the other, inviolable, inaccessibly himself.

"I shared life with you, I belong in my own way to eternity," said Lydia Brangwen, her heart cold, knowing her own singleness.

"I did not know you in life. You are beyond me, supreme now in death," said Anna Brangwen, awe-stricken, almost glad.

This is Everyman, not at all the conventional individualist hero of English fiction; and Lawrence, anticipating perplexity, provided his critics with a long peg on which to hang their theories about *The Rainbow* and *Women in Love*. "You mustn't look," he wrote to Edward

Garnett, who had been disappointed to find no trace of *Sons and Lovers* in the new work, ". . . for the old stable ego of the character. There is another ego, according to whose action the individual is unrecognis- able, and passes through, as it were, allotropic states which it needs a deeper sense than any other we've been used to exercise, to discover are states of the same single radically unchanged element." And he goes on to make obligingly explicit the analogy of diamond-carbon to the mode of characterization he has just begun to feel at home in. Now this tip from the essentially kindly Lawrence to his bewildered English friend is a useful one, for the elucidation of *Women in Love* especially, as Mark Schorer has pointed out. It is nevertheless not so simple, or perhaps even so accurate, as it looks; and it does not indicate anything nearly so unprecedented – if one takes into account Continental fiction – as Lawrence appears to think.

. . . What is revolutionary in *The Rainbow* – what makes Lawrence, in perhaps the most important sense, the only modern novelist – is not the mode of characterization, but the new awareness which finds this mode necessary: the awareness that with the dying away, in the age of technology, of genuine communal relations between men, with the inevitable thwarting of what Lawrence was later to call "the societal impulse," the only hope for man lies in those remaining potentialities of human relationship which depend for their realization on the fullest (not necessarily the most various or complicated) possible real- ization of the sexual impulse. Lawrence, being English, had in this respect no choice but to be revolutionary. English novelists, as spokes- men for the most advanced middle class in the world, had since Defoe been advocating the simplest escape from the intolerable human prob- lems posed by industrialism – the escape into materialist success, the pursuit of what Dickens' Wemmick poignantly euphemizes under the phrase "portable property"; but with the end of the expansive roman- tic phase of English industrialism, no serious English writer could any longer believe in this escape and pursuit, as Dickens and others before and after could believe in it once it had been sweetened by contrition, materialist benevolence, and marital union with another form of portable property. (We cannot imagine a French or an Italian or a Russian Lawrence, just as we cannot imagine an English Dostoevsky, though the awareness of which Lawrence is both creator and instru- ment has, finally, as much to say to the Continent as Dostoevsky has to say to the English.) For Lawrence, then, the hope – in fact the last resort – of modern man is – the unhappy word stares at us as it did at Lawrence's censors – sex: not as cold appetite, not as self-imposed exile from the teeming world, not as the exploiting of sensation or the temporary allaying of an itch, but as the bond of tranquillity and faith between man and woman, those polar opponents, and the last renewable proof of human community.

*The Rainbow* is mid-passage and arrival. Tom Brangwen still has roots, connections, the virtue of quietness in solitude; of these vestiges of community Anna and Will still keep something by, as it were, barely remembering them, Anna in her slovenly cheerful maternity, Will in his mute satisfaction with manual labor or minor artisanship. Only Ursula – modern woman and therefore, in her unforeseen and disastrously unprepared-for homelessness, true representative of modern mankind – has nothing at all of what, outside themselves, sustained the two generations before her. And for all three generations the unmapped territory to be explored, with increasing desperation and hope, is sex.

Tom Brangwen has a real marriage, not withstanding its ultimate vulnerability to the stress of uncomprehended change; his apparently unwarrantable youthful waiting for a strangeness beyond his ordinary experience is rewarded and vindicated, and his life is transfigured by the reality of passion. If his marriage fails to give him everything, it nevertheless gives him much, even enough to make him at length unhappily sensitive to the unknown vibrations of what he must do without.

For Anna and Will, on the other hand, marriage seems at first sunnier and more simple. They have moved very far out of the shadow of the old Brangwen world; Anna, at least, is impatient with established sanctities; and both of them rejoice on their prolonged honeymoon in an uninhibited mutual exploration of sexuality, day after day of vital time-dissolving ease.

. . . In such moments as Lawrence here presents, there can be no "characters" in the conventional fictional sense: the mode of characterization is dictated by the focus of attention, which here is on a core of impulse anterior to personality. It is, of course, easy to misunderstand such a passage in the context of English fiction, especially that sort of woman's fiction of which *Jane Eyre* is a quasi-serious instance: the emotion of romantic love reduces heroine (or hero) to a fluttering impotency – especially in anticipation – that may resemble a reduction to impulse. But the conjugal satisfactions of Tom Brangwen, or Anna, or Will, are not reductive at all; they liberate universal human powers; far from making romantic victims they make those relations between people without which there are only egos in collision and no persons. Nobody, it is true, can live indefinitely at such a depth of impulse; and the comic ascension of Anna and Will to the level of a more mundane appetite testifies not only to the existence of a daylight world in which we are all, more or less, scrupulously differentiated fictional characters, but also to that respect for full human truth which disciplines even the most rhapsodic utterances in this novel. The careful reader never forgets that *The Rainbow* is, in one large and traditional aspect, a great realistic novel: Tom Brangwen's life outside marriage, for example, is registered with an immediacy and resonance that would establish him as one of the great figures in English fiction even if he were nothing more; and one thinks of such superb set-pieces as Tom's efforts at comforting the child Anna while Lydia is bearing his first child, Tom's drunkenly inspired eulogy of marriage, his death in the flood – a luminous pertinence of detail, a fidelity to locale, a sternness of pathos not readily matched in any other fiction. Nevertheless, as the rhythm of the style – always near, when not actually, the rhythm of rhapsodic utterance – persists in implying, life is renewable only and perpetually at the springs of impulse, in celebration and praise, where we are less unique than human; and only to the degree to which we have renewed ourselves there, can we breathe and move as individuals in the daylight world.

Renewal, the gift and aim of life, becomes in modern marriage less and less the gift of repose, more and more pressingly the aim of conscious and personal exploration: woman is less passive and man more anxious, approaching an uneasy identity of roles. Lydia is still withdrawn and enigmatic, a woman of the old dispensation, unharried, immured in domesticity and unamenable to self-questioning; so Tom is the explorer – joyous or baffled – in this first marriage, moving doubtfully at the rim of awareness. Anna, on the other hand, has come awake, because the invasion of all things by mechanism and the conscious mind has made Lydia the last possible woman of her kind: having lost what her mother unquestionably had, Anna must make up for it by becoming explorative in her own right, the free companion of her husband. But, after the shared bliss of the honeymoon, the difficulties of the new dispensation become gradually manifest. When the communal sanction for marriage is dissipated and only free and equal individuals remain, the burden on accidents of personality grows suddenly enormous. The temperamental differences between Lydia and Tom were unbridgeable, and of no significance to Lydia. Yet Will's soft inarticulateness drives the skeptical articulate Anna wild, and Anna's attacks on her husband's temperament drive him into retaliatory fury.

. . . In the perilous colloidal tension of modern marriage, too much depends on merely personal qualities. And – at least for persons living in the delusive afterglow of the old world, still unalert to the swarming problems of consciousness – too much depends on the increasingly elaborate and conscious satisfactions of sexuality: the man, having lost his inherited mastery, comes to depend on these as on a drug, and the woman comes to resent what she will eventually regard as his infantile male weakness. Variety, the avoidance of monotony, becomes more and more a brutal conjugal compulsion. At length, reciprocally excited by Will's brush with infidelity, Anna and Will give themselves to the pleasures of a sort of democratic sexual cannibalism, to the fetishistic daylight fevers of sensuality, the manipulation of bodies as instruments for pleasure; and if Lawrence's imagery in this passage plainly obliges us to find the experience analogous to the Fall, it obliges us also to see the new experiences as a necessary expansion of man's knowledge in the time of another forced departure from the garden. Still, Anna and Will never reclaim their honeymoon fulfilment of passion or seem capable of the reconciliation between passion and sensuality; and their lives dwindle away in subtle disorganization, in the minor consummations and complaints of Anna's role as the fecund housewife and Will's as a woodwork teacher for the town, "very happy and keen in his new public spirit." Since their imperfect truce is the first modern marriage, it is appropriate that they bring into being the first complete modern woman, totally dispossessed and therefore totally explorative.

The child Ursula still has her father's environing and sometimes overpowering love; and she has, also, in conversation with her grandmother, a window on the certainties of the past even as the thought of growing up without such certainties begins to trouble her.

... Lydia's wisdom in old age is wasted on her granddaughter, and reverberates outward into the large implications of the novel. One of the dangers of marriage in the time of a breaking of bonds is, as Lydia suggests, that a man may be driven to seek in a mate not a distinct and different person as generous and needy as himself, but only what will compensate him, somehow, for his sense of loss – though, tragically, he must have both in order to have either. The marriage of Anna and Will is, at last, a deadlock because neither wife nor husband has the generosity and wisdom to acknowledge and accept the unbreakable differentness of the other; and Tom's response to Lydia's strangeness – at the beginning so compelling an attraction for him – is, at last, to drift back into confusion and the oblivion of drink. Moreover, the grandmother's words to the child Ursula are a prophecy; for Skrebensky will desperately seek in Ursula (as Will sought in Anna) only what might make up for his unmanning sense of loss, and Ursula herself will not understand, not at least till very late, that her promiscuity with Skrebensky is no generous gift of love but only a confession of mutual weakness, no passionate resolution but an increasingly unsatisfactory escape into sex from the unprecedented problems of the modern consciousness.

In the new world there are no landmarks or guideposts, the great past is no longer even a memory, everyone is free and dispossessed; so Ursula's life becomes, necessarily enough, a kind of adventure in limbo. Yet it is this concluding section – in bulk, more than half – of the novel that has been most vexatious and unrewarding for readers; and any effort to assess *The Rainbow* bumps hard against it. No doubt, the section is less satisfying than most of what has come before: it is unduly repetitive, it is occasionally content to make points by assertion rather than by incident, it sometimes mistakes mere detailed documentation for thematic illustration and development, its tone sometimes verges on stridency. There are, after all, too many and too similar descriptions of Ursula and Skrebensky making hopeless love; the career of Ursula as a teacher, however interesting it may be in its own right, is recorded at too much length and with too little relevance to the theme of the novel; and when Lawrence, in his haste to dismiss dry book-learning, tries to palm off on us so trivially literary a truism about college life as this:

> College was barren, cheap, a temple converted to the most vulgar, petty commerce. Had she not gone to hear the echo of learning pulsing back to the source of the mystery? The source of mystery! And barrenly, the professors in their gowns offered commercial commodity that could he turned to good account in the examination-room; ready-made stuff too, and not really worth the money it was intended to fetch; which they all knew.

When Lawrence settles for this sort of thing, we are persuaded that he is no longer, for the time being at any rate, attending to the seriousness of his theme. It is perhaps more to the point to agree with Dr. Leavis that Lawrence, his mind already on the very different second novel which had detached itself from his original conception of a single novel on marriage, was trying to finish *The Rainbow* with less sympathy than conscientiousness: in this view, the frustrating account of Ursula's long and strenuous career of frustration may be taken as the result of Lawrence's prudent desire to save her consummation for *Women in Love*.

Still, *The Rainbow* is, finally, not about consummation but about promise. The rainbow that Ursula sees at the very end of the novel need not be dismissed as a despairing symbolic stroke to allow a nominal conclusion and to release Lawrence for *Women in Love*; though the two novels are obviously related in ways more important than the continuance of several characters through the second, it may be that those readers who find the end of *The Rainbow* wanting have turned their minds prematurely to the next book, and are expecting what it is not in the theme of the earlier novel to give. No doubt Lawrence's original intention was to write a single novel which would encompass and illustrate in the lives of a family the great social and psychological change of our century, and which would conclude with a treatment of such individual problems and individual solutions as, indeed, are treated in *Women in Love*. But it must have become eventually clear to him that the breakdown of community was a subject in itself, and that it culminated appropriately in the coming to consciousness of emancipated, modern woman. If Lawrence had ended the novel with modern woman numbed in her grimace of freedom, he would have been merely cynical; if he had ended with Ursula still unsure of her feelings for Skrebensky, the novel would trail off in a puzzle. The novel does, in fact, end as Ursula, having freed herself of her struggle with Skrebensky, is for the first time genuinely free not only of the unrevivable past but of those false ties she has tentatively accepted in place of it. To require any more – at least schematically – is to require an unequivocal happy ending, and even in *Women in Love* or *Lady Chatterley's Lover* Lawrence is not that obliging.

The fault is, then, not of scheme but of execution: much of the last half of *The Rainbow* seems to have been written with a slackening of Lawrence's attention to proportion and detail. Yet much is finely done. Something as difficult, for instance, as the relationship between Ursula and Miss Inger comes off without damage to our sympathy for Ursula, and with strong pertinence to the theme. In a time when the injunctions of community and family have been broken, when the individual is responsible only to himself and to his own impulses, why should not Ursula first admire and then fiercely love the handsome, independent woman who so resembles what she herself wishes to be? And why should the warmth and physical responsiveness of her feelings be curbed? No mere prohibition will do, for sanctions and prohibitions alike have gone under. It is only by living through the experience that Ursula can judge its sinister misleadingness for her: to be free like Winifred Inger is to take pleasure only in the thrill of physiological or mechanical process, to handle and reject, to give nothing, to hate one's humanness and to deny the possibility of relationship – as Ursula discovers during the visit to her uncle's colliery:

> His real mistress was the machine, and the real mistress of Winifred was the machine. She too, Winifred, worshipped the impure abstraction, the mechanisms of matter. There, there, in the machine, in service of the machine, was she free from the clog and degradation of human feeling. There, in the monstrous mechanism that held all matter, living or dead, in its service did she achieve her consummation and her perfect unison, her immortality.

The narcissistic delights of homosexuality are not enough, even for Winifred Inger; even she must make a commitment to something outside herself, and she finds her consummation and her unison, her immortality, in the machine. But Ursula continues to seek hers in the flesh. Perhaps the repetitive savageries of Ursula's sexual encounters with Skrebensky are partly justifiable on the ground that with Skrebensky Ursula's attempt is so much more plausible and at the same time so much more exacerbating: at least Skrebensky is a man and no narcissistic projection of herself, though she can master and break him; at least Skrebensky is not positively evil, though he is weak and inchoate. If we do not lose sympathy with Ursula for her annihilating cruelty toward Skrebensky, it is because we are convinced that she suffers in the grip of an impulse which is, if it can ever be fulfilled, the sanest and most healing impulse accessible to her; if she appears at moments in the guise of a female spider devouring her sexually spent and useless mate, she is in any case obeying a brute instinct more vital than Skrebensky's attachment to political abstractions or Miss Inger's attachment to mechanism. Ursula's quest is desperate, so therefore are her feelings often; but the discoveries she must make cannot be arrived at by theorem, and she has no immediately recognizable allies. To contain and to be blocked from fulfilling so mastering an impulse is, finally, punishment and promise enough, as Lawrence indicates in the marvellous passage in which Ursula has her heart-stopping encounter with the stampeding horses, hallucination or reality.

. . . The new woman is too strong, and the new man is too weak, the woman suddenly conscious of long-sleeping powers and the man suddenly confronted with a rival. It is as if, for the new broken reed of a man like Skrebensky, all the long history of patriarchal Western civilization – its dream of wholeness and community, its exaltation of the family and of romantic love – has been man's dogged postponement of woman's inevitable supremacy. It all leads to Skrebensky, totally dependent, beaten child and rejected lover, hearing his doom on the final morning-after:

> He tapped at her bedroom door at the last minute. She stood with her umbrella in her hand. He closed the door. He did not know what to say.
>
> "Have you done with me?" he asked her at length, lifting his head.
>
> "It isn't me," she said. "You have done with me – we have done with each other."
>
> He looked at her, at the closed face, which he thought so cruel. And he knew he could never touch her again. His will was broken, he was seared, but he clung to the life of his body.
>
> "Well, what have I done?" he asked, in a rather querulous voice.
>
> "I don't know," she said, in the same dull, feelingless voice. "It is finished. It has been a failure."

In this contest – though Skrebensky thinks otherwise – there is no kindness and cruelty, only life and death, all and nothing; the issue is beyond the condescensions of charity, and the time is very late. There must be, somewhere, men to face up to the new dispensation: men like Tom Brangwen, who did much and might have done more had he known better what had overtaken him. Anna, in paralysing contempt of Will when he tried to assert an authority he had already yielded by his unmanly surrender to her flesh, cried out that her stepfather "could put a dozen of you in his pipe and push them down with his finger-end." The new woman is strong in her power to wound and even to kill man's spirit if she has no male counterforce to match her. Yet life somehow continuously renews itself: in a time of human degradation, the unique powers of woman have at last asserted themselves; and such powers, coming so unexpectedly out of the very sources of life, cannot be without a commensurate object and response. What remains, in the compulsive ugliness of modern industrialism, as all values except those preservable by the conscious individual are swept away, is promise.

. . . The pledge of the future is Ursula's knowledge of what is terrible about the present, and her knowledge derives from a power of passion which must at length be consummated because it would otherwise have had no cause to spring into being. Dostoevsky called the Russians the "god-bearing" people, those who carry the secret of life within them and preserve it for that remote apocalypse when all the world will be fit to receive it. At the conclusion of *The Rainbow* Ursula is the single god-bearing person left in the world. It is a tribute to the prodigious optimism and persuasiveness of Lawrence's vision that the secret she holds seems worth the keeping until the world is fit to receive it.[23]

Across the Fifties we can see that the prevailing critical opinion of Lawrence's work had dramatically shifted. Between the 1951 publication of Harry T. Moore's *The Life and Works of D. H. Lawrence*, and the end of 1960, there were 747 articles, books and essays published about various aspects of Lawrence's work and life – nearly seven times the number in the preceding decade. Because of the outstanding efforts of scholars such as F. R. Leavis, Harry T. Moore, Eliseo Vivas, Mark Spilka and Marvin Mudrick quoted here – and notable work by Mark Schorer, Graham Hough, Vivian de Sola Pinto, William York Tindall and many others who began to apply serious thought to Lawrence's novels at the same time – there was, by the turning of the decade, a new attitude to the writer. By 1960, Lawrence's place as a central figure in twentieth-century English literature seemed assured.

Before moving on to examine the treatment of *The Rainbow* and

*Women in Love* during the Sixties, we should note certain important legacies of the Fifties 'Lawrence Revival' and take stock of the critical standing of the two novels at a point just over forty years after their completion.

We began our discussion of the Fifties by noting the influence of an important biography and critical biography, and we should also note the contribution of another major biographical undertaking which spanned the closing years of the decade. In 1957, 1958 and 1959 Edward Nehls published the three volumes of his *D. H. Lawrence: A Composite Biography*, a massive work which presented a judiciously-edited montage of writings by and (mostly) about Lawrence, arranged chronologically to cover his entire life and a short period after his death.[24] The three volumes together present a picture of Lawrence from multiple perspectives, drawing together positive and negative views and opinions, scholarly comments and personal memoirs, sections of letters and parts of published and unpublished works, all arranged around stages of his life. The biography is fascinating for anyone interested in Lawrence, and provides a hugely useful source for scholars of Lawrence's life and work.

The biographical studies of the Fifties are important today because they provide important anchor and departure points for studies of the novels. They are significant also because their publication freed Lawrence's work from the shroud of myth and sensationalism that often prevented public understanding of his ideas and methods – as witnessed in many of the reviews and essays quoted in earlier sections of this book. The academics and critics who discussed the novels were able to proceed with their work much more evenly and productively once the confusion about Lawrence himself had been cleared. In an important way, then, the biographical work undertaken by Moore and Nehls facilitated a clearer focus on the novels themselves.

Another major legacy of the 'Lawrence Revival' was the development – largely by F. R. Leavis – of a hierarchy amongst the novels. Throughout *D. H. Lawrence: Novelist*, and taken up in the work of many other critics of the Fifties, we find a rank-order of merit for the novels becoming firmly established. According to Leavis, it was *Women in Love* and *The Rainbow* (in that order) that stood far above the other novels in terms of their success as 'dramatic poems' and their successful realisation of Lawrence's art. The novel that had haunted the later works, *Sons and Lovers*, was still seen as a fine realist work, but of lesser importance to the canon than the two great sister-works. The novellas, tales and the later novels *Lady Chatterley's Lover* and *The Plumed Serpent* were also beginning to draw more serious critical treatment and recognition as the decade ended.

The Leavisite vision of Lawrence as an intensely moral novelist was important in shaping the view of his works throughout the Fifties and into the Sixties. For many of the younger critics who had been brought up with Leavis's brand of critical practice, the novels became important for their statement of moral resistance to the forces of industrial modernity and capitalism. The early Sixties saw Lawrence's work celebrated for its championing of decency and personal responsibility, and, as Dennis and Fleda Brown Jackson and Marvin Mudrick point out, the novels' frank treatment of sexuality seemed at last to be acceptable to the growing public audience. As we shall see in the next chapter, the 'sexual revolution' that swept Western societies during the Sixties would further contribute to the huge increase of interest in the novels.

# CHAPTER FOUR

# The Sixties and Onwards:
# Acceptability and Dissolution

THE CENSORSHIP actions against *Lady Chatterley's Lover* in the U.S.A. (1959) and Britain (1960) gave a huge boost to sales of all of Lawrence's work, world-wide, right across the Sixties. The mood of the decade was such that Lawrence was now seen as a fighter for individual freedoms, a writer who stood out against hypocrisy and industrial oppression, and a champion of sexual and personal liberation. Many of his ideas seemed to anticipate the concerns of the day, and he seemed to speak directly to a new and vigorous youth-market. There were, predictably, the more gross and exploitative uses of his name to sanction or advertise goods and enterprises the nature of which would have driven him to great fury had he been alive, but in general, the decade saw a genuine broadening of interest in, and understanding of, the novels.

The academic and critical press began to carry a wider range of discussions and analyses of all the novels, in addition to writings on the plays, stories and works of non-fiction. But the overwhelming concern remained with the major novels – and particularly with those established by Leavis as central to the canon: *The Rainbow* and *Women in Love*.

We have already noted that the number of articles, books and essays about Lawrence's work printed during the period 1910–60 is far exceeded by the number published since 1960 – and the total range of publications still grows year upon year. The hundreds of works published during the Sixties pursue a wide range of arguments, the breadth and diversity of which have been given a considerable fillip by the growth of interest in various critical theories during the past thirty years. The academic concerns of the New Critics and Leavisites were, in many ways, overtaken by the work of Marxist and Feminist theorists during the Seventies, and the later debates around structuralism, post-structuralism and deconstruction. This chapter, then, marks the point at which it becomes difficult to follow a strictly chronological ordering of the progress of Lawrence studies, for there must be consideration of some of the major movements in criticism and the resultant range of responses to the novels. Thus, whilst we begin this chapter with a consideration of Lawrence's place at the start of the Sixties, the discussion moves beyond the decade and takes in later works relevant to the central concerns of the chapter.

There are three essential areas of interest around which I have grouped the extracts and commentary that follows. First, we shall consider the earliest re-working of Leavis's 'hierarchy of merit' for the novels, and the mounting of a challenge to the central Leavisite view of Lawrence as a moral novelist, in Eliseo Vivas's work from 1960, *D. H. Lawrence: The Failure and the Triumph of Art*. In the second grouping of the chapter I consider those works primarily concerned with the composition of the novels and the links between the novels and particular ideas found in Lawrence's non-fiction. In this group I place two important works of the Sixties, George H. Ford's 'Introductory Note to D. H. Lawrence's Prologue to *Women in Love*', published in 1963, and Mark Kinkead-Weekes's 1968 essay 'The Marble and the Statue: The Exploratory Imagination of D. H. Lawrence', and from 1973, Frank Kermode's *Lawrence*. Bringing the chapter to a close is an extract from Colin Clarke's controversial but extremely important study of 'the ambivalence of Lawrence's attitude to corruption': *River of Dissolution: D. H. Lawrence and English Romanticism* (1969). By rekindling the debate initiated by Vivas at the start of the decade, and by challenging the orthodox view of Lawrence established during the 'Revival', Clarke's work was responsible for re-invigorating the critical tendency to review and relocate Lawrence's novels – a major feature of the final chapter of this book.

Published in the opening year of the decade, Eliseo Vivas's *D. H. Lawrence: The Failure and the Triumph of Art* divides Lawrence's novels into 'failures' and 'triumphs', and defines the features which constitute the triumph of *The Rainbow* and *Women in Love*. Whilst Vivas's ordering of the novels into a hierarchy suggests an acceptance and reinforcement of the ways that New Critical and Leavisite scholars had approached Lawrence, it is in his view of the qualities of the novels, and of the features that accounted for their 'triumph', that Vivas moves into new ground and distances himself from Leavis.

Vivas was the first critic fully to dispute the Leavisite view of Lawrence's essential morality, and argued in his book that the 'prophecy' and 'message' of Lawrence's philosophising were damaging to the novels, rather than positive. Further, he urged recognition of the darker and more savage aspects of Lawrence's art, rejecting Leavis's moral formalism and arguing instead that the greatness of the art actually lay in its ability to depict and deal with the disintegrative and cruel forces at work in relationships and society. In the scheme of this book, then, Vivas's study (from which a chapter on *Women in Love* is extracted here) represents something of a challenge to the legacy of the Fifties and to Leavis's categorisation of Lawrence as a moral and socially integrative writer.

*The Failure and the Triumph of Art* took as its starting point for an examination of the novels the notion that Lawrence 'did not come into full possession of his poetic power and insight until *The Rainbow* and *Women in Love*. After writing these two novels, his work deteriorated as art – with the exception of a few short stories which, however perfect in their kind, are minor.'[1] Vivas attempted to distinguish between those novels in which the 'prophecy' and 'message' were subordinated to the 'poetry' and 'art', and those in which the didactic intentions and auto-biographical imperatives became dominant. The first group were held as triumphs, the second as failures.

Vivas's book opens with a consideration of *Aaron's Rod, Kangaroo, The Plumed Serpent* and *Lady Chatterley's Lover* – all of which constitute a body of work that 'whatever its many incidental and aesthetic excellences and whatever its ideological value, on the whole fails to come up to the purity exhibited in his two greatest works, *The Rainbow* and *Women in Love*.'[2] In the second part of the book, Vivas discusses the features that make these two novels so successful, and includes also, as a 'triumph', *Sons and Lovers* – though it is recognised that this earlier novel does not 'embody the substance of his vision, as we find it . . . embodied in the later works.' As we have noted above, it is Vivas's contention that perceptions of Lawrence as a chiefly moral novelist were misguided and failed to recog-nise and do justice to his darker side. To Vivas then, recognition of the misanthropy, misogyny, erotic violence and destructive impulses with which the novels deal is fundamental to a full understanding of Lawrence's work.

The extract reproduced here is taken from the chapter entitled 'The Form of *Women in Love*,' in which Vivas considers the ordering and development of the two relationships which provide *Women in Love* with its major theme:

It is an old story that Lawrence was, early in his career, forced to aban-don the classical form of the novel. We remember his explosion in a letter of 1912: "They want me to have form: that means, they want me to have *their* pernicious, ossiferous skin-and-grief form, and I won't." In much of his work Lawrence achieved neither pernicious nor ossif-erous nor any other form. *Aaron's Rod, Kangaroo, The Plumed Serpent* are novels of major pretension that are padded, rambling works, poorly thought and poorly executed. But in *Women in Love* and in a few other of his major novels and in some of his short stories he succeeded in achieving a form appropriate to the substance of his poetry. Of course, his is not the kind of form that can be expressed in simple terms – as one expresses the rhyme scheme of a sonnet. And the reason, as we have seen, is that in the classical sense of the term there is no action or plot in his work. He was interested, mainly, in revealing the quality of experience as experienced and he came as close to success here as is possible. The revelation of experience is undertaken by Lawrence, not merely to give the reader the "feel" of it, but also to exhibit the values discovered and actualised by it. Were he not interested in both experience and its values his work would not be as important as it is for us. The form he achieves is grasped by us when we notice the progress of developing experience: the beginning and gathering of passion, its swelling to flood-strength, its leaping over the dyke or its baffled pounding against it. Because the form of action in the behavioural sense is easier to perceive than the structure of inward experience, a first reading of Lawrence and even a second or third gives us little more than a chaos of incidents and scenes that, however brilliantly presented, seem to lack formal inter-relationships. But persistent search for the structure of the work is at last rewarded. Synoptically we grasp the pattern of an ordered whole. We notice the first signs of nascent desire turning into clearly directed urge and notice the passional urge seeking satisfaction and succeeding or arriving at frustration; we notice the pattern of attraction and repulsion, the harmony of wills or their clash, and back of these harmonies and conflicts we notice the values that these inward commotions seek to realise and succeed or fail in realising. And strange as it might seem, since Lawrence is so frequently dismissed as anti-rational, we notice also the growth in wisdom on the part of his character – or of what Lawrence takes to be wisdom – and the causes for the success or failure of that growth.

More concretely, although *Women in Love* is incredibly rich in detail and dense in substance, its organisation is achieved by means that, formulated in abstract terms, appear to be relatively simple. Its form is given to it by the account of the genesis and development of two contrasting love affairs – that of Birkin and Ursula and that of Gerald and Gudrun. They begin at about the same time but from the beginning they display contrasting qualities which lead one of them to a catastrophic ending and the other to an apparent degree of maturity and fulfilment. There are, of course, between the two affairs, intimate and complex interrelationships. The women, for instance, are sisters, while the men are good friends. Every incident, conversation or scene can be shown to bear on and to support the development of one or both of the love affairs that constitute the novel's main theme. To trace these complex relationships in detail would be an enterprise demanding almost a book. All that I can hope to do now is to sketch the two major lines of development that define the form of *Women in Love*.

Let us begin with the older sister, Ursula, and her lover Birkin. The first time we find Ursula in conversation with Birkin is in Chapter III, the afternoon he visited her classroom in his capacity as school inspector. She has seen him at the wedding, earlier, and had been piqued, attracted and annoyed by him. But although the basis of a relationship is established in the classroom – under the aegis, as Kenneth Burke would put it, of the gynaceous and androgynous flowers – it is not until considerably later on, in Chapter XI, that they meet alone and that Birkin tells Ursula that his affair with Hermione is finally over. From this time on, the development of their love affair runs its stormy course to the inconclusive last conversation with which the book ends. Ursula visits Birkin in his apartment at the mill house and Birkin attempts, but fails, to convey to her that the kind of love he wants and is ready to give is different from ordinary love. But the lovers gradually come to an understanding in spite of their quarrels, or perhaps because of them. Some of their fights are so intense and are reported with such immediacy that the reader is swept into the clash and forced to share in the burning emotions of the conflicting lovers. The proper intransitivity of attention is impossible and an aesthetic spectacle becomes a partisan emotional experience. The poet's power of revelation has betrayed him again, as it did earlier, and does later, into failure. These scenes are followed by moments of peace, of tenderness, of a fulfilment which strains the rich linguistic resources of the poet to convey. But for all its flaws, the account of the affair comes off, for one reader at least with the quick vitality without which poetry turns into soggy journalese. Grasp synoptically the jagged line of development from the beginning of the affair to the heights of erotic satisfaction, down to the depths of hatred, take the relationship in its full span, and you will see how it is the genesis and fruition – such as they are – of their love that informs the substance of the novel. But the love affair is more than an informing agent; it constitutes the substance of the novel and, as it is conceived by both Birkin and Lawrence, it constitutes one of its themes.

We are given the most important clue to this fact in the conversation between Gerald and Birkin, reported in the chapter entitled "In the Train." Birkin introduces the subject by asking Gerald, somewhat abruptly, what he lives for. Gerald, committed to "the ethics of productivity," confesses that life does not centre for him but is artificially held together by the social mechanism. Birkin agrees.

> "I know," he said, "it just doesn't centre. The old ideals are dead as nails – nothing there. It seems to me there remains only this perfect union with a woman – sort of ultimate marriage – and there isn't anything else."

"And you mean if there isn't the woman, there's nothing?" said Gerald.

"Pretty well that – seeing there's no God."

"Then we're hard put to it," said Gerald . . . (Chapter V)

The importance of this passage cannot be over-emphasised and I shall have to refer to it several times in the following discussion. It gives us an early clue to the formal and substantive role that love plays in the book. It is put forth by Birkin as a substitute for God. In what sense Birkin's and Gerald's opinions are borne out and what are the consequences, for each, of the quandaries, it will be our chief business to consider later. At this point it is only necessary to note that the love affair between Birkin and Ursula is *idiotic*, in the original acceptation of the term. Of course they live among friends and in their unconventional way accept the conventions of their group. But they blandly refuse to reckon with established social institutions and Birkin particularly exhibits a strong streak of misanthropy whose fountainhead is not traced in the novel. The fact that we remain in the dark as to the reason for Birkin's hatred of his fellow men constitutes one of the defects of the novel (as it does of many other novels and stories of Lawrence). But let that pass. We are not told what source of income the couple has. Finally, I own, they do marry. But the ceremony is obviously external and unimportant both to the couple and to the novel, for it is only in passing that we are told that it took place. If there is something sacramental in the nature of their union (and the term is not as incongruous as it may seem to those who have not grasped the ethos of *Women in Love*), its sacred character does not come from the ceremonies and rites, the conventions and practices, with which society puts the seal of the sacred on the institution of marriage. It is to be found in the union itself, in the manner in which the lovers for all their difficulties and quarrels, come to respect, even to venerate "the Eros of the sacred mysteries."

But the *idiocy* of their union is not to be interpreted to mean that the lovers "shack up" in a love-nest with the blinds drawn and the doorbell disconnected – in the way in which Will and Anna do after the wedding in *The Rainbow*. Nor does it mean that the love affair can be grasped in its specific quality without reference to the relationships between the lovers and other persons. Indeed, in order to grasp the quality of their relationship Lawrence must give us an account of the collapse of the affair between Birkin and Hermione; and in turn, in order to make this account intelligible, he must give us a comprehensive idea of the personality of Hermione and her friends. He must also introduce us to the bohemian world of Halliday and his friends in London. Thus, the ramifications and dramatic entailments of one love affair are numerous, complex, dense.

With the appropriate changes in detail the same observation holds for the affair between Gerald and Gudrun. Its development is one of the two unifying principles of the novel. And in order to understand the reason for Gerald's failure in love, which constitutes the second major theme of the novel, Lawrence must give us a fairly complete account of Gerald's life, including such information about his past as is relevant, his attitude towards the world and his successful activities as a mine owner – for Lawrence intends us to notice a connection between Gerald's nature and the industrial world that he built and that in turn produced him. To appreciate Gerald's ruthless efficiency, his management of the mines must be contrasted to his father's, whose paternalism was inefficient and finally proved impractical. And in turn to appreciate properly the specious nature of Gerald's success as manager, we must grasp the inadequacy of his attitude towards sex, defined dramatically by the account of the night he spends with Halliday's mistress. Lawrence wants us to see that the weakness of the man is connected with his failure to venerate the Eros of the sacred mysteries. And the point for us is not whether Lawrence's account of Gerald's failure is or is not causally adequate; the point is that Lawrence conceives of the Gerald–Gudrun affair in this manner and uses it – successfully in my opinion – to bring into harmonious unity the multiplicity of incident, the complexity of episodes, the density of dramatic specification which constitutes *Women in Love*.

The assertion that the two love affairs organise or give form to the substance of the novel may be tested by taking each of the episodes or incidents that at first sight do not appear to be related to the main themes and showing how it is in fact related. As already suggested, I shall take only some of the incidents that at first sight may not appear to have any relation to the central themes and show how they are related to them. Some of course will be found to be more closely related to the love affair of Birkin and Ursula than to that of Gerald and Gudrun. But the relations will be found to obtain for each of the incidents, however remote the incident may appear at first sight. Let me begin by showing how the drowning of Diana Crich and the young doctor who attempted to save her are organically part of a harmonious whole.

In order to grasp the connection we must remember Gerald's sense of superiority, his unquestioned conviction that he can dominate men and nature. The conviction is not an altogether empty conceit, for his unquestionable success with the colliers only substantiated his belief and, for a time, ours. But for all his managerial talent and his indisputable masterful will, not only are there limits to his power but there is an inherent weakness in it, which we must be aware of if we are to accept the fact that two persons who do not at first sight seem to possess his strength, Gudrun and Loerke, can be the main agents of his catastrophic ending. Bearing this in mind, let us recall that, as Lawrence takes the trouble to inform us, Gerald is responsible for the water during the part which ended with the drowning. And while in neither a moral nor a legal sense can he be blamed for the drowning, dramatically he fails. For he made a desperate effort to save his sister and her friend. The industrial magnate who thinks of men as mere tools and who wants the pure fulfilment of his own will in the struggle with natural conditions, the high priest of the false idol, the Machine, when he is responsible for the water at the party, a relatively minor responsibility, fails. And the failure draws clearly for us the limits of his power. There are a number of indications throughout the narrative of Gerald's prospective failure; but they would not be convincing or even significant for us if we had not taken the measure of his specious strength. Lawrence wants to tell us that Gerald's failure in his life, particularly in love, has its source in his dedication to the wrong God, the Machine. Whether his intention and the intention of the novel coincide is another question – one that will be considered later.

This is not the only connection of the drowning episode with the rest of the novel. A summary reference to other connections will give us a firmer sense of the closely woven texture of the composition. One of these is ironic and throws us back to Chapter IV, entitled "Diver," in which the sisters, out for a walk, see Gerald diving into the lake and swimming off. In the account the viewpoint shifts – as it does frequently with Lawrence – from the sisters to Gerald and back to the sisters. Watching him swim, Gudrun envies his masculinity almost painfully. She desires the freedom, the liberty and mobility that enables him to do anything he wants, whereas she, a woman, is thoroughly restricted. But it is he who is in fact restricted because weak, and it is she who shows up his weakness and leads him to his death. And this is in part the irony of the situation.

The irony, however, is considerably more complex. The situation in which Gerald is envied by Gudrun for qualities and powers he in fact does not possess is symbolic (in an ordinary semiotic sense of the term). For obvious reasons, water has been thought of by many peoples throughout the world and throughout history as part of a complex which links vegetation, woman, the moon, with fecundity and life. But as it turns out, Gerald is not the source of creativity, fecundity, life; he is bound for destruction. His talents are the talents of destruction and evil, anti-human. Immediately after the sisters resume their walk, having looked at Gerald swimming, Ursula tells Gudrun that Gerald, who is making all sorts of modern improvements in Shortlands, the Criches' home, will "have to die soon, when there is nothing more to improve." And then Ursula tells her sister that Gerald killed his brother when "they were quite boys." This is not the only time that reference is made to Gerald's bearing the sign of Cain. There is a premonitory connection between the drowning of his sister in the water-party chapter, and Gerald's end – for it is by water that Gerald dies. True, it is not the fluid element that kills him, but the vast abstraction of ice and snow up in the Alps; but it is water that kills him nevertheless. Thus we see that the drowning incident is intimately related to the substance of the novel, and not factitiously: the incident is no mere "plant" put there by Lawrence artificially, but is organically and deftly woven into the whole.

It is not altogether irrelevant at this point to dwell on the manner in which Lawrence employs water, and not only in *Women in Love*, but also in *The Rainbow*: not as a symbol of generation and life, but of destruction and death. Thus, the Brangwens' bucolic life is destroyed by the opening of the canal near their farm and we are told that it is the women of the Brangwen family who are different and reject the "blood intimacy" which was the essence of their farming life. And it is by drowning, when the canal breaks and floods the land, that Tom Brangwen dies. Am I being too ingenious? I do not think so. Consider that in *Women in Love*, when Birkin comes back from France after the lapis lazuli incident, the crisis comes to a head after his futile effort to break the image of the moon on the surface of the pond. It is almost as if for Lawrence the symbols of the water and the moon sometimes were reversed. Whether it be true of Lawrence the man or not, of *Women in Love* we can say that neither of the two principal male characters are men who accept love in its full span, as a means for the procreation of life. Neither Birkin's Eros of the sacred mysteries, nor Gerald's Eros of the jaunty "amours," leads to the family with its roots, its stability, and its fulfilment. There is never any question that the Gerald–Gudrun liaison may lead to marriage, the family, and the assumption of the responsibilities of man in society; and the marriage of Ursula and Birkin does not point towards a normal, if eventual and postponed, settled life.

The chair episode, Chapter XXVI, furnishes us with another test of the claim that the novel is closely organised. Ursula and Birkin go to a jumble market to look for furniture. First they notice a young woman who is pregnant and her young man looking at a mattress, and then they discover a chair that attracts them very much and they decide to buy it. But in the conversation that follows the purchase, Birkin tells Ursula that the fact is that he does not want things at all. The thought of a house and furniture is hateful to him and Ursula replies that it is hateful to her too. He makes an emphatic declaration that they will avoid having things of their own, but Ursula points out that they have just bought a chair. They decide they don't really want it, and give it to the young couple whom they had seen looking at the mattress. The significance of this episode is that it serves to reinforce the conversation they had at the inn where they put up after visiting Southwell Minster, in which Birkin tells Ursula that they have to drop their jobs and wander about for a bit.

The connection between the chair episode and the rest of the novel is obvious enough; it is, indeed, directly indicated in the text by Lawrence himself. But the relationship between Chapter XXVIII, entitled "In the Pompadour," and the rest of the story is not so obvious. The chapter contains the scene in which Halliday reads Birkin's ridiculous letter to his friends and Gudrun snatches it from him and leaves with Gerald in the taxi. What does this chapter tell us? While the scene is sharply etched, the relationship between its content and the rest of the story is not at all clear. Surely its central purpose cannot be to give us a picture of Halliday and his friends: for not only has Lawrence already given us an adequate picture of these people, but the incident is really concerned with Birkin. What then is its purpose? It completes, for us, the figure of Birkin. To see how it does, we must go back to the chapter entitled "An Island," Chapter XI, in which a conversation takes place between Ursula and Birkin and in which Birkin expresses his hatred of humanity, a subject on which he has already expressed himself twice before. As I have remarked already, the misanthropy is not elucidated; from the novel it is not possible to discover why Birkin hates mankind as he does. In any case there is no doubt about his feelings in the reader's mind: Birkin tells us he loathes himself as a human being, and believes that humanity is itself dry-rotten, that it is a tree of lies, less than the individual "because the individual is sometimes capable of truth." Ursula watches him rant and decides that she wants him for himself and that she hates the Salvator Mundi, the Sunday-school teacher, the prig of the stiffest kind that in part he is. We are given another picture of this Salvator Mundi aspect of Birkin in Chapter XIV, "Water-Party," in the scene in which Birkin, seemingly for no plausible reason, starts a harangue somewhat similar to that which Halliday is making fun of. He talks of "the other river," and speaks to Ursula of the flowers of dissolution, a progressive process which is the end of the world. Exactly what Birkin is telling Ursula I cannot make out clearly. But this much is clear: that it is this aspect of Birkin that Ursula has seen earlier and disliked because it is the Salvator Mundi side of Birkin. Ursula knows that Birkin "would behave in the same way, say the same things, give himself as completely to anybody who came along, anybody and everybody who liked to appeal to him." But we have only Ursula's word for it, and we do not see, until Halliday reads the letter, in precisely what manner Birkin would give himself away to people who would ridicule him for it and who, we have already been shown, are a rather shabby lot of bohemians. In Chapter XXVIII, "In the Pompadour," we see the degree to which Birkin was ready to expose himself. Gudrun had reason to be angry, for the letter made a fool of Birkin. But whatever her reaction, by the scene Lawrence showed this aspect of Birkin's nature without pity.

When we view the novel in this manner, I believe we must agree with Lawrence when he exploded against the "pernicious, ossiferous skin-and-grief form," which critics wanted him to have. For the traditional form of the novel he has substituted his own form, and one which answered adequately to the demands made by the substance of the novel, which is no longer defined by character and action . . . His best work does have form, but it is a form which is organic with the substance informed and not one copied from earlier work.[3]

As mentioned in the introduction to this chapter, I wish to consider, in this second section, the growing critical interest in the composition of the novels and the links between the novels and Lawrence's non-fiction prose. The general rise of interest in Lawrence through the late Fifties, and the more general acceptance of his place among the major authors of the century, led to a broadening and diversification of critical activity concerning the novels. As a result, during the Sixties, more scholarship was devoted to examining the peculiar process of composition out of which the novels had emerged, and the relationships between these two major works and other less well-known works of the same period.

George H. Ford's investigation of early manuscript drafts of 'The Sisters', *The Rainbow* and *Women in Love* led to the publication for the first time, in 1963, of a discarded 'Prologue' chapter to *Women in Love*, together with a 'Note' from Ford which addresses many of the issues raised by earlier critics of the novel, and several of the points already discussed by Middleton Murry, Aldous Huxley, F. R. Leavis and Mark Spilka in this volume.[4] In addition, Ford's comments on Lawrence's tendency towards moral and dramatic ambiguities are to be picked up and explored more thoroughly in the extract from Colin Clarke's *River of Dissolution*, in the last section of this chapter. (Ford's 'Note' is reprinted in full in the Macmillan Casebook on *The Rainbow* and *Women in Love*, edited by Colin Clarke.)

Ford was one of the many critics and academics who began to investigate the relationships between manuscript versions of the two novels during the Sixties. Running alongside the interest in the manuscript drafts of 'The Sisters' and 'The Wedding Ring' and their eventual reworking as *The Rainbow* and *Women in Love*, was a growing interest in the works wherein Lawrence tested and developed his philosophy during the long gestation process for the two novels. Seeking to address some of the more complex questions about Lawrence's thinking on corruption, marriage and the nature of male and female relationships, a number of academics turned their attention to the two studies Lawrence wrote whilst he worked on the novels: *Study of Thomas Hardy* and *The Crown*.

The *Study of Thomas Hardy*[5] was written after Methuen had rejected Lawrence's first version of *The Rainbow*, which he completed in February 1914, and before he re-worked the novel into its finished form in March 1915. During the time he worked on the *Study*, the First World War began, and Lawrence's response to its horrors is plain in both the *Study* and the subsequently re-worked version of the novel. Though the first draft of *The Rainbow* has not survived, it is generally thought that it contained much material from what is now *Women in Love*. In addition, the second version of *The Rainbow* is significantly influenced by the thinking that went into the *Study* and its vision of oppositions and possible unities between the sexes. For critics seeking some useful keys to the concerns of the novel, then, the *Study* offered rich ground for exploration and inquiry.

In the first full-length study to concern itself with the links between Lawrence's essays and novels, H. M. Daleski's *The Forked Flame: A Study of D. H. Lawrence*[6] (1965) made a significant contribution to what was to become a central area of interest for later critics. Daleski considers the 'dualism' of Lawrence's thought in relation to *Sons and Lovers*, *The Rainbow*, *Women in Love*, *Aaron's Rod*, *The Plumed Serpent* and *Lady Chatterley's Lover*, and makes strong links between the 'expository writings' and the novels, to the extent that he is able to claim that readers should 'regard the expository writings not as laboratory reports on experiments successfully concluded, but as signposts to a road which is finally travelled only in the art'. In the novels, Daleski argues, there is a consistent and uneven attempt on Lawrence's part to 'reconcile the opposed elements within himself', which springs chiefly from his own knowledge that he is more attuned to the 'female principle as he himself defines it in the essay on Hardy'. Where Lawrence manages to develop some statement of opposition or workable polarity between the male and female principles, the novels are successful – as with *The Rainbow* and *Women in Love*. Where there is an effort to attune himself artificially with the male principle through his fiction – as in the later novels – the work is weakened as a result.

Daleski's work in *The Forked Flame* was developed further with the publication, in 1968, of Mark Kinkead-Weekes's essay 'The Marble and the Statue: The Exploratory Imagination of D. H. Lawrence.'[7] Kinkead-Weekes's discussion of the relationships between *The Rainbow* and *Women in Love* and their links with, respectively, *Study of Thomas Hardy* and *The Crown*[8] made a huge contribution to the understanding of Lawrence's creative process and imaginative powers. The essay is based on meticulous research of manuscript fragments and drafts, and analyses the arguments and thought-processes which shaped the studies and the two novels. The language and symbols used by Lawrence in the two studies are examined, and the development between the two, and their linked novels, is made clear: where the *Study* looks for a hopeful reconciliation of opposites as achieved in *The Rainbow*, *The Crown* deals with corruption and discord:

... although *The Crown* was a rewriting of the *Study*, the differences go even deeper than the attempt to replace Christian language, pare away the whole apparatus of history, art criticism, and literary criticism, and write in more popular terms for a public audience. The essential difference is that the *Study* was positive, while *The Crown* is an attempt to diagnose disintegration.[9]

Kinkead-Weekes finds that the chapter of *The Crown* entitled 'The Flux of Corruption' affords a vision of the imaginative world out of which *Women in Love* was born, and holds the key to the differences between Lawrence's mood as expressed in the *Study* and *The Rainbow* and its much darker realisation in the later works. In his focus on the dissolution and corruptive elements of *The Crown* and *Women in Love*, Kinkead-Weekes prepares the ground for many later discussions of the novel, as we shall see in the extracts from Colin Clarke's book which close this chapter. Kinkead-Weekes's essay is a central work in Lawrence criticism, and although too long for reprinting here, should be read by any serious student of the novels.

Since the publication of 'The Marble and the Statue', Lawrence's two essays have been universally acknowledged as the philosophical templates for *The Rainbow* and *Women in Love*, and are generally seen as providing a key to many of the symbolic and structural elements of the novels.

Six years after the publication of 'The Marble and the Statue', Frank Kermode published a brief yet informative and highly readable book on Lawrence's novels and longer tales: *Lawrence*.[10] In his chapters on *The Rainbow* and *Women in Love*, Kermode makes a point of considering the importance to the novels of Lawrence's two essays. His accounts of the *Study* and *The Crown* provide useful summaries of the dominant symbols and oppositional forces in each essay. The short sections on each of the studies are reprinted here:

### The *Study of Thomas Hardy*

*Hardy* is about possible plenitude of life, symbolised by the poppy: disregarding time, the poppy flares its uniqueness even as it prodigally scatters its seed; it attends to being poppy and the rest follows. This is an example of what we should be, but instead we go in for the wrong kind of self-preservation: the law, the movement for female suffrage which will result only in women making more laws – these are mechanical and life-destroying substitutes for poppy-like self-fulfilment; and their consequence is war. The only good of the war is that it can convince us of the need for a revolution in the heart; it won't matter if many die so long as there is afterwards 'alive in the land, some new sense of what is and what is not, some new courage to let go the securities, and to be, to risk ourselves in a forward venture of life, as we are willing to risk ourselves in a rush of death' (*Phoenix*. I. pp. 407–8).

Lawrence is again talking about the need to let go, and hinting at the perverted female force of law which prevents the race from doing so, as his mother prevented him. He attacks the cult of work, an expression of that law; work is bad unless it extends human consciousness. The doctrine is evolutionary: with the right kind of human effort – but that must be wholly unmechanical – the ascent of man from undifferentiated tissue to mammals, 'from mammals to man, from man to tribesman, from tribesman to me' (*P*. I. 432) may continue till every man is as distinct an individual as an angel: each man a melody, and, with his neighbours, a harmony. This happiness can come only from the rebirth of the individual; which, according to Lawrence, should occur at twenty or thirty years of age. One is reborn not by taking thought, but by letting go – by a 'fall into the future', or a movement 'to the edge of the unknown' (441).

The means is love. The sexual act is the leap into the unknown; the deposition of seed for continuance of the race is a consequence, not a cause, of this poppy-like fulfilment. 'That she bear children is not a woman's significance. But that she bear herself, that is her supreme and risky fate' (441). So with man; it is not the seed that remains but the expense of the whole spirit that matters. Procreation is the accidental tribute of these momentary immortals to time; the union of male and female, are two distincts which, undivided, generate 'the complete consciousness' (444). Man is hub (did he mean rim?) and woman is axle; his motion portrays her motionlessness, and their perfect union is a frictionless union of motion and rest, time and eternity. Lesser unions are unstable, unsatisfying, the man inhibited from his leaping by the insecurity of the woman, the woman unstable because the man cannot be depended upon to convey stability into motion. For 'life consists in the dual form of the Will-to-Motion and the Will-to-Inertia, and everything we see and know and are is the resultant of these two Wills' (447). Perfect duality is 'as yet unthinkable'; thus in races as well as in marriages one Will predominates.

Here, at the point where Lawrence's sexual teaching shades over into racial theory, as it almost invariably does, we may reflect that certain basic insights on 'letting go', on the polar distinctions and tensions between the sexes, on the rebirth of the self – excited in him the need not only to express them in art, but to develop them into a world system. The Hardy study and its successors soon proceed from sex to more abstract considerations, which are then embodied in very elaborate and systematic structures of thought . . . Thus the reconciliation of the two Wills, of man and woman, will create a third thing, standing to Law and Love, or Woman and Man, as the Holy Ghost stands to the Father and the Son. This is Lawrence's habitual trinitarianism. The imposition of the idea of separate and contending forces on any situation that will accept it is equally characteristic; we shall see how, in applying it to a diagnosis of the decline and rebirth of cultures, Lawrence is willing to let it generate very extreme opinions.

The Hardy study is an important indication of the way in which Lawrence used these principles to explore areas apparently unrelated to his main interests: race, for instance. From the doctrine of Wills emerges the statement that the Jews, being weak in maleness, allowed female inertia to overbear them, and so led in the rush to degeneracy. Monotheism, the Law, are – as we might guess from the Preface to *Sons and Lovers* – female; 'the great assertion of the Male was the New Testament' (452). The New Testament contains the command to be born again, into distinct identity: love and multiplicity invade law and the Jewish monism. The Father and the Son are reconciled by the Comforter. Europe followed the Male Christ; for a moment of perfection at the Renaissance Male and Female were perfectly fused, and Botticelli signals that fusion. But usually there is more of one than the other. Lawrence seeks the fulfilment of the Law in Love, the flesh in the spirit; but 'since the Renaissance, disappointed in the flesh, the northern races have sought the consummation through Love; and they have denied the Father' (468). It is time the Flesh of the Law and the Spirit of Love were again united.

Such is the mixture of art-history, heterodox trinitarian theology and literary criticism, that Lawrence produces in *Thomas Hardy*. It is only a beginning; for the notions of the surrender of male to female in individuals, and in races; of a dissociation between flesh and spirit since the Renaissance; and of the radical modern error of using love for functional purposes, not for the leap into the unknown, have many further implications. Lawrence found in Hardy's Sue Bridehead an image of the 'ghastly sickness of dissolution', and in her husband Phillotson [in *Jude the Obscure*] another, of that excremental death flow which horrifies us because of its proximity to the flow of generation; and these also reflect a phase of cultural history as well as personal disaster. This is not an age when the Consummate Marriage reflects the power of the Holy Spirit to unify Love – the man – with Law – the woman. It is rather that we are at the end of an age of Love, the first having been that of Law; and we shall enter the third only when Male and Female find themselves, unite, and usher in the Holy Ghost. The art of that age is like the Consummate Marriage, knowing 'the struggle between the two conflicting laws and . . . the final reconciliation' (515–516). But at present we have only that apocalyptic pause, 'the pause of finality' (513) which is 'not the end'; the end is the reign of the Holy Ghost.

All this Lawrence will develop further, though never with the same optimism. The notion of personal and historical regeneration working in parallel gives rise to a tripartite apocalyptic world-history, which in turn endows the moment of writing – the early war years – with cosmic significance. The decadence of the spirit is almost contemporary with the moment of its regeneration; the new age, the renovation of time, is born out of the death struggles of the old. As with Yeats's historical cones, the tip of one emerging from the base of the other, the moment of transition is a moment of annunciation. In the midst of the Terrors, a sign; after the flood, a rainbow. If this seems an alarming programme for a novelist we may take heart from Lawrence's confidence that 'artistic form is a revelation of the two principles of Law and Love in a state of conflict and yet reconciled . . .' (477).[11]

### The Crown

Lawrence now decided that the Hardy study needed expansion. He was changing; meeting new people, for example Bertrand Russell and Lady Ottoline Morrell; becoming more vehement about his charismatic role, more apocalyptic in his talk. The war, he often said, killed him, and he awaited resurrection (*Collected Letters* 310); 'being risen from the dead, I know we shall all come through'. Early in 1915 he felt that he had been 'dead as a corpse in its grave clothes' (*C.L.* 314), but now he was 'waking'. *The Rainbow* had rescued him; 'I am coming into my full feather at last'. And the Utopian future seized him; Rananim, his ideal society, could be England, its inhabitants those whom an earlier English apocalyptist had called 'God's Englishmen'. He saw the need for revolution to achieve this (*C.L.* 317, to Russell) but it would be a revolution primarily in the relationship of men and women, a break with an old world of sex, which he thought of as relying on masturbation, or on sex merely as a substitute for it. He also advocated the abolition of private property (*C.L.* 322); and as his programme expanded he entered into his disastrous association with Russell, and decided to rewrite *Hardy*. His object, as he told Lady Ottoline, was simply to procure the regeneration of the race, to 'give a new Humanity its birth' (*C.L.* 325). Russell persuaded him to abandon the Christian terminology of the Hardy study; he began the new treatise in March, gave it up, resumed it in April, finished it in May, and rewrote it between June and September [1915]. Three of its six chapters were published in Middleton Murry's short-lived review, *The Signature*. The whole thing was eventually included in *Reflections on the Death of a Porcupine* (1925).

*The Crown* is what the lion and the unicorn are fighting for, but in Lawrence's allegory they represent the stability of two equal and opposite forces, so that neither should win it. The lion is our dark nature, the unicorn our light; the strife and equilibrium is the third of the trinity, reconciling the two eternities between which we exist. The argument is not fundamentally different from that of *Hardy*, but it is more rapt. In a person, or in an epoch, Law or Love may predominate; but perfection lies in their balance of the two opposing tendencies or streams; there is a possible moment, as of eternity, when Beginning and End and all other opposites are reconciled. At the moment of writing they were not: 'For the stiffened, exhausted, inflexible loins of our era are too dry to give us forth in labour, the tree is withered, we are pent in, fastened, and now have turned round, some to the source of darkness, some to the source of light, and gone mad, purely given up to frenzy . . . then began chaos, the going asunder' (*Phoenix*. II. 371–2).

The Going Asunder is the critical epoch of *Women in Love*. The war is the meaninglessness which persists when the two floods of night and day are asunder, when there is no 'iris between the two floods' (*P*. II. 373). The appearance of the rainbow must be delayed; so must the eternal union of man and woman.

One theme is more positively stressed than before: indeed Lawrence gives it a chapter to itself. This is 'The Flux of Corruption'. In accounting for the degree to which the going asunder had progressed he speaks of the dark returning to the dark after knowing light, as the cabbage, having aspired to flower, grows rotten at the heart. This is our corruption; our effort at flowering goes into corruption instead. We even 'enjoy . . . this being threshed rotten inside. This is sensationalism, reduction of the complex tissue back through rottenness to its elements. And this sensationalism, this reduction back, has become our very life, our only form of life at all' (*P*. II. 388). Sex is 'frictional reduction', and the same sensationalism is expressed in the war. So potent are the forces of dissolution that our consciousness and civilisation are held together only by a sort of evil rind: 'so circumscribed within the outer nullity, we give ourselves up to the flux of death, to analysis, to introspection, to mechanical war and destruction, to humanitarian absorption in the body politic, the poor, the birth-rate, the mortality of infants . . . It is the continued activity of disintegration' (392).

The imagery of corruption now took increasingly hold of Lawrence's mind (he often compared people he disliked to beetles, messes inside carapaces). To assume that the world is merely what is inside the case is modern egoism. But when movement forward to a new epoch seemed blocked, Lawrence entertained the idea that one way to make it possible was to make everything get worse. Looking around him, seeing frictionally reductive sex, the women trying to look like children, the cinema with its phoney heroines (he always thought of the cinema with loathing, as a sort of masturbatory brothel), he concluded that the Holy Ghost, who would lead us into the blossoming time, was missing: the first victim was sex, and true sex had been usurped by a deathwish, as the war showed. Perhaps corruption and destruction must be the way forward. 'In corruption there is divinity . . . in the soft and shiny voluptuousness of decay, in the marshy chill heat of reptiles, there is the sign of the Godhead . . . decay, corruption, destruction, breaking down is the opposite equivalent of creation' (402). Corruption, then, will 'break down for us the deadened forms' (P. II. 403), break the rind. Its emblem is the snake, 'the spirit of the great corruptive principle, the festering cold of the marsh' (407). By sinking deeper into corruption, we may break out of our false universe, and begin again.

This new obsession is a measure of the changed tone of Lawrence's second apocalypse, *Women in Love*. As the war went on he developed it. In 'The Reality of Peace', published in 1917, once again under the sign of the snake in his 'festering marshy border' (P. I. 678), he speaks of the serpent and the marsh as 'within me'. The desire for creation and the desire for dissolution balance in the psyche and in the body. 'How shall it be a shame that from my blood exudes the bitter sweat of corruption on the journey back to dissolution; how shall it be a shame that in my consciousness appear the heavy marsh-flowers of the flux of putrescence, which have their natural roots in the slow stream of decomposition that flows for ever down my bowels?' (P. I. 679). The processes of generation and corruption – of the life and the death-flow – are now explicitly related to genital and excrementatory functions. Here is the battlefield; here a third force will reconcile them. The obsession grew stronger: Lawrence often returns to this theme, which is of great importance in his finest polemical work, *Pornography and Obscenity* (1929); but the first and most important manifestation of the revised and now darkened metaphysic was to be *Women in Love* fittingly, since art is still the great image of the Comforters, the reconciler of the two tendencies or streams.[12]

As discussed in the introduction to this chapter, the final work for discussion is Colin Clarke's *River of Dissolution: D. H. Lawrence and English Romanticism* (1969). Clarke's book (which deals centrally with *The Rainbow* and *Women in Love*, though it also features a short discussion of

*The Plumed Serpent* and *Lady Chatterley's Lover*) is centred upon the argument that we need to develop an awareness of the duality and ambivalence in Lawrence's presentation of corrupting and reductive forces in the novels. In his introduction to the book, Clarke makes his position clear:

It needs to be demonstrated . . . that paradoxes about corruption are dramatized at *every* level, that the strategy is directed *throughout* to affirming but also calling into question (often simultaneously) the dichotomies of decadence and growth, purity and degradation, the paradisal and the demonic.[13]

Clarke's study drew much criticism and was energetically disputed by those who supported the moralistic Leavisite view of Lawrence's writing. The argument that Lawrence owed a 'debt to the English Romantic poets', whose attitudes to corruption and decadence had been essentially ambivalent, was wholly antithetical to the moral vision of the novelist propounded since the publication of Leavis's *D. H. Lawrence: Novelist.*

Clarke was clearly aware of the vast differences of view and interpretation that existed between his own and Leavis's reading of Lawrence's works. Again, in the introduction to his study, Clarke sets out what he feels to be a 'blind-spot' in Leavis's account of the novels' morality, tone and moral purpose. Having quoted a passage from *D. H. Lawrence: Novelist*, in which Leavis asserts that a 'strong normative preoccupation, entailing positives that are correctly present in many ways (we have them . . . in the phrases "the goodness, the holiness, the desire for creation and productive happiness") informs the life of *Women in Love* . . . ', Clarke is clear about his objective in *River of Dissolution*:

How much this leaves out of account, I hope to show. The satanic Lawrence, the Lawrence who finds beauty in the phosphorescence of decay, will be sought in vain in the pages of *D. H. Lawrence: Novelist.*[14]

According to Clarke, the fascination for images of corruption and decay in the novels – and in *Women in Love* particularly – is representative of Lawrence's search for a 'creative-destructive' collapse of the ego, out of which may emerge a new and essentially fuller and more productive being. Throughout *River of Dissolution*, we find Clarke drawing upon the language of the novels, their rich images of decay and their correspondence to the arguments of *The Crown*, with its ambiguous mixing of regenerative and destructive forces. Early in the chapter entitled '*Women in Love*: "The Rhetoric of Corruption"', we see the influence of studies of *The Crown* and *Study of Thomas Hardy* on Clarke's reading of the novel, and we notice just how much he sees *Women in Love* as the natural successor to *The Rainbow*, building upon and developing the darker, more ambivalent aspects of Lawrence's creative interests:

It is clear not only from the final pages of *The Rainbow* but also from the tenor of the argument in *The Crown*, which is work of much the same date, that the metaphor of young life stirring under an old husk, to be revealed suddenly at the due time, was likely by itself to do much less than justice to the complexity of Lawrence's evolving conceptions; for *The Crown* does not make that absolute distinction between creation and corruption which the image of the husk cannot but imply. What is most in question rather is the distinction between corruption that is creative and corruption that is not.

> When the swan first rose out of the marshes, it was a glory of creation. But when we turn back, to seek its consummation again, it is a fearful flower of corruption.

> And corruption, like growth, is only divine when it is pure, when all is given up to it. If it be experienced as a controlled activity within an intact whole, this is vile. When corruption goes on within the living womb, this is unthinkable.

From now on this kind of rhetoric is habitual with Lawrence. He does not cease to oppose growth sharply to decay or destruction; but this antithetical pattern is apt now to be overlaid by, or to overlay, more complicated patterns.

Clarke continues his analysis of the novel, focusing particularly on the relationships between Ursula, Gudrun and the town of Beldover, quoting Lawrence's description of the mining community with its:

wave of disruptive force, that was given off from the presence of thousands of vigorous, underworld, half-automatized colliers, and which went to the brain and the heart, awaking a fatal desire, and a fatal callousness . . .

They belonged to another world, they had a strange glamour, their voices were full of an intolerable deep resonance, like a machine's burring, a music more maddening than the sirens' long ago.

As the argument progresses, Clarke points out that:

The machine takes over something of the age-old glamour of coal, and its mysterious cruelty is half-sanctioned and half-repudiated. If Gudrun, suffering from her fascination and resisting, is nevertheless compelled by the callousness and disruptiveness, this is a token of her vitality as well as of something worse. And if the colliers are half-automatized, it is also true that the dark, disruptive force which they mediate is an elemental life-energy. And finally, if Ursula is unresponsive to these equivocal resonances, if at this stage in the story she shows no faculty for this knowledge in corruption (effectively she is not present in the scene, though at the beginning we know her to be at Gudrun's side) then so much the worse – as well as the better – for her.

Throughout this commentary I have tended to absorb the concepts of corruption and disruption into each other; and I have done this always with a full sense of being justified by the text. It is as though the phonetic connection alone, and the derivation from a common root (*rumpere*) held for Lawrence its own suggestiveness (the same applies to the phonetic connection between 'reduction' and 'destruction'), setting in motion that process by which more complex and significant kinds of identity-in-difference are linguistically realised . . .

The examination of the reductive/destructive and corruptive/disruptive elements of the novel continues throughout the chapter on *Women in Love*, as Clarke deals with the correspondences and conflicts surrounding the Gerald/Loerke characters, the 'African statuettes' so beloved of Leavis, and finally the images of fecundity and vegetable decay which are used to provide richness and colour in so many of the novel's more memorable scenes.

At the close of the chapter on *Women in Love*, we are left to consider the full possibilities of Clarke's reading – a reading which confronts the liberal Leavisite reclamation of the novel and opens a path for new, perhaps more vigorous, readings:

Leavis has spoken of 'the "spontaneous-creative fullness of being" out of which *Women in Love* comes'.[15] It is a way of making his point that has probably proved quite as harmful as corrective. For it tends to imply – whether what is in question, primarily, is the artefact or the endowment of the artificer – that the only impulses that make for health or wholeness are the pure, creative impulses. (It is in keeping with this attitude that Leavis should affirm, without any qualification, that 'The West African statuette . . . represents something that we are to see as a default, a failure'.) 'The creative-*destructive* fullness of being out of which *Women in Love* comes' would be a happier way of putting it.[16]

We have already noted the powerful social forces that helped give a new impetus and acceptability to the reading and study of Lawrence's novels during the late Fifties and Sixties. With the firm establishment of a critical reputation and place for Lawrence in the canon of English literature, critics (through the agencies of writers like Clarke – despite the often hostile responses to his work) were able to transfer their energies away from a rigid and often embattled defence and justification of his novels to focus more on the *sort* of reputation his work deserved.

The extracts and essays discussed above provide evidence of a widening of scope in the discussion of the novels, such that the contributory essays, works of philosophy and even personal experiences of the writer could be reconsidered at a safe distance from the overheated atmosphere of analysis and biographical fixation that overshadowed Lawrence criticism in the Thirties and Forties. With the freedom to range more broadly across areas of critical concern, the recognition that there were distinct moral ambiguities in the work was inevitable. Where once the Leavisite defence of Lawrence as a moral and wholly reconstructive novelist was paramount to the safety of his reputation, critics now seemed able to move away from such a restrictive view, to explore new arguments about the certainty and dependability of Lawrence's moral vision. As we move to consider the later assessments of Lawrence's novels, we shall see how the initial widening of debate during the Sixties is accelerated with the development of feminist and Marxist critical theories in the Seventies and Eighties.

# CHAPTER FIVE

# Phallic Pride and the Politics of Sex: Feminist Criticism

TO DISCUSS Lawrence's critical standing and reputation at any time beyond the Sixties is to encounter not a single body of thought, but a range of perspectives and often conflicting, often coincident, theoretical positions. In this chapter we shall see how, even within an area so confidently titled 'feminist criticism', there are a number of approaches to, and understandings of, Lawrence's work. In the extracts and essays reprinted here, I have attempted to offer a range of responses to Lawrence's major novels and to provide a useful selection from the huge number of ideas and arguments that have emerged from the feminist critical perspectives of the last quarter-century.

With the sexual freedoms of the Sixties and the resultant shift in power-relations between men and women came a change in the understanding and acceptance of literary conventions and attitudes amongst readers of Lawrence's work. Hailed as the poet of sexuality and sex-relations by the generation of readers who first turned to his works in the Sixties, by the beginning of the Seventies Lawrence's reputation was undergoing a major revision, and he was being questioned and attacked for his phallocentrism and misogyny by a number of powerful feminist writers.

The view of Lawrence as the prophet of an essentially masculine sexual order may actually be observed in its most consistent form as far back as 1949, with the publication, in France, of Simone de Beauvoir's pioneering study of womanhood and gender relations, *Le Deuxième Sexe*. Translated and published outside France for the first time in 1953, *The Second Sex* was the first work to raise the contention that Lawrence celebrated the phallic at the expense of woman's reality and being. The central concern of the book is with the male representation of woman as the 'Other' throughout history and in the present, in life, myth and art. The section of the book which deals with Lawrence is sub-titled 'Phallic Pride', and discusses the ways in which Lawrence (as one of five authors) uses his characters to promote and justify the 'Myth of Woman' that has been for so long a feature of the relations between men and women in most cultures.

In the extract below, de Beauvoir responds to her own question about the reciprocity of relations between male and female in Lawrence's work. She has discussed some moments of the relationship between Gerald Crich and Gudrun Brangwen, and arrived at the point where Lawrence appears to be arguing for a mutuality and balance between man and woman:

Reciprocal gift, reciprocal fidelity: have we here in truth the reign of mutuality? Far from it. Lawrence believes passionately in the supremacy of the male. The very expression 'phallic marriage', the equivalence he sets up between 'sexual' and 'phallic', constitute sufficient proof. Of the two blood streams that are mysteriously married, the phallic current is favoured. 'The phallus serves as a means of union between two rivers; it conjoins the two different rhythms into a single flow.' Thus the man is not only one of the two elements in the couple, but also their connecting factor; he provides their transcendence: 'The bridge to the future is the phallus.' For the cult of the Goddess Mother, Lawrence means to substitute a phallic cult; when he wishes to illuminate the sexual nature of the cosmos, it is not woman's abdomen but man's virility that he calls to mind. He almost never shows a man agitated by a woman; but time and again he shows woman secretly overwhelmed by the ardent, subtle, and insinuating appeal of the male. His heroines are beautiful and healthy, but not heady; whereas his heroes are disquieting fauns. It is male animals that incarnate the agitation and the powerful mystery of Life; women feel the spell: this one is affected by a fox, that one is taken with a stallion, Gudrun feverishly challenges a herd of young oxen; she is overwhelmed by the rebellious vigour of a rabbit.

. . . Thought and action have their roots in the phallus; lacking the phallus, woman has no rights in either the one or the other: she can play a man's role, and even brilliantly, but it is just a game, lacking serious verity. 'Woman is really polarised downwards towards the centre of the earth. Her deep positivity is in the downward flow, the moon-pull. And man is polarised upwards, towards the sun and the day's activity.'[1] For woman 'the deepest consciousness is in the loins and the belly'.[2] If this is perverted and her flow of energy is upwards, to the breast and head, woman may become clever, noble, efficient, brilliant, competent in the manly world; but, according to Lawrence, she soon has enough of it, everything collapses, and she returns to sex, 'which is her business at the present moment'[3].[4]

By far the most concentrated and well-known assault on Lawrence's 'Phallic Pride' came in 1970, with the publication of Kate Millett's *Sexual*

*Politics* – a work which did much to alter, in a permanent way, the perception of Lawrence as a writer on sexual relations and gender issues. A work of polemical nature, *Sexual Politics* takes up the core of de Beauvoir's arguments and develops them into a full-blooded assault on Lawrence's 'sexual consciousness', naming him as a proponent of the view that 'sex is for the man'.[5]

Millett considers *Lady Chatterley's Lover, Sons and Lovers, Aaron's Rod, Kangaroo* and *The Plumed Serpent*, in addition to *The Rainbow* and *Women in Love*, in the chapter of her book devoted to Lawrence, and effectively presents a structured, though sometimes wayward, reading of all the major novels which is in keeping with her view of Lawrence as a writer of *male* fiction. Millett's work put Lawrence's sexual politics on the critical agenda in the Seventies – and there it has remained to the present.

The feminist treatment of Lawrence has been understandably negative for the most part. In the early Seventies, still reverberating to the shockwaves of Kate Millett's attack, Lawrence's reputation amongst feminist critics stood at a very low ebb. By the end of the decade, however, a number of studies appeared to return a slightly less hostile impression of the works.

In the extract below, taken from *Lawrence and Women* (1978), a collection of essays edited by Anne Smith, we find Philippa Tristram considering Lawrence's treatment of women in *The Rainbow* and *Women in Love*. Throughout her consideration of the novels, Tristram also draws on Lawrence's philosophical works *Psychoanalysis and the Unconscious* (1921) and *Fantasia of the Unconscious* (1922), setting these against Freud's *Civilisation and its Discontents* (1930) to provide some element of triangulation for her assessment of Lawrence's attitudes and treatment of his female characters. (There is also a short section of the essay dealing with *Aaron's Rod*, which has been cut from the text reprinted here.) The tone of the essay is much more measured than was the case with Millett's work, yet, at base, there are many shared conclusions:

When Anna and Will are married in *The Rainbow*, Tom Brangwen, Anna's stepfather, "wanted to make a speech":

For the first time in his life, he must spread himself wordily.

"Marriage," he began, his eyes twinkling and yet quite profound, for he was deeply serious and hugely amused at the same time, "Marriage," he said, speaking in the slow, full-mouthed way of the Brangwens, "is what we're made for."

"Let him talk," said Alfred Brangwen, slowly and inscrutably, "let him talk." Mrs Alfred darted indignant eyes at her husband.

"A man," continued Tom Brangwen, "enjoys being a man: for what purpose was he made a man, if not to enjoy it?"

"That's a true word," said Frank, floridly.

"And likewise," continued Tom Brangwen, "a woman enjoys being a woman: at least we surmise she does."

"Oh, don't you bother," called a farmer's wife.

"You may back your life they'd be summisin'," said Frank's wife.

"Now," continued Tom Brangwen, "for a man to be a man, it takes a woman."

"It does that," said a woman grimly.

"And for a woman to be a woman, it takes a man," continued Tom Brangwen.

"All speak up, men," chimed in a feminine voice.

"Therefore we have marriage," continued Tom Brangwen. (p. 127)

On similar occasions every reader must have sat uneasily through such wordy paternal spreadings and wished them well over. Although Lawrence despised "the old stable ego of the character", few novelists can capture with more precision the essence of the everyday. But the scene does not rest at observation merely: Lawrence, as [Ford Madox] Hueffer remarked, is an "investigator into the bases of the normal".[6] That episode engenders much more than an all-too-familiar discomfort: it is a drama in little of the tensions, the uneasy compacts, between the sexes. The assurance of the men, so firmly rooted in their masculinity, is evident: a man clearly enjoys being a man. But do the women equally enjoy being women, as Tom "surmises"? Their comments are oblique and barbed, answering not to their own sense of themselves, but to men's view of them.

In writing on Lawrence's treatment of women, I do not, like Kate Millett, want to attack him as "a counter-revolutionary sexual politician"; equally, I do not want to affirm with Mailer that he "understood women as they had never been understood before."[7] One could adopt either position, at different times and on different levels of his work; that scene could itself be engaged in both causes. My own feelings about Lawrence are divided, both admiration and anger finding their focus in his attitude – or rather attitudes – to women. I admire deeply the observer's insight in the first two generations of *The Rainbow*, which penetrates beneath the "stable ego" of Lydia and Anna to the instabilities, the flux and the profound continuities of life. I grow uneasy with the Ursula of the third generation, and positively angry with the two sisters in *Women in Love* – though that novel has often been acclaimed as his greatest work. There the observer's distance is abandoned: "I don't so much care about what the woman *feels* – " Lawrence writes to Garnett in 1914. "I only care about what the woman is – what she IS – inhumanly, physiologically, materially." This anatomizer, vivisectionist, is a kind of Frankenstein, who creates in that novel the woman he does not find in life; and then, understandably recoiling from his creature, seeks to destroy it. "Your hatred of me," he writes to Cecil Gray in 1917–18, "like Frieda's hatred of me, is your cleavage to a world of knowledge and being which you ought to forsake." His women (those of the novels) "though in a cringing, bad fashion . . . represent none the less the threshold of a new world, or underworld, of knowledge and being . . . like Magdalene at her feet-washing." It may be no exaggeration to say that the "bad fashion" of those Magdalenes ultimately sickened Lawrence.

From his first novel to his last, Lawrence is of course deeply concerned, in varying modes and degrees, with sexual relationships . . . *The Rainbow* is first drafted March–June 1913; *Women in Love* April–June 1916 . . . *The Rainbow* is therefore substantially a pre-war novel, *Women in Love* a war experience . . . These years also coincide with Lawrence's interest in Freud, though they are not quite coextensive with it. Lawrence was first introduced to Freud's ideas by Frieda in 1912, in time for those ideas to influence the final version of *Sons and Lovers*. His knowledge of Freud was largely at second-hand, though in 1914 he became acquainted with some professional Freudians. Between December 1919 and July 1921 he made his peace with psychoanalysis – by declaring war upon it in the two tracts, *Psychoanalysis and the Unconscious, Fantasia of the Unconscious.*[8]

Lawrence resented Freud's "adventure into the hinterland of the human consciousness" more, perhaps, because an explorer does not like to feel that his journey has been anticipated, than because, as Frieda alleged, their maps were different. The overt argument was, however, based upon that difference. "In attributing a sexual motive to all human experience," psychoanalysis, Lawrence contended, was "out, under a therapeutic disguise, to do away entirely with the moral faculty in man." In the later *Fantasia*, Lawrence modified his position slightly:

> We are thankful that Freud pulled us somewhat to earth, out of all our clouds of superfineness. What Freud says is always partly true. And half a loaf is better than no bread. But really, there is the other half of the loaf. All is not sex. (p. 11)

It is possibly an impatience to get on with that search for the other half of the loaf which leads Lawrence to assail his female characters in *Women in Love* . . . Lawrence died in 1930; Freud's *Future of an Illusion*

and *Civilisation and its Discontents*, published in 1927 and 1930 respectively, came too late to modify his opinions. Had he lived longer, he
might well have felt that Freud, in the aftermath of one war and the
approaching shadow of another, was mapping a territory more exten-
sive and familiar than he had at first supposed. But quite likely
Lawrence would have continued to resent that coincidence. Where
Freud sought to know, Lawrence sought to be. Where Freud felt that
men needed to bring the forms which moved in darkness into the light
of consciousness, Lawrence was convinced that they must "forsake
that world of knowledge" and discover their true being in "pristine
unconsciousness":

> Long ago we watched in frightened anticipation when Freud set
> out on his adventure – into the hinterland of human conscious-
> ness. He was seeking for the unknown sources of the mysterious
> stream of consciousness. Immortal phrase of the immortal James!
> Oh stream of hell which undermined my adolescence! I felt it
> streaming through my brain, in at one ear and out at the other . . .
> Horrid stream! (*Psych. & Unc.*, p. 199)

Where Lawrence fought the cerebration of psychoanalysis as the
enemy, Freud always allowed that the experience of literature had
anticipated him, and more fully. He concluded his tentative lecture on
"Femininity" by observing: "If you want to know more about femininity,
enquire from your own experiences of life, or turn to the poets."[9] Since
criticism, at least, is cerebral, it seems not unfair to redress the balance
a little by allowing Freud's own observations to illuminate Lawrence's
novels on occasion.

It is doubtful, however, that Freud can throw much light upon the
early *Rainbow*; which is to say that Lawrence, in the first two generations of Brangwens, needs no expositor. The delightful early work of
Freud's, *The Psychopathology of Everyday Life*, might offer some clues to
*The Rainbow*, but their use would be limited. Where Freud speculates,
say, on the breaking of an inkstand, Lawrence's insight into such
insignificant everyday events has an unstated significance. During
Anna's childhood, for example, it emerges that on market days Tom
Brangwen "loved buying things, odd things that he thought would be
useful". On Anna's betrothal to Will, Tom "suffered agony – . . . Oh, he
was ashamed. He trampled himself to extinguish himself." He makes
his peace with "odd things", abetting Anna's nesting:

> With more particular thought [than Will he] spied out what he
> called handy little things for her. He appeared with a set of new-
> fangled cooking-pans, with a special sort of hanging-lamp, though
> the rooms were so low, with canny little machines for grinding

> meat or mashing potatoes or whisking eggs . . . On market days there was always a long thrill of anticipation. (pp. 120–21)

This is the Lawrence of a letter of 1913:

> "I got the blues thinking of the future, so I left off and made some marmalade. It's amazing how it cheers one up to shred oranges or scrub the floor."

At another extreme, Tom's gifts of "odd things" express, without stating, much that Freud perceived of the relations between daughters, fathers and husbands.

At this period in his writing, Lawrence made actual women his study. He would ask the women he knew to write down what they felt in certain situations, and he would use their accounts as source material for his novels.[10] "The great living experience for every man is his adventure into the woman" Lawrence wrote to [Bertrand] Russell in 1915. "The man embraces in the woman all that is not himself." That experience of sexual otherness is finely captured in *The Rainbow*, when Tom observes Lydia, unaware with her child, through the bright kitchen window at the vicarage:

> The wind boomed strongly. Mother and child sat motionless, silent, the child staring with vacant dark eyes into the fire, the mother looking into space. The little girl was almost asleep. It was her will which kept her eyes so wide. (pp. 35–6)

Lawrence marvellously understood the distinct nature of maternal love. Its "visceral" characteristics are finely delineated in *Psychoanalysis and the Unconscious*:

> Child and mother have, in the first place, no objective consciousness of each other, and certainly no *idea* of each other. Each is a blind desideratum to the other. The strong love between them is effectual in the great abdominal centres, where all love, real love, is primarily based. (p. 227)

Freud might have agreed. Certainly, he asserts the sexual nature of maternal love, as against "'pure' love" ("ideal behaviour", "love in the head" as Lawrence would say), and defends the former as Lawrence does: the mother "is only fulfilling her task in teaching the child to love."[11]

In the Foreword to *Fantasia*, Lawrence writes: "I do not believe in evolution, but in the strangeness and rainbow-change of ever-renewed creative civilisations." For the early *Rainbow* itself, one might substitute the word "relationships" for "civilisations". No theory, or need, or willed conclusion imposes itself on the relationships of Tom and Lydia, Will and Anna:

All things about her had become intimate, she had known them near and lovely, like presences hovering upon her. What if they should all go hard and separate again, standing back from her terrible and distinct, and she, having known them, should be at their mercy? (p. 158)

Intimate, separate; complements, opposites; now lovers, now enemies – the relationships of men and women answer to a rhythm beyond their comprehension. If Freud and Lawrence both asked the question – was femininity created in nature, or made in culture – then the early *Rainbow* seems to answer: created in nature.

Ursula's story, in the later *Rainbow*, is, however, a different matter. Throughout the novel Lawrence writes at a level other than that of the conscious mind; yet in the earlier, stable world of the first two generations, the movement between cerebral and "visceral" convictions, between articulacy and the inarticulable, is scarcely perceptible, save as a recurrent rhythm. In *Psychoanalysis and the Unconscious*, Lawrence writes:

The term unconscious is only another word for life. But life is a general force, whereas the unconscious is essentially single and unique in each individual organism; it is the active, self-evolving soul bringing forth its own incarnation and self-manifestation . . . And consciousness is like a web woven finally in the mind from the various silken strands spun forth from the primal centre of the unconscious. (p. 241)

These sentences finely express the process of the early *Rainbow*. Things "may go hard and separate" in Anna's environment, but they may equally return to intimacy, "near and lovely"; in the worlds of Cossethay and the Marsh Farm, the soul is enabled to evolve, to incarnate and manifest itself. But Anna's daughter enters upon that wider world which her forebears only glimpsed distantly, and the abrasive environment of the "man's world" of Brinsley Street School leaves her at the mercy of things incurably hard and separate. Bereft of a context that nurtures personal life, neither Ursula nor Lawrence can achieve that finely woven, silken web of consciousness. The final sequence in which Ursula encounters the horses calls for the kind of exposition and comment which Freud offers in his case history of little Hans.

This process, both in the writing and in the heroine, is continued in *Women in Love*, for, where *The Rainbow* is rooted in nature, its successor is deracinated in culture. It is not only that the generations of Brangwens move out from the inarticulate, instinctual life of the Marsh Farm, into the over-articulate, moribund culture of London and Europe: one must not forget that *Women in Love* is a war book. If *The*

*Rainbow* was banned as pornography because of Lawrence's attitude to war rather than to sex, as has been claimed, one might also suspect that his engagement in its successor was with war rather than women. In the Foreword to *Women in Love* Lawrence himself asserts:

> It is a novel which took its final shape in the midst of a period of war, though it does not concern the war itself. I should wish the time to remain unfixed, so that the bitterness of the war may be taken for granted in the characters.

The reminder is timely. Freud's words in *Civilisation and its Discontents*, written at a later date but in recoil from the same experience, might form an epigraph for *Women in Love*:

> The meaning of the evolution of civilisation is no longer obscure to us. It must present the struggle between Eros and Death, between the instinct of life and the instinct of destruction, as it works itself out in the human species.[12]

He glosses this statement in 1932, in his open letter to Einstein, "Why War?":

> Neither of these instincts is any less essential than the other; the phenomena of life arise from the concurrent or mutually opposing action of both.[13]

These statements will be taken into the novel shortly; at the moment it is only necessary to observe that Eros, in *Women in Love*, is strictly male, and Death female. Even the novel's most fervent admirers, like Dr Leavis, have demurred at the phallic insistence of its prose:

> With perfect fine finger-tips of reality she would touch the reality in him, the suave, pure, untranslatable reality of his loins of darkness. To touch, mindlessly in darkness to come in pure touching upon the living reality of him, his suave perfect loins and thighs of darkness, this was her sustaining anticipation. (p. 311)

Leavis's comment on a related passage formulates this characteristic weakness:

> In these places Lawrence betrays by an insistent and overemphatic explicitness, running at times to something one can only call jargon, that he is uncertain – uncertain of the value of what he offers; uncertain whether he really holds it – whether a valid communication has really been defined and conveyed in terms of his creative art.[14]

But one might also observe that the loins, which figure so insistently in the prose, are always male. His women do not have them. They have stockings.

Such stockings – and in all colours! On the second page Gudrun's are "emerald-green", and they cause comment amongst the "common people" at the church door: "'What price the stockings!'" Gudrun "would have liked them all annihilated, cleared away, so that the world was left clear for her." Hermione wisely sticks to "brownish-grey" on the same occasion, and Gudrun, perhaps in response, confines herself to "dark green" when she visits Breadalby. But in the "coal dust" of home, the sisters flame out again:

> Ursula had an orange coloured knitted coat, Gudrun a pale yellow. Ursula wore canary yellow stockings, Gudrun bright rose.

A young miner assesses "'her with the red stockings'" as worth a "'week's wages for five minutes'", and on this occasion Gudrun merely "loathes" these "sinister creatures". But even her father feels her garments call for comment when she dons "pink silk stockings" for the water-party, to set off her black, pink and yellow clothing: "'Don't you think you might as well get yourself up for a Christmas cracker, an' ha' done with it?'" It seems significant that at the Pompadour, when Gudrun makes her gesture on Lawrence's behalf, her stockings should be merely "silver-grey", whereas scarlet and royal blue, each time in contrast with her skirt, become a positive uniform for her confrontations with Gerald, which lead ultimately to his destruction. It also seems significant that, before the sisters part, Gudrun, with sacramental intensity, confers stockings on Ursula:

> Gudrun came to Ursula's bedroom with three pairs of the coloured stockings for which she was notorious, and she threw them on the bed. But these were thick silk stockings, vermilion, cornflower blue, and grey, bought in Paris. The grey ones were knitted, seamless and heavy. Ursula was in raptures. She knew Gudrun must be feeling very loving, to give away such treasures.

> "I can't take them from you, Prune," she cried. "I can't possibly deprive you of them – the jewels."

> "Aren't they jewels!" cried Gudrun, eyeing her gifts with an envious eye. "Aren't they real lambs!"

> "Yes, you must keep them," said Ursula.

> "I don't want them, I've got three more pairs. I *want* you to keep them – I want you to have them. They're yours, there – "

> And with trembling, excited hands she put the coveted stockings under Ursula's pillow.

"One does get the greatest joy of all out of really lovely stockings,"
said Ursula.

"One does," replied Gudrun; "the greatest joy of all." (pp. 427–8)

"'Jewels?'" "'Lambs?'" "'The greatest joy of all?'" One cannot help
feeling that stockings, like loins, are receiving undue emphasis. The
"over-explicitness" which Leavis notes seems produced by a need to
assert a significance which Lawrence cannot fully account for. One
might suggest, in Freud's terms, that, where male loins emphasise the
neglected Eros, female stockings repudiate carnality and the instinct
for life; they allure men to an embrace which will destroy them. That
assured movement in the early *Rainbow* between the self and the
world which encompasses it, enables the expression of unconscious
states without their rationalisation. But in *Women in Love* that
expressiveness has gone, because the realities of the external world
have simply collapsed; in "the bitterness of war" everyday objects
assume a distorted significance.

One has only to recall Anna's nesting with Tom's "odd things" in
*The Rainbow*, and then to consider the corresponding chapter, "A
Chair", in *Women in Love*, where Ursula and Birkin determine that they
will not nest. The chair itself recalls a past which can no longer exist,
as Birkin remarks:

> "When I see that clear, beautiful chair, and I think of England,
> even Jane Austen's England – it had living thoughts to unfold
> even then, and pure happiness in unfolding them. And now, we
> can only fish among the rubbish-heaps for the remnants of their
> old expression. There is no production in us now, only sordid and
> foul mechanicalness." (p. 347)

Ursula protests against Birkin's nostalgia for the past, but wishes that
the chair "'had been smashed up when its day was over'". She is "'sick
of the beloved past'", but, as Birkin retorts, "'not so sick as I am of the
accursed present'". The egg whisks, potato mashers and meat grinders
of *The Rainbow* were still, one may remember, "canny little machines",
not "'foul mechanicalness'". They can be humanised as offerings by the
inarticulate Tom to the daughter he once loved and was ashamed, in her
marriage, to hate. The chair is a symbol, which Ursula wants to destroy,
and Birkin to decline. In the end they give it away to a "common" couple, forcibly betrothed in the old mode because the woman is
pregnant. "'I won't aid and abet them in it.'" Birkin demurs. "'Oh yes,'
cried Ursula. 'It's right for them – there's nothing else for them.'"

"'There's nothing else for them.'" The phrase should be allowed to
reverberate a little. From its first page, *Women in Love* presents the
desolation after the cataclysm, the battlefield strewn with the wreck-

age of a former order. The old containing continuities and securities of *The Rainbow* are gone: neither sister wishes to marry or bear children, regarding a domestic destiny as "'the end of experience'". The un-enlightened may continue to mate and breed because there is nothing else for them, but is there, in this desolate world, any more for the enlightened? *Women in Love* pursues that question down a cul-de-sac, and predictably arrives at no conclusion.

For Lawrence, the "front line" existed in art. "After all," he writes to Garnett in 1914, "this is the real fighting line, not where soldiers pull triggers." If he claimed at that time to Harriet Monroe, "I am much too valuable a creature to offer myself to a German bullet gratis and for fun", he was willing to expose himself to the bullets of public opinion in his writing:

> It is the business of the artist to follow the war to the heart of the individual fighters – not to talk in armies and nations and numbers – but to track it home – home – their war – and it's at the bottom of every Englishman's heart – the war – the desire for war – the will to war – and at the bottom of every German heart.

As his letter to Einstein shows, Freud would have agreed: if life were produced by an incessant struggle between Eros and Death, then no League of Nations could put an end to conflict. The malaise of a civili-sation is continuous with the malaise of a relationship, or, as Lawrence was later to think, of an individual. But in *Women in Love* the battle between Eros and Death is polarised into male and female. Men possess the instinct for life; women the instinct for destruction.

It is not difficult to glimpse this paradigm in Gerald and Gudrun, or to foresee its outcome in Gerald's death. From the moment of their meeting, the Eros in Gerald's "fair sun-tanned type" is prospectively frozen. "In his clear northern flesh and his fair hair was a glisten like sunshine refracted through crystals of ice." He is "pure as an arctic thing." "'Is there really some pale gold, arctic light that envelopes only us two?'" Gudrun speculates. Gerald has traded his instinct for life for "foul mechanicalness"; he is the murderee who, in Birkin's view, invites his murderer. When Gudrun flashes her stockings at him, he reacts – the cliché is unavoidable – like a bull to a red rag:

> Her fingers had him under their power. The fathomless, fathom-less desire they could evoke in him was deeper than death, where he had no choice. (p. 324)

In this kinship of the corrupt there is little to choose, except that Gerald has a chance and Gudrun doesn't.

Ursula, though another modern woman "nerve-worn with con-sciousness", has other possibilities. She is not entirely a creature of destruction: after an impulse to destroy it, she gives the chair away; she wishes that Gerald would spare his mare, when Gudrun cries "in a strange high voice, like a gull, or like a witch screaming out from the side of the road: 'I should think you're proud.'" But if Ursula is not to be a destroyer, the woman in her must be mastered, as Birkin warns her:

> "And woman is the same as horses: two wills act in opposition inside her. With one will, she wants to subject herself utterly. With the other she wants to bolt, and pitch her rider to perdition." (p. 132)

Undeterred by Birkin's assurance that subjection is "'the last, perhaps highest, love-impulse: resign your will to the higher being'", Ursula, at this stage, elects to bolt. But later, despite occasional spurts of resistance, she allows Birkin to school her in his image of womanhood. His programme is graphically outlined in *Fantasia*:

> Let her learn the domestic arts in their perfection. Let us even artificially set her to spin and weave. Anything to keep her busy, to prevent her reading and becoming self-conscious. (p. 83)

> Make her yield to her own real unconscious self, and absolutely stamp on the self she's got in her head. Drive her forcibly back, back into her own true unconsciousness. (p. 188)

> When once she . . . knows that the loneliness of waiting and following is inevitable, that it must be so; ah, then how wonderful it is! How wonderful it is to come back to her, at evening, as she sits half in fear and waits! How good it is when the night falls! How richly the evening passes! (p. 190)

Those statements have an all-too-familiar ring.

"The chief clue to *Women in Love*," John Murry wrote, is "the endeavour to force upon the woman a sexual or sensual homage to the man." It is a clue certainly, but Murry's explanation of this "endeavour" seems rather less certain: Lawrence, he claims, is a covert homosexual, whose "loathing for women only grew with the years". In consequence he argues that "*The Rainbow* is, radically, the history of Lawrence's final sexual failure."[15] I certainly do not share that suspicion of *The Rainbow*, nor do I think his view of *Women in Love* more than partially true. One might recall Freud at this point: "In all of us, throughout life, the libido normally oscillates between male and female objects."[16] It is true that Lawrence will not permit that oscillation in women: Ursula's relationship with Winifred Inger in *The Rainbow* is clearly debased in "foul mechanicalness"; where the chapter "Man to Man" in *Women in Love*, is centred upon the true affections of Gerald and Birkin, "Woman to Woman" focuses the animosities of Ursula and Hermione. It is rather *because* the women in the novel come to personify the instinct of destruction, that Birkin's need for Gerald, and Gerald's for him, is only the instinct of life in another guise. "'He should have loved me,'" Birkin says of the dead Gerald, looking at Ursula "with dark, almost vengeful eyes." Ursula, the destroyer, retorts:

"What difference would it have made!"

"It would!" he said. "It would."

It is also clear that, for the moment at least, that search for the other half of the loaf which is not sex, has failed. The novel ends with Ursula disputing:

"You can't have two kinds of love. Why should you!"

"It seems as if I can't," he said. "Yet I wanted it."

"You can't have it, because it's false, impossible," she said.

"I don't believe that," he answered.

It is not necessary, however, to believe that this other impulse is simply another kind of love, for a man. That is not centrally what Birkin needs to draw him from a dead world into life again. The emphasis is not upon alternative relationships; it is upon singleness. Thus Birkin rebukes Ursula:

"I don't want love, . . . . I don't want to know you. I want to be gone out of myself, and you to be lost to yourself, so we are found different." (p. 179)

To Gerald he makes a similar proposal: "'An impersonal union that leaves one free.'" (p. 199). Between these two proposals, he reflects:

Sex is subordinate, but perfectly polarised. Each has a single, separate being, with its own laws. (p. 193)

When he wrote *Women in Love*, woman, or indeed man, was for Lawrence the way back from "knowing" into "being" oneself, a ground for complaint in Ursula's view of Birkin:

He said the individual was more than love, or than any relationship. For him, the bright, single soul accepted love as one of its conditions, a condition of its own equilibrium. (p. 258)

Woman is thus no more than the way back from consciousness, as she was the way into it: "She is the door for our in-going and our outcoming. In her we go back to the Father . . . blind and unconscious."

It is not surprising that the door should so often seem to slam in

Birkin's face, or that he, and Lawrence too, should have become impatient with their uncooperative creations. If women will not facilitate the search, they necessarily impede it. It is true that Birkin wishes Ursula to achieve "a single, separate being" as well; but a return to *Fantasia* suggests she had grounds for hesitation:

> Once man vacates his camp of sincere, passionate positivity in disinterested being, his supreme responsibility to fulfil his own profoundest impulses, with reference to none but God or his own soul, not taking woman into count at all, in this primary responsibility of his own deepest soul; once man vacates this strong citadel of his own genuine, not spurious, divinity, then in comes woman, picks up the sceptre and begins to conduct a rag-time band . . .

> Of course there should be a great balance between the sexes. Man, in the daytime, must follow his own soul's greatest impulse, and give himself to life-work and risk himself to death. It is not woman who claims the highest in man. It is man's own religious soul that drives him on beyond woman, to his supreme activity. For his highest, man is responsible to God alone. He may not pause to remember that he has a life to lose, or a wife and children to leave. He must carry forward the banner of life, though seven worlds perish, with all the wives and mothers and children in them. (pp. 97–8)

In one mood that can sound very much like Milton: "He for God only, she for God in him." In another, one may notice that, if Lawrence had left women out of it altogether, and had used "man" in the generic sense of "mankind", the impulse (if not its conditions) could give no cause for quarrel. That endeavour to rise out of destruction, "to give oneself to life-work and risk oneself to death", is surely admirable. No doubt Lawrence was right to draw the "fighting line" in the self. He was mistaken to identify the enemy with women, not with the enemy within. It impeded his search.

The . . . novels that have been discussed are, on one level, the account of personal crisis – the lapse from a secure state of being in *The Rainbow*, into the total disorientation of *Women in Love* . . . On the other level, that of an author's genius, the stories form an account of Europe itself in that traumatic period; and if I consider that *Women in Love* has mistaken the enemy, so too perhaps did the colliding forces in the First World War: it was a battle that no one could win.[17]

The final extract for consideration in this chapter is taken from Carol Siegel's *Lawrence Among the Women: Wavering Boundaries in Women's Literary Traditions* (1991). Siegel's fascinating book attempts to review 'women's literary traditions through a consideration of D. H. Lawrence's work' – a project that Siegel herself admits may seem at first sight to be 'deliberately bizarre, even perverse'. Her method is well-grounded, however, for there is much that binds Lawrence to the traditions of women's writing:

Lawrence often wrote in response to directions from his women friends, represented himself as the inheritor of Victorian women novelists, and influenced his literary female contemporaries' thinking about women's creativity. He also affected the development of the next generation of women writers, as both a precursor and a figure for the male artist. He still contributes to our concept of a gendered literary heritage, through the role he plays as a subject of feminist criticism.[18]

It is not Siegel's intention in *Lawrence Among the Women* to offer a deliberately 'friendly feminist reading of Lawrence' – the treatment of Lawrence and his work is always subordinated to concern for an understanding of the growth and development of women's literary traditions.

In the following extract, from Siegel's chapter entitled 'The Battle of Tongues', we find an investigation of the phenomenon that Lawrence himself pointed out in several of his essays and letters – the ability of a text to speak with its own voice despite, perhaps, the intentions so often ascribed to the author:

Lawrence's work is particularly resistant to any reading that dismisses the importance of authorial intention because, since the banning of *The Rainbow* in 1915, his intentions have been a recurrent topic of legal discourse. It is also hard to think of a writer about whom more biographical material has been written than D. H. Lawrence, but easy to see why this is so. The greatest difficulty presented by Lawrence's work – that he continually contradicts himself – is exactly paralleled in what we know of Lawrence's life. Moreover, the contradictions in Lawrence's work and in his life cluster around the same issue: the relations between men and women. Perhaps the greatest mistake that a reader of Lawrence can make is to treat the contradictoriness of his writing as an unconscious intrusion of personal conflicts. Such readings seem based on the assumption that Lawrence wished to produce texts that would communicate coherent, unified statements, that he tried but failed to make his works speak with one voice. On the contrary, some of Lawrence's nonfictional writing reveals his dedication to allowing what he perceived as an external, female voice intrude into his work to challenge the voice he identified with himself.

It is true that in 1914, when Lawrence wrote his *Study of Thomas Hardy*, he said the most difficult problem faced by fiction writers was "reconciling their metaphysic, their theory of being and knowing, with their living sense of being."[19] In his specific comments on the novels, Lawrence makes it clear that he is most disturbed by the gap he sees between Hardy's implicit theorising about gender relations and his depictions of female characters. Whether Lawrence ever believed that these two aspects of a text could be brought into harmony remains doubtful, however. He seems unable to think of an author who successfully aligns metaphysics and art. In the 1918 version of "The Spirit of Place," Lawrence sees as "one of the outstanding qualities of American literature: that the deliberate ideas of the man veil, conceal, obscure that which the artist has to reveal."[20] Again, Lawrence shows us compelling female characters veiled by their authors' socially prescribed statements of their meaning. By 1923 he had revised the passage to emphasise the universality of the writer's inability to communicate with one voice: "Truly art is a sort of subterfuge . . . The artist usually sets out – or used to – to point a moral and adorn a tale. The tale, however, points the other way, as a rule."[21] To believe that Lawrence makes such statements in hopes that his critics will save the truth of his own art from the lie of his metaphysics is naïve. Nothing in Lawrence's work or life gives the impression that he was so humble about his talents or his role as an author.

In Frank Kermode's study of the conflict between doctrine and art speech (what Lawrence calls the metaphysic and the tale) in the novels, he demonstrates that Lawrence is aware of the contradictions in his works; indeed, that he emphasised them with complex techniques of narration.[22] Kermode shows that Lawrence's best fiction is governed by the standard articulated in the *Study of Thomas Hardy*: "The degree submitted to criticism within the work of art makes the lasting value and satisfaction of the work" (*Study*, 476). Lawrence's apparent scepticism about his own beliefs is not the unifying force that Kermode suggests it is, however. Like most artists, Lawrence often calls upon his reader to accept some apparent contradictions as part of the mystery of life, which is made up of many truths, but he also presents us with voices within his fictions that make assertions which cannot be simultaneously accepted as truths.

As Wayne Booth points out, "Again and again, Lawrence simply surrenders the telling of the story to another mind, a mind neither clearly approved nor clearly repudiated yet presented in a tone that seems to demand judgement."[23] However, Bakhtin's dialogics, which Booth draws on to explain Lawrence's "double voiced" texts, seem less useful than Dale Bauer's modification of the theory into feminist dialogics, because Lawrence's voices in opposition are almost always also oppositely gendered. As Bauer asserts, dialogic community, which inheres in the struggle of competing voices, "does not exist without the tension between the marginal and the central, the eccentric and the phallocentric," positions that are always gendered.[24] And in Lawrence's texts this tension is foregrounded as the battle for reader identification going on between male and female voices. For instance, Ursula and Birkin in *Women in Love* can be seen as having equally plausible views of their shared experiences, but only one of them can be right when they disagree, at the end of the novel, over whether or not it is possible to "have two kinds of love."[25] Ursula's criticism of the doctrine does not simply modify our understanding of the doctrine; if we accept the criticism as correct we must reject the doctrine.

E. M. Forster amusingly describes the sort of demands Lawrence's fiction makes on the reader by categorising Lawrence as both visionary prophet of nature and annoying preacher.[26] This complaint is not an adequate assessment of the conflicting demands of Lawrence's fiction, because it implies that the reader is forced to put up with the preacher in order to enjoy the prophet, read through the metaphysic in order to see the art, when, in fact, we are presented not with a sermon, but a trial which the hectoring author insists we judge. Although Lawrence's lyrical evocations of nature are often gratingly disrupted by his outbursts of narrowly moralistic interpretation, this may annoy but should not confuse the reader. Many writers before Lawrence found "sermons in stones" and insisted on preaching them. There is no intrinsic conflict between an author's ability to describe the physical world delightfully and his propensity to philosophise tediously about it.

The characters in Lawrence's landscape, not the landscape itself or the sermonising about it, jumble Lawrence's message. Forster's metaphor of a man divided into two (male) selves is inaccurate because he leaves out the fundamental conflict in Lawrence's fiction: the discrepancy between male and female world views. Still, in describing Lawrence's conflicting voices as conflicting personas and linking the more attractive and artistic persona to Lawrence's celebrations of nature, Forster does, although unknowingly, draw attention to one area in Lawrence's work where real female voices successfully compete with Lawrence's dictatorial male pronouncements. Lawrence frequently used material written by his female friends as sources for his famous descriptions of nature.[27] Nonetheless, Lawrence's fiction does not present us with a female representation of nature lying helpless in the grasp of a hermeneutics of male supremacy, but, instead, with female characters who, as Kermode points out, consistently undercut the doctrinal pronouncements of both the author and his fictional spokesmen.[28]

In accordance with sound rhetorical practice, Lawrence seems to present what he imagines to be his opponent's argument in order to destroy it. What is so unusual about Lawrence's use of this rhetorical technique is that he usually makes such a good case for the opposition that he is unable to refute it. F. R. Leavis sees the oppositional female voices in Lawrence's fiction as representative of his wife's criticisms ("the voice is unmistakably Frieda's") and takes it as a sign of Lawrence's brilliance that he represents that voice as "unanswerable" in novels like *Aaron's Rod* and *Kangaroo*.[29] Certainly Lawrence's honesty in these instances is admirable, but it also causes him to cut the doctrinal ground right out from under himself. This effect is not limited, as Leavis suggests, to Lawrence's weakest novels. *Women in Love*, *The Lost Girl*, *The Plumed Serpent*, and *The Fox* all have major female characters who assert their own wills against men who apparently speak for Lawrence in demanding that women submit to male authority.

In each of these novels, the view of life Lawrence gives us seems to support the women's final assertions. For example, in *Women in Love*, Lawrence never shows that it would be possible for Birkin to add a blood brother to his ménage, and he gives us every indication that Ursula's instincts are superior to Birkin's. Moreover, in the other three stories the woman is the protagonist, and in all four her common-sensical views further invite reader identification. While Lawrence associates the major male characters with death, he depicts the women as wholesome. Their unanswerable criticisms of male authority are presented as intrinsic to a healthy will to survive rather than the "deadly female will" Lawrence so often rails against in his essays. Thus, even if we want to believe that Lawrence wrote his fiction with misogynous intentions, the texts confound us because of their presentation of patriarchal discourse within not only what Booth calls "a chorus of voices, each speaking with its own authority,"[30] but also a feminized cosmos that most often seems to affirm a female character's point of view.[31]

In the extract from Siegel's book, we see evidence that the earlier feminist views of Lawrence as a prophet of 'phallic consciousness' have given way to a wider range of considerations. Many of the feminist critics of the late Seventies and Eighties argued for a recognition of the number of perspectives and 'voices' active in the novels, and argued that Lawrence frequently presents his female characters (as is the case with Ursula Brangwen) as moving towards a level of self-determination, individuality and self-awareness that is far out of reach of most male characters.

Siegel's comments demonstrate, also, the distance that feminist criticism had travelled between the start of the Seventies and the Nineties, in terms of the extent to which there has been an interaction with other key theories of criticism. The strength of Millett's early revisionist arguments – and their origin in de Beauvoir's comments on Lawrence – persists, but has been transformed and subsumed into a wider movement of criticism that draws additional strength from the interrelations of structuralist, semiotic, Marxist and post-structuralist argument.

Siegel's references to Bakhtin's dialogics gives us a view of the range of readings to which Lawrence's work has been subject in recent years. The mere mention of Bakhtin's ideas invokes a whole pattern of critical debate, whereby Bakhtin's position is set against the work of Russian Formalists, Saussurean linguists and latterly, pure Structuralists – and it is both against and through the interplay of these theories that some of the more recent feminist arguments are formulated. Feminist criticism's modification and redefinition of other critical perspectives is clear in Dale Bauer's reworking of the Bakhtin position to promote the expression and recognition of 'feminist dialogics', that is itself utilised in Siegel's argument.

In the final chapter of this book, the range of views on Lawrence's work is further developed along other theoretical lines, leaving us with a sense of the postmodern Lawrence of the Nineties.

# CHAPTER SIX

# Materialism, Ideology, Myths and Histories – a Number of Lawrences

THE THREE essays that make up this final section of the collection are linked by a number of factors: first, they offer, between them, a useful view of the sorts of directions in which Lawrence scholarship has moved in the past two decades; second, they all share, though in interestingly different ways, a postmodern concern with the past and its relation to the present; third, they all set out to re-read the novels and – again in different ways – offer up a 'new' Lawrence, who may be seen and understood in the light of the readings to which his works are accessible.[1]

In the first of this final group of extracts, Graham Holderness turns his attention to *The Rainbow* in an attempt to offer a revision of the primarily Leavisite view of Lawrence as a recorder of social history 'with an unrivalled insight into individual life'.

Holderness sets out from a materialist perspective to address the shortcomings of the novel-as-social-history view of *The Rainbow*. He sets out the core of his thesis with absolute clarity in the introduction to his book *D. H. Lawrence: History, Ideology and Fiction*, arguing that 'all literary productions (whether or not they have an ostensible historical content or make a direct reference back to their own history) can be understood completely only by relating them to a historical and ideological context.'[2] It is Holderness's view that Lawrence adapts the realist form to develop an 'assault on bourgeois society', found in its clearest form in the closing stages of the novel. According to such a reading, the prevailing critical judgement of the final chapters as 'weaker' than the early parts of the book derives in part from the strength of Lawrence's 'assault on bourgeois society' in these closing sections. Further, it is Holderness's view that *The Rainbow* does not offer readers an historical chronicle, but a series of separate and separable *myths* about which the novel is focused, and around which its supposedly realist/historical movements are played out:

*The Rainbow* does not, then, preserve the realist totality at all, since its 'evolving generational structure' has no realist or historical content. It merely presents three different settings for dramas of personal relationship: agricultural pastoral, rural village, and industrial city. Clearly, if the original rural society is mythical rather than historical, it cannot possibly contribute to an authentic presentation of historical evolution.[3]

The extract that follows is taken from a chapter entitled 'Transition', in which Holderness argues that the non-fiction work *Study of Thomas Hardy*, the novella *The Fox* and *The Rainbow* represent a stage in Lawrence's fiction when he was not only 'laying aside the realist conventions' of earlier works, but was 'temporarily abandoning the tragic mode', to which he would eventually return with *Women in Love*. The extract reproduces only that part of the chapter dealing with *The Rainbow*.

The most interesting argument advanced in Terry Eagleton's brilliant but brief sketch of literary ideologies from Matthew Arnold to D. H. Lawrence is his view that 'the fissuring of organic form is a progressive act', and one of the most interesting hints thrown out in his provocative but undeveloped passage on Lawrence is his suggestion that the development from *Sons and Lovers* to *Women in Love* is a progressive development:

> The 'symptomatic' repressions and absences of the realist *Sons and Lovers* may be recuperated in the ultra-realist forms of *The Rainbow* – a text which 'explodes' realism in its letter, even as it preserves it in the 'totalising' organicism of its evolving generational structures.[4]

*Women in Love* continues to enforce this 'progressive' discontinuity with a realist lineage already called into profound question by *Jude the Obscure*. Eagleton points out that such a position conflicts with 'a Marxist aesthetic tradition heavily dominated by the work of Georg Lukács'; he seems to remain unconscious, however, of the extent to which his evaluations align suspiciously with those of bourgeois critical orthodoxy. I would like to examine *The Rainbow* in the light of these comments and argue that the novel neither preserves nor explodes realism, but substitutes for it, in the form of metaphysics and mythology, a textual ideology of a peculiarly pure and non-contradictory kind. Ideology is not, in *The Rainbow*, set into conflictual relationship with history; ideology is, simply, offered as an alternative to history. Far from creating a progressive discontinuity with realism, *The Rainbow* surrenders literature almost completely to the domination of ideology.

*The Rainbow* (1915) is such a different kind of novel from *Sons and Lovers* that critical discussion has generally been conducted on a different terrain. Lawrence saw his more 'analytical' technique as a way of penetrating deeper into the lives of people than the realist novel – preoccupied with 'external' features of living, social existence and relationships, morals and manners – could ever hope to do. The method of *The Rainbow* certainly attempts this, and on the face of it, such intensive 'depth psychology' must inevitably make the social world of the characters recede and diminish in importance. But the book is no 'stream-of-unconsciousness' novel where individual characters are so detached from their society that it hardly seems to exist at all. On the contrary, as Eagleton points out, the form of the novel is, apparently, historical in a very large and impressive way: the three central figures, Tom, Anna and Ursula Brangwen, with their respective partners, Lydia, Will and Anton Skrebensky, represent three generations who live through a historically changing social world between 1840 and about 1905, and clearly the transition from the agricultural life of the Brangwen farmers to Ursula's life as a wage-earner in an industrial town is historically significant. At first glance *The Rainbow* seems to offer the ideal method for exploring human life in both its communal and individual dimensions: a form or structure which dramatises large-scale historical changes, and a manner or style which is able to explore very deeply the lives of the individuals living through this historical process.

This view of the novel is, of course, embodied in Leavis's study, where Lawrence appears as an 'incomparable' social historian with an unrivalled insight into individual life. And many other critics have been more than happy to accept the contention that these 'deeper', unconscious levels of experience are the more 'essential' reality of human existence. That kind of criticism we can leave to its own devices; it is the view (shared by both Leavis and Eagleton) that *The Rainbow* offers a significant attempt to interpret historical change that I wish to challenge.

'Where *Women in Love* has that astonishing comprehensiveness in the presentment of contemporary England (or the England of 1914), *The Rainbow* has instead its historical depth. As social historian, Lawrence, among novelists, is unsurpassed.'[5] Leavis's strategy is subtle but obvious: by concentrating on the *values*, the 'spiritual heritage' of a society, he is able to conflate individual with social existence and effectively negate history altogether. The essential aspects of a 'culture' and 'civilisation' are those values which live in the moral conscious-ness of individuals. But there can be little doubt that Leavis sees *The Rainbow* as a valid (and true) account of a society in transition, from 'organic' rural past to urban industrial present. Marvin Mudrick, argu-ing along similar lines, adds an important term to Leavis's analysis – the concept of 'community':

> In his historic moment, Lawrence has before him the life of the last
> English community . . . a life rich in productive labour and in con-
> tinuity with the passing seasons . . . a life seemingly permanent yet
> fated to pass away in the general breakdown of codes and commu-
> nities . . . It is this process, over three generations, which is the
> subject and theme of *The Rainbow*.[6]

This is the conventional view of *The Rainbow*, as a historical chronicle
dramatising and enacting in its aesthetic form a transition from organic
community to alienated individual; and I think Eagleton does little
more than reproduce it in a different language. It is necessary therefore
to examine more closely the novel's pretensions to a 'historical-
chronicle' form, and to show how Lawrence's adaptation of that form
provides an ideological basis for the assault on bourgeois society contained in the later stages of the novel: an ideology of individualism
which contains the social criticism and draws its form into complicity
with the very society it challenges.

*The Rainbow* is a radical novel of criticism and protest against the
values of Lawrence's contemporary society; a protest launched, let us
remember, in the early years of the 1914–18 war (the novel's suppression in 1915 was undoubtedly, in part at least, political). The common
critical consensus that the later stages of the book are artistically weak
no doubt has some connection with the concentrated and comprehensive assault against bourgeois society which they contain.

Ursula's experiences take her through a wide range of social
realities, and gradually compose in her consciousness into a comprehensive view of industrial bourgeois society as a 'mechanised' system
in which all institutions, practices and codes seem to have their
subordinate function. Through her relationship with Skrebensky,
Ursula develops a profound dissatisfaction with the ethics of bourgeois democracy, imperialism and war; teaching in a school, she finds
a 'hard, malevolent system' (377) which reproduces the general
relations of society; at college she discovers education to be a 'ware-
house of dead unreality', a 'little side-show to the factories of the
town'. (434) Her major decision, made as the novel closes, involves
the rejection of a bourgeois marriage. At the very heart of this system
is industrial capitalism, and the primary image of that civilisation is a
colliery town, Wiggiston.

Wiggiston is Lawrence's Eastwood, seen now from a radically
alienated (indeed, by now, expatriate) perspective, and transmuted
into symbol by the language and imagery of that 'organicist' tradition
of social criticism studied by Raymond Williams in *Culture and Society*.
Whereas the mining landscapes of *Sons and Lovers* and *Odour of
Chrysanthemums* are always seen and known from within, here for the

first time in Lawrence's work such a landscape is seen only from an external perspective (or rather two – that of the colliery manager, and that of the female dissident who attacks his values). Both perspectives are external: the system viewed cynically and irresponsibly from above; the system viewed passionately and antagonistically from outside.

The 'description' of the mining town is not at all realist in manner; it registers Ursula's point of view and reproduces terms familiar from the Romantics, Carlyle and Dickens: the town is uniform and monotonous ('homogeneous') shapeless ('amorphous') and 'rigid'. There is no concreteness or sensuous definition in the language; it is almost wholly analytical: 'abstract', 'sterile', 'meaningless', 'unreal'. The abstraction is itself a way of defining the nature of Wiggiston: the colliery is 'mathematical', another term from the vocabulary of Romantic social protest. Abstraction is also part of the method to indicate that Wiggiston is unreal, not amenable to realist presentation: it is a kind of dream or nightmare. It appears like an apparition; it is inhabited by 'spectres'; it is a 'vision of pure ugliness', 'some gruesome dream'.

At the heart of the town there is a blank space, an 'absence': 'In the middle of the town was a large, open, shapeless space . . . There was no meeting place, no centre, no artery, no organic formation.' (345) It is from that empty space, that social and human absence in the centre of industrial society, that the myth of pre-industrial society – the myth of Marsh Farm – is generated. Marsh Farm has no closer or more direct relation to history than that.

Wiggiston is the negation of community. It is dominated by the 'proud, demon-like colliery'; the miners are subdued to that dominion – they have to 'alter themselves to fit the pits'; each man is 'reified' to a function of the machine, one of Ruskin's 'unhumanised' labourers. Personal and social life are subordinated to the machine; the values of the community have disappeared. 'The pit was the great mistress.'

Ursula views the place with horror and distaste, from a carefully preserved distance. She also feels (in a passage which anticipates *Women in Love*) the powerful allurement of the system: 'There was a horrible fascination . . . human bodies and lives subjected in slavery to that symmetric monster of the colliery. There was a swooning, perverse satisfaction in it . . . Hatred sprang up in Ursula's heart. If she could she would smash the machine.' (349–50)

That decision is defined as Ursula's 'growing-up'. She sees Wiggiston as a vision of unreality, recognises it as meaningless; and 'departs' from it – rejecting the machine, denying its power over her, and adopting a position of refusal, denial and resistance. The decision involves a comprehensive rejection of society as a whole: she enters a 'great loneliness, wherein she was sad but free' – the isolation of a life displayed and excluded from the social totality.

The style of presentation is now quite different from the realism of *Sons and Lovers* and *Odour of Chrysanthemums*. The industrial mining society is not a solid reality at all, but a kind of dream or nightmare. On the one hand there is a radical split between the conscious, perceiving subject and the external, objective society from which she excludes herself. On the other hand Wiggiston is Ursula's nightmare. The 'communal narrator', who in the realist *Sons and Lovers* assures the reader that the society is always more complex and comprehensive than any one character's perspective, has disappeared. Wiggiston is a record of Ursula's perceptions, not a social reality but a bad dream. And, of course, from a dream one can always awake.

The posing of that contradiction – that bourgeois society is a subjective nightmare, which yet has an objective existence and a sinister and alien power over the individual who dreams it – is, of course, a valid and important revelation of a genuine social experience. It is a reflection of real historical contradictions – emerging in the intensification of human subjection to enormously violent and alien forces, industrial, imperialist and military, in the years immediately preceding the war. It also expresses an ideological crisis: 'the strange death of liberal England'; the ideological crisis of liberal humanism; the tortured conscience of an individualist society which has enslaved the individual and left him in possession only of a bad dream. But the reflection of real historical contradictions, and the expression of ideological crisis, are articulated into a specific aesthetic form; and this brings us to the real 'ideology' of *The Rainbow*.

If we measure the distance between this style and the realism of *Sons and Lovers*, we can see that although Lawrence is still here primarily concerned with the relation between individual and community, and although the image of community is still the mining town of his birth and upbringing, the vision of society is now both expanded and radically fractured. The colliery now holds sway over the whole of society; but the individual resists incorporation into that society, denies her own social existence, and therefore begins to see society as a dream, unreal, from which the sleeper can, by conscious effort and choice, awake. That is the contradiction. What *The Rainbow* does is to substitute a pleasant pastoral dream for the nightmare of bourgeois society. Into the blank space between living, conscious subject and alien, 'reified' society the novel inserts the organism of a myth which effectively seals that breach, ideologically resolving the glaring contradictions of historical reality. That myth is the myth of rural England: Marsh Farm.

I am proposing that we read *The Rainbow* backwards, from Wiggiston to Marsh Farm, rather than the other way round. We should see the novel not as a record of historical process, with Wiggiston as the culmination of a real history of social decline, but as mythology, where the 'history' is deduced from the present and cast backwards into the past. Marsh Farm is a myth created to fill that blank space in the centre of Wiggiston, that human absence at the heart of the modern community; a myth created to seal the painful breach between individual and community so clearly revealed in Ursula's vision of Wiggiston.

Marsh Farm – the first of the novel's three stages – is not an actual historical society at all, but a simple inversion of Wiggiston; a 'developing' of the photographic negative into colour and life. In Wiggiston society is mechanical and dehumanised; at Marsh Farm it is organic and human. In Wiggiston human beings are subdued to an impersonal collectivity; at Marsh Farm the individual is sovereign and autonomous (a clear distortion of history, which I will be discussing below). In Wiggiston labour is alienated and men reduced to industrial functions; at Marsh Farm work is creative and fulfilling, and although Tom Brangwen is not exactly the figure of the 'harmonious man',[7] he becomes a figure of organic harmony in his marriage to Lydia.

How, then, does the presentation of the mining town here compare with the realism of, say, *Odour of Chrysanthemums*? I have acknowledged that realism has its suppressions and absences; but I would wish to argue against Eagleton that there are *degrees* of suppression, and it is possible for art to reduce a social totality to such an extent that its contradictions are completely negated. In Wiggiston the working class is excluded as a dramatic presence, as an active agent, as a human force; the industrial system operates by its own laws, which deny and negate all value. Values can be introduced only from above or below within the system: either from the liberal paternalism of the owner, or from the struggle of the workers (such an interaction is explored very interestingly in the chapter 'The Industrial Magnate' in *Women in Love*). Where the bourgeoisie itself is excluded, and the managerial class is empty of value and devoid of humanity, and the working class is present only as passive and exploited victims – then the social totality appears, simply, as a myth of a negative kind, which drains a society of its contradictions, establishes it as a hollow deadness, and proceeds to fill its absences with retrospective and elegiac mythology. Contradiction can take place only between the society and a displaced individual; and Ursula, as we shall see, is actually rescued from that society and incorporated into the alternative myth.

I will now examine that alternative myth, the supposedly 'historical' society of the elder Tom Brangwen. The first image of society presented in *The Rainbow* (in the first part of Chapter 1) is, explicitly, not a realistic one at all: it is defined, in fact, as a 'poem'. There are no individuals here, but a collective 'race' of Brangwens. Only the sexes are differentiated: the men satisfied with their lives as agricultural producers, the women cherishing ambitions and aspirations extending beyond it. But these aspirations are actually fulfilled *within* the rural community *itself* – by the existence of a superior (gentry) class: 'The male part of the poem was filled in by such men as the vicar and Lord William . . . The wonder of the beyond was before them.' (11) The rural 'village' society is a 'poem' because within it imaginative needs are fulfilled; every part is organically articulated into a unified whole, and all contradictions are resolved. There is a complete circuit in which aspiration is automatically fulfilled, a complete harmony of parts corresponding to the bourgeois conception of aesthetic perfection:

> The lady of the Hall was the living dream of their lives, her life was the epic that inspired their lives. In her they lived imaginatively, they had their own Odyssey enacting itself. (11)

This model of society is a myth in the strictly philosophical sense: an ideological harmonising and resolution of real social contradictions. There is no conflict here between individual and community, because the Brangwen race is an unindividualised, collective entity; there is no conflict between 'society' and 'nature', because human life and the natural world are mediated by agricultural labour; there is no class conflict between gentry and yeomanry, no tension between human aspiration and an impoverished social environment.

The passage openly declares itself as myth, by its explicit self-definition as a 'poem' and by its declamatory rhetoric and biblical cadences, and it resists the temptation to site itself in real history. It is a deliberate evocation of an imaginary, pre-industrial, quasi-feudal organic community (the Brangwen women aspire to belong not to the cultured and educated bourgeoisie, but to a 'fighting host' – a touch of feudal romance). It makes no attempt to describe a society that ever existed, but presents itself as a myth constructed negatively in response to the conditions of Lawrence's own contemporary society. In keeping with the aestheticism which pervades Lawrence's earlier writing, it defines social harmony in terms of aesthetic completeness and perfection – poem, epic, Odyssey.

As the second part of Chapter 1 begins, myth gives way to 'historical-chronicle' ('About 1840, a canal was constructed across the meadows of the Marsh Farm . . .' (11)), and we are really entering a different world, a world of change and mobility. Early industrial developments – canal, railway, colliery – approach Marsh Farm. Tom's brother Alfred leaves the farm and works as a lace-designer in Nottingham, becoming a classic example of industrialised life. So Tom's decision to perpetuate the old agricultural life is made in a context of alternatives and possibilities; but the 'continuity' he chooses sets his own life into connection with that original myth rather than with history. The industrial world is sheared away, and Tom occupies a pastoral world irradiated by the illumination of that introductory social 'poem'.

There is actually no rural community at all in this earlier part of the novel: there is only a family. The family is, of course, as Eagleton says, 'at once social institution and domain of intensely interpersonal relationships';[8] but this family exists as an autonomous unit, with as little connection with a contingent or contextual community as a country house in Jane Austen – and without even other similar families to connect with. The elder Brangwen generation die, and all other members of the family move away, before the real beginning of Tom's history, his meeting with Lydia, at which point he stands completely alone, isolated in time and space.

Tom is presented as the only person who works the farm. We learn from a single reference that there are 'farm-hands' (85), but these labourers have as little existence in the novel as servants in Jane Austen: they are simply not there. Tom's profitable farm could not be run without those absent people, but for Tom and Lydia they do not exist, and the narrator does not wish to accord them any more significance, or give them any more substance, than that. Lydia Lensky is scarcely aware of other people at all: she perceives 'people who passed around her, not as persons, but as looming presences' (55); and Tom himself 'liked people, so long as they remained in the background'. (102) That is their privilege; but the novelist clearly shares and endorses their point of view. When Tom and Lydia marry, the wedding is pared right down to its 'core' of significance – the 'religious' binding of two people. As a social ritual or communal experience it has no existence; 'the guests' are shadowy presences whose 'being' both characters and novelist ignore. (57–8)

Tom Brangwen's work is hardly ever given real substance, and there is certainly very little attempt to connect that aspect of social life with his emotional problems and crises. Leavis lights on a pair of examples from very few instances, notably the beautiful but 'set-piece' description of Tom taking the child Anna into the barn. Here a conflictual relation within the family is resolved in association with nature, the connection mediated by work. The dramatisation of this convergence is impressive, but 'community' exists only in Tom's recollections of childhood – 'community' is a function of the memory:

> He looked down at the silky folds of the paisley shawl. It reminded him of his mother. She used to go to church in it. He was back again in the old irresponsibility and security, a boy at home. (79)

Even the family (apart from its single-generation nucleus), which defines the range and limits of 'community', exists only in Tom's memory. The old rural society, then, exists only within the individual; 'community' has been internalised and embodied within the self. Tom is a model of pre-industrial society: 'organic' society is incorporated in the 'organic' individual. The marriage between Tom and Lydia forms an image of the original social 'poem': her 'foreignness' fulfils his aspiration, and the unified couple constitutes a symbol of wholeness and harmony (the arch) which stands for an 'organic' society. The family, whole and complete within itself, floats in a social vacuum free of the pressures and determinations of a real history:

> They were a curious family, a law to themselves, separate from the world, isolated, a small republic set in invisible bounds. The mother was quite indifferent to Ilkeston and Cossethay, to any claims made to her from outside . . . She was mistress of a little native land that lacked nothing. (103)

The form of the novel actually ratifies this isolation: it automatically negates 'claims from outside', suppresses Ilkeston and Cossethay, and detaches the family from its contingent socio-historical context. 'Community' is an absence, not a presence, in the text.

The novel's narrative technique works to confirm this abstraction of individual and family from community. Scenes of family life are narrated from a neutral point of view, dramatising the experience of several consciousnesses. In Chapter 3 a wider *social* life is evoked: the world of market town, inn, pub, cattle-yard and eating-house, where Brangwen's acquaintances become dramatic presences, and where a genuine world of work, commercial activity and sociable relationships is fully rendered. But the presentation is done from the point of view of the child, who is specifically alienated from that social world. Even at this early stage of the novel, and even though it is the pre-industrial, 'organic' community that is being dramatised, the 'privileged consciousness', the chosen viewpoint, is that of the outsider who looks at society as an external object from a radically alienated perspective.

Let me compare this first stage of *The Rainbow* with a more classically realist account of the life of an agricultural proprietor: that of Constantine Levin in Tolstoi's *Anna Karenina*. Naturally the differences between the life of a member of the Russian landed nobility and that of an English Midlands farmer obscure the comparison, but they do not adequately explain the difference of method. Levin's life on his estate is not at all individualised, and not at all reduced to a simple 'pastoral' setting. Levin lives in the midst of a busy and active network of social relationships: with members of his own family; with his servants; with other landowners; and, above all, with the peasants whose labour supports his life. It is the problem of relationship with them that preoccupies Levin as the most pressing problem of his life.

And we actually see Levin (the aristocrat) working his farm more often than Tom Brangwen. All Levin's deep emotional problems (his marriage, his struggles with death and religion) are intimately connected with the lives of others in an effective working community. Of course, Tolstoi does not tell any 'whole truth', and *Anna Karenina* suppresses a great deal of Russian rural history. But the presentation has enough fullness and complexity to reveal a 'genuine' alternative society, complete with its own contradictions, whereas Lawrence succeeds only in composing a myth.

In abandoning realism, Lawrence rejected more than 'the certain moral scheme' and 'the old, stable ego of the character' to which he objected in Tolstoi and the traditional novel. And it is not necessary to agree entirely with Lukács's conservative view of realism to want to withhold consent from Eagleton's argument that Lawrence's development beyond realism was 'progressive'. Considering what Lawrence lost in embarking on the experiment of *The Rainbow*, it is possible to conclude rather that the attempt was ultimately sterile and directionless. (For example, he lost the power to create an imaginative synthesis of individual life and actual history, such as that achieved in *Odour of Chrysanthemums*; he lost the power to present the complexity and contradiction of his own society and social existence, as in *Sons and Lovers*; and he lost the technique of the 'communal narrator' (derived from the realist novel and applied to a working-class community), which creates the necessary complexity of viewpoint and social experience – a method which is in *The Rainbow* replaced by a subjectivist narrator who constantly collapses into the immediate experience of individual character.) A historical criticism should surely take account of such losses before evaluating any specific example of the movement beyond realism.

*The Rainbow* does not, then, preserve the realist totality at all, since its 'evolving generational structure' has no realist or historical content. It merely presents three different settings for dramas of personal relationship: agricultural pastoral, rural village, and industrial city. Clearly, if the original rural society is mythical rather than historical, it cannot possibly contribute to an authentic presentation of historical evolution.

Neither does the novel 'explode' realism in a progressive way, exposing and calling into question the concealed ideology of the realist method. In fact its form and method amount to a denial of history and an affirmation of ideology. Its images of society are not the kinds of myth which balance, resolve and disclose contradictions; its form is rather a montage of myths, which never actually enter into dialectical conflict and connection, because they occupy different spaces, temporal and theoretical. The separate myths are organised loosely into a sequence corresponding to the theory of history sketched in *Lady Chatterley's Lover*: 'This is history. One England blots out another . . . The industrial England blots out the agricultural England. And the continuity is not organic, but mechanical.' (163) The myth of Marsh Farm *grows through* the solid nightmare of Wiggiston, in the presence of Ursula, as grass (to use one of Lawrence's favourite metaphors) grows through a concrete pavement, and effectively negates it.

The vision of society transformed which concludes *The Rainbow* is simply a substitution of pastoral dream for the myth of industrial nightmare. Ursula has rejected 'Skrebensky's world', all 'the old, dead things'; in her vision of the rainbow that world disappears, and she awakes into an alternative dream. The rainbow, symbol of organic social harmony, encompasses and unifies the regenerated society; beneath its arch symbols of organic growth ('fruition' and 'germination') stir into vitality. In structure and content the new society reproduces the old. Ursula is the organic descendant of the Marsh Farm myth, bearing its values within her as her grandfather did; her individual consciousness reaches out and embraces the real social world, transforming it, binding it around with the rainbow, fertilising its internal essence. The two meanings of 'organic' – unity of natural growth, and structural totality – here fuse into one. The novel's ideological images of social completeness, harmony and fulfilment – arch and rainbow – were offered as symbols of the old organic society, and were permitted, by the mythological mode, to stand unmolested by real history. They appear again in the novel's conclusion; and they are not set into conflict with real history at all. History, in fact, is explicitly cleared away, leaving ideology standing, firm yet evanescent, in a seductive nakedness of beauty. A completely unqualified ideology of individualism replaces the imagery of social harmony which was the pastoral ideology of Marsh Farm; the individualising, historically suppressive manner of the novel achieves, by an extraordinary ideological *tour de force*, a synthesis of those utterly contradictory structures: if the individual cannot be at one with society, then society will be incorporated into the individual and reproduced in her image.

This is the fundamental reason for Lawrence's abandoning, at this stage of his writing, not only of realism, but also of the tragic mode as a form for the novel. At precisely that moment, in 1914, when the tragic view of society should have appeared with new urgency and insistence, Lawrence's art denied and refused that recognition. In *The Rainbow* real historical forces are abstracted into separable myths, and the myths arranged into the sequence of an 'organic/mechanical' theory of history, while the organic continuity of the Brangwen race runs through Tom, Anna and Ursula in a *separate*, parallel evolution. The social tragedy enacted by the novel's mythological structure –

from organic past to industrial present – is therefore in practice evaded by the characters. Tragedy is therefore never seen as a true historical process, and never really lived through, in *The Rainbow*. So the 'affirmative' conclusion is not an arbitrary note of optimism gratuitously tacked on, as Leavis maintained, but the true consummation of the novel's form, the symbol for its explicit refusal of historical tragedy.

Powerful ideological images of social harmony and reconciliation are snatched from actual history and encoded within specifically mythical context, where they can exist and flourish unmolested by the stubborn conflicts and contradictions of that actual history. It is hardly surprising that despite initial suppression and subsequent neglect, *The Rainbow* was incorporated very easily into the canon of 'classic' modern literature, its powerful social challenge already absorbed by its own ideology.

A text, according to Eagleton, produces ideology by setting it into conflict, not with itself (there can be no contradictions within ideology, since its precise function is to deny them), but with history. *The Rainbow* does not do this: it fills its absences with myth; and its individualist ideology is never exposed, as the unreality of the social world permits the individual consciousness to replace it. History disappears; ideology itself stands before us: 'And the rainbow stood on the earth . . .' History has to be 'swept away' before this vision can be achieved, a vision in which ideology, incarnate, descends from the heavens and unifies a fractured world.[9]

In the second extract of this closing chapter, 'The Sense of History in *The Rainbow*', by Mark Kinkead-Weekes, we find a fascinating response to Graham Holderness's Marxist/materialist reading of the novel. Kinkead-Weekes's essay was originally delivered as a paper to a symposium marking the centenary of Lawrence's birth, at the University of Nottingham in 1985. (The essay is collected, with eleven others, mostly by eminent Lawrence scholars, in the volume from which this piece is extracted.[10]) The setting and the nature of the centenary event itself are significant in providing a focus for the essay, which sets out to present a view of *The Rainbow* as an historical novel. The argument raised by Holderness, that the novel 'has no realist or historical content', is refuted by Kinkead-Weekes by recourse to a wide range of tightly-controlled and intricately-linked references to events, locations and circumstances which establish that the novel does function effectively as a depiction of 'the major changes in provincial middle-class life between 1840 and 1905'.

We have already discussed (in Chapter 4) Kinkead-Weekes's major contribution to Lawrence studies with his essay 'The Marble and the Statue', in which he made clear the links between the two essays *Study of Thomas Hardy* and *The Crown*, and *The Rainbow* and *Women in Love*. The same level of painstaking scholarship that marked out 'The Marble and the Statue', by means of careful textual analysis and wide research of manuscript and contemporary sources, is evident in the essay that follows. Kinkead-Weekes establishes dozens of links between the actions and activities taking place in the novel and those that actually occurred in the region in which the novel is set, building a convincing argument (almost against his own wishes, as suggested in the opening paragraphs) for seeing *The Rainbow* as '"historical" fiction':

*The Rainbow* is an historical novel – and if we have not read it so, it is despite the hint, in the pointed division of the opening chapter, which clearly asks for a double focus. From one angle, we are to see archetypal Men and Women in a timeless nature, outside history. The Brangwens, farming their borderland, reveal modes of being that are universal and 'from the beginning'; oppositions that provide a basic language for all the individual persons and particular conflicts that follow, so that we can compare and contrast three generations of lovers in unchanging terms and grasp the underlying nature of their relationships. However, the second section of the chapter begins pointedly with a date, 1840, and a marked change affecting the daily consciousness of the Brangwens, the cutting of the Nottingham Canal across their lands. The novel will turn out also to be very much concerned, though in Lawrentian ways, with major changes in English life between 1840 and 1905: with effects of industrialism and urbanisation, with education, the emancipation of women, the decline of religion. From this angle the structure looks quite different. Instead of seeing the same conflicts reorchestrated (and so understanding them better), we have now to see each generation as very differently affected by historical development and social change. Moreover the movement *into* history is an important theme. We shall not find the 'hungry forties' or the Chartists in the world of the beginning: Tom's Marsh Farm is still relatively isolated and Lydia comes there as a refugee from history; but we can watch Anna and Will begin to enter the mainstream of their time; and Ursula and Skrebensky live in a fully historic world.[11]

It is not of course surprising that criticism should have concentrated on the archetypal ahistorical view. That is where the art seems most challenging and newly imaginative, sounding chords the whole work will orchestrate: there is the rich earth on which the Men are at one with the whole of nature, so that the life of each participates and is reflected in the other; there, conversely, is the road, the church tower on the hill, pointing up, out, beyond, to the town, the civilisation, the world of awareness, individuation, the separate self. Can the opposed visions, the conflicting impulses, the breadth and the height be

*married*? We set out to discover how and why the marriage of opposites – present anytime, in everyone – becomes creative or destructive
in the personal stories of Tom and Lydia, Will and Anna, Ursula and
Skrebensky, as these shed light on one another; and we find a new
kind of vision, demanding a new kind of art, a new attitude to 'character', new dimensions of symbol, rhythm, language. It is hardly
surprising that we should tend to concentrate on such dimensions.
But, for once, I propose to take the other view, and ask how exactly the
novel sees the major changes in provincial middle-class life between
1840 and 1905, and in what sense one might make a serious claim for
it as 'historical' fiction, in those terms.

The first surprise is to find an elaborate chronology. From three
fixed points – the Polish insurrection of 1863; the wedding of Anna
and Will on Saturday 23 December 1882;[12] and the outbreak of the
Boer War in October 1899 – one can work backward and forward,
using a multitude of particulars, to show that (apart from four easily
explicable mistakes), Lawrence had a remarkably accurate sense of
when as well as where he was on every page, far more than was necessary for novelistic purposes. Confidence grows when one works out
that Ursula must have passed her London matric in 1900, and then
finds 'June 1900' on her application form in the manuscript, though
this has disappeared from the first edition. More extraordinarily, the
novel might even help to date events outside. Lawrence based the
outer shape of Will's career on that of Alfred Burrows, father of his
fiancée Louie. James Boulton, writing of Alfred's woodwork classes in
Cossall, and supposing Lawrence right that 'he' was about thirty at the
time, puts the date at 1894.[13] But the novel's chronology says 1891 –
and Wright's directory for 1891 mentions the new reredos carved for
Cossall Church by 'the carving class'.[14] There may of course have been
two carving classes; but one then discovers why a class might have
begun in 1891; because it was in that year that such evening classes
first became eligible for grants, so that there was a remarkable flowering just then.[15] It is not often that one can use a fiction to suggest the
possibility of a factual correction to one of the most meticulous of
scholars. Moreover, several revisions seem sensitive about chronology.
For instance, Lawrence rightly decides that Skrebensky could not
have hired a taxi to take Ursula for a drive in 1899.[16] Indeed, it is only
by reading historically that one realises quite how exciting a 'coup'
and a 'romance' that ride was meant to be. It was only just possible for
the son of a Baron-Vicar of a local church to have got hold of a car from
one of only three suppliers in Nottingham, and there were only 125 in
the whole shire four years later.[17] But it was possible, because
Nottingham was remarkably progressive; indeed several motor-cars
had been locally manufactured before 1900, when the Automobile

Club's famous expedition to popularise the motor-car came to town. Again, Lawrence oddly designates one of the books that Ursula and Maggie read in their lunch-break as 'some work about "Woman and Labour"'. He has a particular book in mind (hence the inverted commas), but also knows that Olive Schreiner's *Women and Labour* was not published until 1911, when he sent it to Louie, and this is a decade earlier.[18] Such concern for accuracy is remarkable, and there are very few anachronisms.[19] Lawrence does displace, by two or three years, some details of the Ursula story where it most closely approaches his own experience. Her accurately described tram-ride, for instance, from Ilkeston station to 'St. Philip's School Brinsley Street' in 1900, obviously draws on Lawrence's own twice-weekly journeys to the Pupil Teacher Centre – but the tram-service only opened in 1903. Since he knew this very well, however, the licence is deliberate. Yet even if one conceded a tendency to displace memory to that extent, one would still be testing a fiction by extraordinary standards. Of course we need not think of him as some painstaking local historian – he could clearly draw for his third generation on his own memory; for the second on all he knew or had heard of the Burrows family; and for the first he had points of reference in well-known locals like the Polish refugee Baron von Hube, Vicar of Greasley,[20] and the Fritchley family who had farmed outside Cossall for 'over two hundred years' (as both Trueman's *History*[21] and *The Rainbow* put it). What does need insisting on, however, is that Lawrence's imagination was as densely 'historical' *in its nature* when he wrote *The Rainbow* as it was archetypal and 'mythic'.[22] There will therefore be a myriad of details which could say more than they seem to now, if only we hadn't lost the sense of date that Lawrence commanded. Tom Brangwen associates a Paisley shawl with his mother, precisely because the pattern had its great vogue in the 1830s. More important, when Will rides a motorbike into 'Beldover'/Eastwood in 1902, an unworldly man has become remarkably up-to-date. (There were only 40 in the shire in 1903.[23]) Readers in 1915 could fine-tune as we cannot; and local readers still more so. Of course little Anna and her step-father found Derby's indoor market attractive. It still is, but when they went it was gleaming new.[24] And of course young Anna, determined to be a lady, would want to model herself on Princess Alexandra – for all Nottingham was full of her after the Prince opened the Castle Museum in 1878, when Anna was fifteen.

Given that his imagination was historical then, with what sense of pattern and diagnosis does Lawrence draw his Portrait of an Age?

'About 1840', canal, colliery and railway come together, to alter the life and consciousness of the Brangwens. The date may seem approximate short-hand, for a more gradual and complex process, but Lawrence chooses an actual spot – one can stand on it today[25] – in order to dramatise in a single vivid picture the essentials of industrial progress, and the picture turns out to be more accurately dated than appeared at first. A canal goes over a road on embankments and a bridge; through the arch is a colliery; there is a railway at the foot of Ilkeston hill; and a farm tucked away behind the embankment in pre-industrial England, yet within constant sight and sound of the Industrial Revolution in the midst of the countryside. Actually, 1840 was nearer the end of the canal-building age than the beginning; the Nottingham Canal had opened in 1796, and, with the Cromford and the Erewash canals, had opened up markets that gave the Erewash Valley coal-owners a competitive edge.[26] But when they were faced with the threat of a railway in Leicestershire which might turn the tables, the Valley coal-owners met at the Sun Inn in Eastwood, and as a result the Midland Counties Railway opened, in 1840, with an Erewash spur a few years later.[27] Vast new markets became available and an extraordinary mining, industrial, trading and population expansion began. So new bits of canal and new coal seams were opened, about 1840. Barber, Walker & Co. had taken over Cossall Colliery by 1844;[28] and it even seems that by 1836 a new route for the canal may have been cut (replacing a loop on the other side of Cossall Marsh whose embankment broke in 1823),[29] more steeply banked, and hence involving a narrow-arched aqueduct across the road which for the first time shut the Marsh Farm off from Ilkeston. Both Nottingham and Derby began a rapid industrial expansion. The Nottingham lace-curtain, that essential feature of Victorian respectability, went into factory-production in 1846, to be followed by bicycles, sewing-machines and motorbikes, all of which duly make their appearance in *The Rainbow*. Ilkeston had grown by only 1000 people in the fifteen years before 1846, but grew nearly as much in the next five. By 1881 (just before Will marries Anna) the 4500 of the 1840s had leapt to over 14,000; and in 1891 (when Will began those evening classes) it was nearly 20,000. Eastwood had 'the greatest increase of any parish in Nottinghamshire during the 19th century in population per square mile'.[30] So those houses spreading across the skyline at the end of the book were quite as spectacular and ugly a development as *The Rainbow* suggests.

On the other hand, the prosperity of the Marsh Farm, supplying that growing urban population, becomes readily intelligible. Though Lawrence does not spell it out, it is clear how there is business enough for a separate family butchery, and why the farm Brangwens, as they prosper, go up the social ladder. If one reads historically, what seemed insignificant detail reveals a chain of implication. Take, for example, the generational significance of the engine. We now know why a demand for lace-designers for machine-production took Alfred

Brangwen into the factory, to be followed by his son Will, until he escapes. But Tom's son, studying engineering in London via Nottingham High School, becomes a technocrat and manager. The prosperity that made Tom squire-like buys the education that turns his sons into gentlemen, on terms with the Big House. But we can also see an irony in making Skrebensky an engineer in the third generation, or rather, a Sapper. For in his world the Industrial Revolution has turned to war. The novel may end in 1905, but we know Anton will have to return from India to help engineer the destruction in Flanders. The passages which deal with the sprawling ugliness on the skyline, and the dehumanisation of the miners' lives in Wiggiston where Tom junior is manager, are the one area where the book's sociohistorical insight has been discussed. However, it has far too often been in isolation from the actual complexity of the fiction. The Lawrence of 1914–15 was by no means simply 'agin' the machine, as the *Study of Thomas Hardy*[31] made clear, and *The Rainbow* is very much aware of how the widening horizons of Ursula's generation relate to the mine and the factory. She has no intention of being poor; Lawrence knows perfectly well what has produced her mother's sewing machine, and the bicycles on which Ursula and Maggie tour the countryside. Most of all, we shall not understand Lawrence's diagnosis of the ills of industrialism and urbanisation without seeing how these connect with the revolution in education, which followed.

The first generation of Brangwens are only half-educated. Alfred goes to school in Ilkeston in the 1840s, but it is only in drawing that he shows any talent, hence the factory – though we see later that there was more to him. Frank soon goes into the butchery, and their sister marries a collier (there is no talk of her education). But the mother has ambitions for Tom and sends him to Derby Grammar School, which dates from the sixteenth century and offers the classical education of the old foundation. However, Tom cannot articulate, argue, or become mentally conscious. He has strong and delicate feelings, and an instinct for the order of mathematics; but he seems unable to develop intellectually, and is glad to give up and take over the farm at seventeen. Lydia had a governess in Poland but she too, despite the seeming progressiveness of having been a nurse, is a physical and mystic being rather than an intellectual one. So their marriage, though the most successful in the book, carries in all its richness a sense of limitation, of human resources that have not yet opened out.

The second generation have far wider horizons. Young Tom we saw going to Nottingham High, another sixteenth-century foundation; but in this more scientific age he goes on, not to classical Oxbridge, but to London, almost certainly the Royal School of Mines which, with the School of Science, became Imperial College. There, in the eighties, 'some of the most energetic scientific and mathematic people' were indeed to be found, notably Huxley. We measure the contrast with his father, and how young Tom and his brother have become gentlemen. In the other family Will, pulled into the lace factory behind his father, is neither a gentleman nor a success. Yet he too escapes his background because of the intensity of his self-education in the arts, which aligns him with another side of the new times. Fred may read Ruskin, but Will is an enthusiastic practitioner of the Gothic and the Pre-Raphaelite. His woodcarving becomes the link with the Morris-inspired Arts and Crafts movement, and he is ready for his chance when it comes. What had seemed peripheral and private turns out to be in the mainstream of its time. Out of the evening classes and the summer holiday schools comes the post of Art and Handwork Instructor for the new County Education Department; experimental classes in new Swedish methods of teaching manual dexterity in schools; and a role in the education of the underprivileged.

What still lags is the education of women; and here the chronology holds ironies which I for one had missed. Anna is better educated than her mother, and has a more developed and critical intellect, but she is born just too early to get the education she deserves. In 1872 she is sent to a Dame School, in ironic juxtaposition to the Education Act. She goes on to 'the High School' in Nottingham, founded in 1875, only the sixth to be created by the Girls' Public Day School Company,[32] but in its very earliest years when it still resembles a young ladies' seminary. Even so, as Anna and Will argue about art and religion, we have a dramatic measure of how the consciousness of the second generation of Brangwens has altered, and is becoming articulate. But in the third generation the change is spectacular. In 1892 Ursula is at no Dame School but one of the new kindergartens pioneered in Nottinghamshire by the progressive Inspector Abel, who makes an appearance in the novel.[33] Then she and all her siblings attend, as they now must, a state school made free since 1891 – which is as well, since there are eight of them! Next, the eldest three go on to the Girls' High, now risen in the world and firmly established in a handsome lace-manufacturer's house – once again we see connections between industry, wealth and education. Gudrun is headed for Art College, unlike her father, and his. Ursula's London Matriculation will qualify her as a teacher, then take her to the 'Gothic' grandeur of the new University College of Nottingham with the chance of a degree – and we measure the full contrast with her mother, and her grandmother. The difference in the position of the three generations is carefully and dramatically plotted. Of course, Ursula's two years as a teacher also expose the seamier side of the coming of free and compulsory education. The pushing-up of the leaving age to 12 in 1899 (13, by bye-law, in

Nottinghamshire)³⁴ created desperate over-crowding. That is why in 'St. Philips' the big-room has been glass-partitioned and three classes of 55–60 children each are being taught simultaneously. Both school and (Ursula thinks) university have become like factories. So though the story of *The Rainbow* is essentially of widening circles – hence the two chapters thus entitled – the most highly educated of all the Brangwen women is deeply disillusioned by her experience.

And the same is true of the other New Women, for we have also been talking about female emancipation. This had been central to the novel from its earliest stage *The Sisters*, whose germ, Lawrence told Garnett, had even then been 'woman becoming individual, self-responsible, taking her own initiative.'³⁵ Ursula and Gudrun are only two of a number of emancipated women who, in professional independence, freedom of ideas and morals, and the demand for the vote, proclaim new conceptions of womanhood. Winifred Inger seems the most 'advanced': the science studies at Newnham, the contempt of men, the critique of religion, the friends who seem to conform to a smug provincial society but are inwardly raging. Her lesbian relation with Ursula is finally rejected by the girl, yet she had been a liberating and enriching influence. But there is something half-hearted which emerges when she settles, open-eyed, for marriage with Tom Brangwen the mine manager; for domesticity within a system, both of which she had condemned. This says something about her times, but also something about her: she is a compromised Diana, somehow only half-formed. Maggie Schofield has also become a competent professional in a man's world, but in order to do so has had to divide herself in two, so that paradoxically 'there was something like subjection in Maggie's very freedom'.³⁶ Her personal life exists quite separately from her working life. And though she has advanced ideas of love – that it is beyond law and must be plucked where it is found – she is unfulfilled, brooding, melancholy . . . Of all these, however, Ursula seems to embody the New Woman most powerfully. Her life seems to include them all with greater intensity than any: the education, the struggle for independence through work, the freethinking, the liberated sexuality, above all the passionate pursuit of the liberty to be herself and shape her life to her own wishes. This is the constant impulse beneath all the violently contradictory phases of her life: as she rides above the crowd or defines herself against her young love; in her female relation with Winifred or the male world of Brinsley Street School; in the world of the senses with Andrew Schofield or the world of the mind at university; in the passionate sexuality with Skrebensky or the even more passionate aspiration which turns against and destroys him. In every phase the New Woman demands the freedom to create herself and her life. So when she staggers up the hill at the end, to miscarriage and breakdown, she seems a bitterly ironic comment on the impulse towards new life of the Brangwen women at the beginning.

But to see why, and to establish the ultimate basis for Lawrence's diagnosis of what had happened since 1840 – from which one might hope to connect up his critique of industrialism, of the ugliness of urbanisation, of the malaise of education, and the nonfulfilment of feminism – I think we need to see how it was the decline of the religious sense that was the most significant of all to a writer who called himself 'a passionately religious man'.[37] The world of Tom and Lydia is destroyed by flood, but far from having been sinful, it was a world in which the forces of divine creativity could build, in the human relation of man, woman and child, a House for the Lord. It was also a limited world in which whole dimensions of human potential had not yet opened. But as a result of the 'widening circles', as the century wears on, we see in the novel how rational scepticism and scientific materialism not only bring about the decline of the church but also of the religious sense itself. Anna pits against both a newly sharp critical intellect, exposing the reduction by the Victorian church of religion to morality, and turning against Christian symbols and mysteries a scientific, literal materialism, to which her less intellectual and articulate husband can find no answer. In Lincoln Cathedral her resistance to Will's religious ecstasy and self-abandon reaches a climax, as she sets out to destroy his sense of mystic unity, in the name of humanism, multiplicity, freedom. Her brother Fred studies Huxley's agnosticism. Her brother Tom, the scientist and engineer, moves beyond the agnostic to the atheist. He becomes cynic and hedonist; sardonic observer of the wife-swapping of the Wiggiston miners and the reduction of their personal and family life in subjection to the machine. His own display of domestic feeling, Ursula thinks, is a kind of sentimentality based on no commitment to any system of value. Winifred, scientifically educated, directs at religion the other form of demythologising intellect, 'comparative religion'; seeing all religions as the deifying of man's own values, and his own impulses to submit to or identify with what are no more than aspects of himself. Dr Frankstone, teaching biology at university, will recognise nothing mysterious about the creative processes of life, which science will sooner or later explain and codify. The mystic and religious side of Ursula rebels against all these, her mother, her uncle, Winifred; and turns from Dr Frankstone to see the cell under her microscope as a mysterious and gleaming triumph of infinity. But she also makes love in her father's church, and listens in scorn to the old hackneyed tale of Genesis and the Flood and the Rainbow; for Ursula is a ferment of contradiction. Like Anna with Will, she reacts against too-ready self-abandonment or inadequate selfhood in Skrebensky; but her own aspiring self-assertion turns out to be even more destructive, beaked, like a harpy. Where the religious sense is not destroyed, it seems perverted.

As the novel's history moves into the twentieth century, then, it is not merely that the great promise of Victorian progress and opportunity seems to have gone sour, or even that individuals have become hollow or destructive, marshy or brittle. Something seems to have gone wrong with the very springs of human life. But to seek below the symptoms for the innermost cause, is to be steadily forced back to the *other* way of looking, the archetypal vision of the Beginning. History, for Lawrence, is only to be finally understood in terms of the timeless deep-structure within personal stories, those basic and opposite impulses within all people and relationships: the impulse to be at-one with all created nature through the body and the senses; the opposite impulse to become individual, to know, and act upon the 'other', in separateness and differentiation. In one, we are aware of ourselves only in togetherness with nature and fellow man or woman; the other defines the self against the not-self, a process of individuation, self-conscious thought and utterance. One is stable; the other holds in change both threat and promise. As archetypal Men and Women give way to Tom and Lydia, the personal stories reveal both impulses conflicting in each, and both individuals unfulfilled. But with strange beauty and power they are drawn magnetically together like opposite 'poles'; and experience in marriage a kind of death and rebirth. Sexual relationship is a crucible of conflict, and it is intensely painful to 'die' to the old self and be transformed through the 'other'; yet from conflict and self-abandon springs rich new life. Out of the ashes of dead selves the lovers rise like phoenixes, more themselves each time; separate individuals, strangers, yet indissolubly bound together. Biblical language and symbol insist that we see this marriage of opposites as a religious mystery. In continual Genesis, man and woman create and recreate each other, and the tree of knowledge, by marrying the divine forces within and between them. They journey through the wilderness from exile, but meet as pillars of cloud and fire, passing through each other to create a rainbow-arch, a doorway to the Promised Land of new life beyond; with new freedom for man, woman and child. In marriage, rather than stone or wood or scroll, they build a House for the Lord to dwell in. Though a flood destroys their 'Old Testament' world, and Tom/Noah is drowned, he and she have laid hold of eternity.

Anna and Will partly re-enact this archetypal pattern – but with new strain on both sides. Anna tends to resist the movement towards the other: her greater individuality, wary intelligence, more developed self-consciousness make it harder to give or risk herself, as Lydia had done. Conversely Will, who seems assured because he is so unselfconscious, is over-ready to abandon himself and merge into the other, which betrays insufficiency of self. As she resists, he becomes insistent, clutching, predatory. As he demands, she resists more strongly. The creative conflict of opposites turns into a battle for domination which Anna, the more self-assured articulate individual, is bound to win. But having conquered, she dances her own fertility to the Lord, against the shadowy man in the doorway. She builds a house for herself on Pisgah, but doesn't enter the Promised Land or open it for Will. Indeed, as she pushes him off, he nearly drowns in the flood of his insufficiency, and only gradually develops some independent selfhood. Now we see how directly the greater potential and the lesser achievement are *related*. New dimensions and tensions of religion and art, intellect and spirit, opening out through history, mean that there is more to marry in the second generation – but also that it is more difficult to marry. The polarities become more extreme, and the increased one-sidedness in each begins to turn the conflict from creation to destruction.

Ursula in the third generation embodies all the opposites of her family at peak intensity, and with greater awareness than any. She is intensely visionary and intensely sceptical, spiritual and fleshly, arrogant and unfixed, emancipated and primitive, and it is her fate because of her generation to be conscious of herself in all these aspects. She also wins new freedom of choice. So we watch her trying continually to resolve her contradictions by pursuing one aspect of herself to the exclusion of others, but never finding the way to marry them: 'always the shining doorway was a gate into another yard, dirty, and active, and dead'.[38] She reacts one way and another, but none can fulfil because each reduces her complex being. In the three crises of her affair with Skrebensky we measure the escalating difficulty of the marriage of opposites, and the still greater antagonism that comes from asserting partial selves. When the young lovers dance at the wedding, it becomes a destructive contest in which Ursula, like her mother, is victrix. When Skrebensky returns from Africa, some years after the Boer War, Ursula is reacting against university and the life of the mind, and they achieve a purely sexual kind of consummation, mating their 'darker' sides. Inevitably, however, reaction sets in, and the terrible scene on the beach shows how Ursula cannot be satisfied while her infinitely aspiring 'bright' side is denied. Under an incandescent moon, beside a brilliant sea, she tries to force the opposite of what they had had, some consummation of intense awareness – and succeeds only in destruction, like a harpy. Then she tries to settle for domesticity, but that is to reduce herself still more. She has tried all the reductive ways; only the inclusive one remains, and Lawrence confronts her with it in that powerful last scene with the horses.

. . . Yet for Lawrence the creative sources of life are always there, in challenge and promise, and that is why Ursula must be made to meet them in the end. The encounter with the horses confronts the educated modern city girl, so ready now to deny the elemental forces in herself, with the unitary landscape of her grandfather, the big wind, the earth and looming trees, the rain, the power of animals, the fire from their nostrils. But the summons is not to the merely elemental; it is, as always, to the marriage of opposites. The horses are an intensity of conflicting energies that cannot be denied or reduced, and must not be, in Ursula. But she now finds nature terrifying, and she cannot meet the abiding challenge to meet the 'other' and 'come through' to new life, beyond – which has always meant an agony like death in the self. At first she does manage to walk on, towards 'the high-road and the ordered world of man'[39] through the horses, but only by refusing to look or think or know, following her feet blindly and instinctively while her nerves and veins 'ran hot, ran white hot, they must fuse and she must die'.[40] But Ursula's modernity has everything to do with awareness, and to become aware of the horses is to increase the terror of self-risk. The old ways of instinct are gone by, but she *cannot* go through again in full consciousness. She runs away, climbs a tree, collapses, 'like a stone at rest on the bed of the stream'.[41] This is her Flood, and it almost destroys her. On the 'realistic' level she is pregnant, terrified, in shock, and she miscarries. But on a deeper level Lawrence suggests that she has failed, not only because of the inadequacy of Skrebensky, but also because she herself has seemed incapable of the marriage of opposites. Yet in her illness she diagnoses what is wrong: her self-projections and relationships have all been unreal entanglements, forced by her will. She must 'die' to her own self-assertion, and at last let go, trust herself nakedly to the sources which feed all life, but she is then reborn into a new world, the mysterious work of divine creation, as in Genesis. She must no longer try to manipulate herself, or others, but wait for the coming of a Son of God, from the infinite and eternal to which she now belongs, 'within the scope of that vaster power in which she rested at last'.[42] The Rainbow is not achieved – but as she sees the sign in the sky it remains covenanted like the one in the Bible. Perhaps the promise is not the logical outcome of the story but an assertion of Lawrence's own revolutionary optimism breaking through in a language of assertion; but the one in the Bible was also gratuitous, and seen only by the reborn soul that has died to its old self in the Flood.

Finally the two kinds of reading are also dialectic, and to be married. The deep-structure view of men and women has to be embodied in personal stories, and these in turn seen as moments of consciousness and crisis in the whole inner and social history of their time. But conversely, consciousness in time, and of history, must always for Lawrence be transfigured by consciousness of the timeless and archetypal, or man will perish from an inadequate conception of his own nature and his world.

Yet to recognise the richness and power of fusing archetypal with historical vision in *The Rainbow*, is to recognise a degree of loss thereafter. For that richness of texture came from Lawrence's sense of still *belonging*, to a place, a culture, a history; and also to a literary community, an audience which could share and understand. The denunciation and destruction of the novel shattered these conditions for ever. No fiction like *The Rainbow* could come from Lawrence again. What did come, even in the 'continuation' of *Women in Love*, is not only another story but necessarily another kind of story, which overtly renounces the sense of date and historical precision.[43] Of course there is gain as well as loss, a new apocalyptic and mythic intensity; a new sharpness of diagnosis and separation; and might-have-beens are always unprofitable but a kind of imaginative loss there is, and only a fully historic reading of *The Rainbow* can bring out its nature and extent.[44]

In the final extract of the chapter we focus on an essay which sets out to consider both of Lawrence's major novels in a new light, and free from many of the preconceptions and assumptions that have been the lot of critical readings post-Leavis. Alistair Davies's essay also provides a fitting conclusion to this collection, for it draws together much of the argument that has run through the extracts included in previous chapters, and it provides a neat example of the postmodern ability to move towards the future from a re-reading of the past.

The Cambridge critic F. R. Leavis has, for many, provided in his *D. H. Lawrence: Novelist* (1955) the definitive readings of Lawrence's *The Rainbow* and *Women in Love*.[45] According to Leavis, Lawrence presented in *The Rainbow* a broad but intimate social history of England at the crucial points of its transformation from an agricultural into an industrial society. He described this process from first-hand experience, and as he described, he also enumerated the losses, in community, in human relationships, in contact with Nature, which the change entailed. Indeed, to Leavis, it is as a recorder of the social and cultural traditions, of the modes of life, of a certain nonconformist civilisation in English history, at the moment when industrial England interpenetrated and destroyed the old, agricultural England, that Lawrence has most value. In the modern period, Lawrence was, Leavis argued, 'as a recorder of essential English history . . . a great successor to George Eliot' (p. 107). *The Rainbow* was in the tradition of *Middlemarch* and might have been written:

to show what, in the concrete, a living tradition is, and what it is to be brought up in the environment of one. (As to whether the tradition qualifies as 'central' I will not argue; I am content with recording it to have been that in the environment in which George Eliot, too, was brought up.) We are made to see how, amid the pieties and continuities of life at the Marsh, the spiritual achievements of a mature civilisation . . . are transmitted. (p. 105).

Lawrence, however, did not simply memorialise the nonconformist tradition out of which he (and George Eliot) had come. He showed, through the history of three generations of the Brangwen family, that the tradition was not only a shaping and sustaining power, but that its pieties and sanctions remained, even in the contemporary world, a living presence. Ursula's quest for spiritual fulfilment was in no essential measure different from that of her predecessors. The new kind of civilisation which had obliterated the world of Marsh Farm had not obliterated its spiritual heritage, its particular sacredness of vision. It was this vision which Lawrence had preserved and transmitted through his 'marvellous invention of form' which rendered 'the continuity and rhythm of life' (p. 144). If the final section of the novel dealing with Ursula often seemed tentative, if her final prophetic passages were 'wholly unprepared and unsupported' (p. 142), the achievement of Lawrence's novel as a whole was undiminished. He had described, and, more importantly, had enacted 'the transmission of the spiritual heritage in an actual society' (p. 145).

*Women in Love*, Leavis continued, was a more complex work, in terms of its fictional technique and of its social vision. There were 'new things to be done in fiction, conceived as a wholly serious art, and it was for his particular genius to do them' (p. 147). Lawrence created here a panoramic novel of Edwardian and Georgian England before the sickness which he diagnosed within it had precipitated the country into the destruction of the First World War. 'After reading *Women in Love*, we do feel', Leavis asserted, 'that we have "touched the whole pulse of social England"' (p. 173). Lawrence's powers as a novelist lay in exploring the essential, or the inner spiritual history of England, and he presented with brilliant insight the brutality and self-destructiveness of Gerald, the perversity of Gudrun, and the positive and creative drives of Ursula and of Birkin. Yet, if his diagnosis was first-rate, his solution to the problems diagnosed was less satisfactory. Ursula and Birkin may have discovered, as a couple, a realm of values and of being which allowed them to withdraw from the downward rush to destruction of the civilisation around them, but their personal quest for salvation, a quest which led them to abandon England, was, Leavis acknowledged, perplexing and contradictory in a novelist so committed to social renewal. Lawrence perhaps had been defeated by the difficulty of life.

Leavis intended his study to champion Lawrence's peculiarly English vision, his peculiarly English genius, and in this, he was brilliantly successful. With *D. H. Lawrence: Novelist*, he established Lawrence's reputation in English and American criticism as the foremost English novelist of the century. Moreover, he drew attention not only to Lawrence's merits as a novelist but also to his importance as a modern thinker. Lawrence, he argued, had analysed the problems and the dilemmas of our present phase of civilisation, when industrial society and industrial values were becoming paramount, with an insight which no other modern thinker possessed. Yet there was a paradox in Leavis's approach, for while he related Lawrence's work to a definite historical moment, he did not concern himself with the precise literary, social or political context in which the novels were written. He did not have, it is true, the advantage of the textual histories of *The Rainbow* and *Women in Love* which have been produced since his study was first published. We now know in detail, for example, not only how Lawrence reworked *The Rainbow* and *Women in Love* from an earlier work, "The Wedding Ring," but also exactly how he redrafted *The Rainbow*, after the outbreak of the First World War, giving (among other substantial changes) much greater prominence to Ursula's quest for freedom and independence. Even so, Leavis's disregard for the way in which the outbreak of the First World War might have affected Lawrence's reworking of *The Rainbow* and *Women in Love* is strange in a critic otherwise so conscious of the historical and social pressures upon Lawrence's writing.

It is a disregard which, in due course, led to a curious imperceptiveness in Leavis's reading. When Ursula, for instance, recovers from her illness, at the end of *The Rainbow*, she insistently repeats: "I have no father nor mother nor lover, I have no allocated place in the world of things, I do not belong to Beldover nor to Nottingham nor to England nor to this world, they none of them exist, I am trammelled and entangled in them, but they are all unreal" (p. 492). These are hardly the words of a Dorothea Brooke, for Ursula does not believe that she should submit, as does George Eliot's heroine in *Middlemarch*, to the forms and limits of local and of national life, but seeks rather to find her identity by rejecting and transcending them. The contrast, indeed, is instructive: the importance of Ursula's quest lies precisely in her refusal to accept such forms and limits. How are we, therefore, to understand her words – and the quest for freedom which, in the last and longest section of the novel, inspires them? They have profound implications for Ursula's private life; but they have no less profound implications for her (and for our) political life as well. It is impossible to ignore their subversive intent. We need, Lawrence suggests, if we are to become free, if we are to become truly ourselves, to reject all national values, all national perspectives and all those human ties which, under present conditions, uphold the nation-state. *The Rainbow* was not simply a novel rewritten during the First World War: it became, in the process, a novel about, and in opposition to, those forces which made war possible.

... The England of Ursula's early adulthood is a world of Jingoism, of imperialist war, of a new and sinister morality of the nation-state, all implicit, in Ursula's words, with 'a great sense of disaster impending' (p. 328). As the Boer War begins, and Anton Skrebensky, Ursula's lover, leaves for war, she 'knew the huge powers of the world rolling and crashing together, darkly, clumsily, stupidly, yet colossal, so that one was brushed along almost as dust.' She wanted 'so hard to rebel, to rage, to fight' (p. 326). But with what? Ursula's sense of helplessness was compounded by the fact that her friends and acquaintances had all seemed to have committed themselves . . . to the ideals of the nation-state. Anton Skrebensky, 'to his own intrinsic life . . . dead', had no qualms about fighting in Africa. He had quite literally dedicated himself to the State, to the army, as an instrument, as a tool:

> Who was he, to hold important his personal connection? . . . He was just a brick in the whole great social fabric, the nation, the modern humanity. (p. 326)

Winifred Inger, Ursula's teacher, was committed to scientific socialism, with its own idealisation of the powers of the State. Winifred and her radical friends, 'various women and men, educated, unsatisfied people' were, however, 'inwardly raging and mad' (p. 342). Ursula's Uncle Tom, the manager of one of the local collieries upon which England's political and industrial power was founded, had married Winifred, but his only mistress, we learn, was the machine. At the National School in which Ursula had her first teaching post, the teachers coerced the children 'Into one disciplined, mechanical set, reducing the whole set to an automatic state of obedience' (p. 382). Even the college she later attended as a student had a sinister, coercive function, for it was simply 'a little, slovenly laboratory for the factory' (p. 435).

Ursula, understandably, feels crushed; understandably, she wishes to rebel. But what are to be her means? She significantly refuses the chances offered by the Suffragette Movement, for she does not want, she says, simply a mechanical freedom, a freedom within the existing nation-state. It is spiritual freedom she desires and spiritual health, for she believes that the commitment of her friends and acquaintances to the nation-state reveals their spiritual sickness, their submission to an external system which satisfies dimly understood needs either for power and significance, or for freedom from self-responsibility. It is, however, only when Anton Skrebensky returns from Africa, after several years of service, first in the Boer War and then in the administration of Empire, that Ursula finds the opportunity to express her spiritual rebellion, to begin her quest for spiritual freedom and spiritual health. Anton's new-found cynicism gives her the confidence to formulate her own dismissive thoughts. Civic ideals, she told herself, disguised the rage and the frenzy of the impotent and the unfulfilled:

> 'What are you, you pale citizens?' her face seemed to say, gleaming. 'You subdued beast in sheep's clothing, you primeval darkness falsified to a social mechanism.' (p. 448)

Ursula's renewed relationship with Anton, however, does not bring her freedom or health. A servant of Empire, finding in the bullying discharge of his duty the means to keep at bay his terrifying recognition of inner emptiness, Anton inescapably sets a limit to Ursula's quest for self-realisation and for freedom. The very system Anton serves is the one which she must reject. She significantly feels her dissatisfaction with him most acutely when walking by the sea in Lincolnshire, where they holiday together before their proposed marriage. 'The salt, bitter passion of the sea, its indifference to the earth, its swinging, definite motion, its strength, its attack, and its salt burning, seemed to provoke her to a pitch of madness, tantalising her with vast suggestions of fulfilment' (p. 477). By comparison with the sea, with its 'vast suggestions of fulfilment', Anton seems puny and constricting. There was an essential element of 'reality' – evoked by the power and the motion of the sea – of which Anton had no knowledge and from which he would exclude her.

Accordingly, Ursula rejects Anton, and returns to her parents' home. It is a moment of defeat, for Ursula not only finds herself pregnant by Anton, but brings herself, on reflection, to write submissively to him asking *no more than to rest in your shelter all my life'* (p. 485). Her energy, we are told in a suggestive image, was frozen, and her defeat, we can see, lies in the degree to which she denies within herself that sense of mystery, that sense of fulfilment which she had glimpsed while walking on the beach. Yet her defeat is not absolute. The remainder of the novel – with its account of her struggle with the horses amidst the blinding rain on the Common, with its account of her illness and miscarriage, with its account of her tenacious and willed recovery, in effect describes the processes by which that energy becomes unfrozen, by which Ursula is released from her old ego to a sense of true Individuality. On the heath, amidst the dissolving rain, she becomes conscious – as she had upon the beach – of the forces of life, and, as a result, she sheds the old ego which had tied her to family and to place, to lover and to nation-state:

> I have no father nor mother nor lover, I have no allocated place in the world of things, I do not belong to Beldover nor to Nottingham nor to England nor to this world, they none of them exist, I am trammelled and entangled in them, but they are all unreal. I must break out of it, like a nut from its shell which is an unreality. (p. 492)

As Ursula rejects her allocated place in the world of things, as she frees herself from her entanglements in a world which is for her spiritually unreal, she achieves Individuality, and with that achievement, she comes, in her final prophetic vision, to an understanding of the universality of mankind, both in its present suffering and in its future glory.

The story of Ursula's spiritual revolt, of her struggle to free herself from the determinations of the nation-state, of her journey towards self-realisation, provides the essential aspect of the last sections of *The Rainbow* . . . Ursula knew that 'the sordid people who crept hard-scaled and separate on the face of the world's corruption were living still', but she also hoped that they would cast off 'their horny covering of disintegration, that new, clean, naked bodies would issue to a new generation . . .' (p. 495).

. . . Lawrence, I believe . . . presented a powerful satirical account of England's decadent intellectual, political and cultural circles . . . but also stressed that the future lay alone in the hands of those great individuals who might extricate themselves from the present destructive system of nation-states. There was indeed, amidst the catastrophe of war, an even greater sense of urgency that such men and women should emerge, and an even greater conviction that the old forms of life were irremediably rotten. It is not, therefore, surprising that Lawrence should, in *Women in Love*, concentrate upon those few who, he believed, might escape from the present shipwreck of civilisation and found – at a later date – a new world.

In the first chapters of *Women in Love*, Lawrence gives us a panoramic view of England – of the industrial England of Gerald Crich, of the intellectual England of Hermione Roddice, of the *avant garde*, bohemian England of Rupert Birkin and of the *habitués* of the Café Pompadour – but quickly the focus of the novel shifts to Ursula who, even as she is drawn into the worlds of Shortlands and of Breadalby, maintains a distinct aloofness and distance. Indeed, in the major scenes in which the characters reveal themselves through actions or words, Ursula is present, providing resistance to and judgement upon the worlds into which she has been drawn: Birkin and

Hermione in the schoolroom, Gerald bathing in the lake, the weekend at Breadalby, Gerald on his horse at the railway crossing, Birkin repairing his damaged punt near the Mill House, and finally, the water-party at Shortlands. Her aloofness, however, is not simply a formal device to provide a perspective from within the novel, for her strength and steadfastness serve the larger purpose of suggesting that there are individuals able to live through and counteract the present sickness. Ursula, on account of her self-realisation in *The Rainbow*, is free from the drift and decadence of her contemporaries. She is, we see immediately, one of those fitted to be a constructor of the future.

Necessarily, the critical distance which Ursula maintains to the worlds into which she is drawn qualifies the reader's response to Rupert Birkin. When Birkin expounds his philosophy to her, after they have met while he is repairing the punt, Ursula dismisses as self-important exaggeration his fanatical desire to save mankind. For all his 'desirable life-rapidity', there was, she felt, 'this ridiculous mean effacement into a Salvator Mundi and a Sunday-school teacher, a prig of the stiffest type' (p. 122). Significantly, Ursula refuses to accept Birkin's desire to encompass all mankind in the curative process of destruction, and her refusal is doubly important. Firstly, Ursula throws doubt upon Birkin's imagery of apocalypse, suggesting that apocalypse is not the inevitable fate of mankind, but the nightmarish imagining of those who had lost contact with the mystery of life and had fallen into a deathly, catastrophic view of the future; secondly, she refuses altogether Birkin's view that all mankind must be saved. She herself knew, Lawrence writes, suggesting that Birkin did not, 'the actuality of humanity, its hideous actuality' (p. 120). It is enough for Ursula that men and women – the few, exceptional men and women who recognise the spiritual crisis of the present – should save themselves, and it is to this task that she dedicates herself, seeking, after a serious relationship with Birkin begins during the fateful water-party at Shortlands, to extricate herself and the strange, remarkable, but seemingly doomed man she now loves, from the disaster which she knows will engulf the world in which they live. Mankind as a whole had gone too far, too irretrievably, into hideousness.

After the drowning which interrupts the water-party at Shortlands, Ursula and Birkin (who leaves for France) take stock of their lives, for the fact of death compels them to review their hopes and purposes. At first, Ursula feels that 'her life . . . was nearly concluded' (p. 183), but her mood of depression is a temporary one, for she recognises that her frustration, and her helplessness, are common experiences and come from the corrupt values and oppressive realities of the world of the nation-state in which she is condemned to live: '"A life of barren routine, without inner meaning, without any real significance," she felt. "How sordid life was, how it was a terrible shame to the soul, to live now!"' (p. 185). Those who controlled the political and economic life of the nation-states had turned the sea:

> into a murderous alley and a soiled road of commerce, disputed like the dirty land of a city, every inch of it. The air they claimed too, shared it up, parcelled it out to certain owners, they trespassed in the air to fight for it. Everything was gone, walled in, with spikes on top of the walls, and one must ignominiously creep between the spiky walls through a labyrinth of life. (p. 185)

Ursula traces her sense of nullification to the mode of existence demanded of her within the world of nation-states, and, for the first time, contemplates abandoning altogether the country in which she has been brought up. It seems impossible for the individual – not least one who has achieved the kind of realisation and insights Ursula has achieved – to remain permanently oppressed within this soiled and soiling world. When she meets Birkin again, he asks her if she had done anything important while he had been away. Her reply is direct and startling: 'I looked at England, and thought I'd done with it' (p. 241). Although she denies that this scrutiny is important, it is – in the trajectory of the novel – profoundly so, for Ursula realises now that the only way to save herself, and to save Birkin, is to leave England – England as a nation-state, as one part of a system of nation-states. He is less certain: 'It isn't a question of nations,' he asserts, 'France is far worse' (p. 241). Birkin makes such a qualification because he hopes, on account of his personal ties with Hermione Roddice and with Gerald Crich, to reverse England's 'race-exhaustion' and to call England back again to new life. For Ursula, however, this remains a false and grossly misguided belief: all ties with England, with Hermione and Gerald, had to be broken.

It is while visiting the jumble-market in Nottingham to buy furniture for Birkin's house that the underlying differences which separate them become manifest. As Birkin looks at the wares on sale, he comes across an 'arm-chair of simple wood, probably birch, but of such fine delicacy of grace, standing there on the sordid stones, it almost brought tears to the eyes' (p. 347). Birkin buys the chair because it seemed to express, in its line and strength, the spirit of England, but Birkin's sentimental nostalgia angers Ursula: 'I wish it had been smashed up when its day was over, not left to preach the beloved past to us. I'm sick of the beloved past' (p. 348). Ursula insists that they give the chair to a young couple whom she had seen at the market, 'so secretive and active and anxious the young woman seemed, so reluctant, slinking, the young man' (p. 346). He was, she realised, going to marry the young woman because she was pregnant. Birkin, however,

remains uncomprehending, thinking that Ursula wants to divest herself of possessions, of a fixed habitation; but her motive is infinitely more
complex. She was, we are told, attracted to the young man, who was:

> a still, mindless creature, hardly a man at all, a creature that the
> towns have produced, strangely pure-bred and fine in one sense,
> furtive, quick, subtle. His lashes were dark and long and fine over
> his eyes, that had no mind in them, only a dreadful kind of subject,
> inward consciousness, glazed and dark. (p. 350)

The only outlet for his vitality, she thought, as he settled down to marriage,
to a position within the nation-state, was furtive and subterranean,
with 'the stillness and silkiness of a dark-eyed, silent rat' (p. 350). Yet
there was, for all his furtive rat-like vitality, an element of meekness,
of defeat about him, for he had made a compact with the society which
had produced him. It was a society, Ursula realised, in which the
individual could not live, in which individuality was completely
crushed. By giving away the chair, Ursula symbolically rejected her
own engulfment within such a society, the society of the nation-state.
As they journey home on the tram, Birkin himself suddenly but
decisively understood her motives. "'I want," he agreed, "to be disin-
herited"' (p. 354).

Birkin and Ursula marry, their marriage taking place on the understanding that they will leave England afterwards. As they journey
across Belgium, Ursula sees a man with a lantern coming out of a
farm-building. A familiar sight in her childhood, it reminds her of
Marsh Farm, of the old intimate farm life at Cossethay. Its strange context, however, informs her of how far she had been projected from her
childhood. As they arrive in the Tyrol, she accepts that she had now no
'anterior connections':

> She was with Birkin, she had just come into life, here in the high
> snow, against the stars. What had she to do with parents and
> antecedents? She knew herself new and unbegotten, she had no
> father, no mother, no anterior connections, she was herself, pure
> and silvery, she belonged only to the oneness with Birkin, a one-
> ness that struck deeper notes, sounding into the heart of the
> universe, the heart of reality, where she had never existed before.
> (pp. 399–400)

She had finally achieved that desire she had formulated at the end of
*The Rainbow*, that refusal of an *allocated* place in the world of things,
and although her decision to leave England cannot be separated from
her rejection, in the name of individualism, of mass, democratic
society, it is a decision, within the perspective of *The Rainbow* and of
*Women in Love*, which is not negative but positive, not destructive but

creative. She had finally managed to struggle free of the destructive forces of nationality and of nationalism; she had shed that special brand of Englishness from which neither Birkin nor Gerald could, without great – and in Gerald's case – fatal efforts, free themselves. At the end of the novel – in the saga of Birkin's contradictory but powerful love for Gerald, of Gerald's death upon the mountain-side – it is clear that Birkin could not make the easy break with the past which Ursula had made, but he had come to appreciate that Gerald could not have found his way to the positive renewal which he, under Ursula's guidance, had tentatively made. We are left in no doubt that Ursula's way to self-realisation, to true individuality, by leaving England is the only way; nor are we left in any doubt that it is a way which involves the complete rejection of 'English' identity for something more real, more universal and ultimately more constructive.

There is much in Lawrence's novel, if this reading is correct, which is unsatisfactory, but before evaluation can begin, we need to be sure that we have managed, as fully as possible, to describe the kind of fiction Lawrence actually wrote, or the kind of perspectives he actually put forward, or the kind of rhetoric he actually used. When we consider that *Women in Love* was written in 1916, during a period of extraordinary political and military crisis, we might find his work, with its stress upon the survival of the exceptional individual amidst the collapse of modern civilisation, a profoundly inadequate, even a contemptible response. Certainly, F. R. Leavis, otherwise the most stalwart defender of Lawrence, felt himself profoundly perplexed by the conclusion of *Women in Love*. Yet we need to reserve such censure until we have weighed fully the significance of Ursula's triumphant break from 'anterior connections' . . .

What is at issue, of course, is no longer simply a literary question, but an historical, a cultural, a political one as well. Would *The Rainbow* and *Women in Love* provide support for war-resistance, for conscientious objection, for a refusal of the State? Or do we find in them the last, desperate assertion of Individualism at the very moment when the conditions of Liberalism had been finally eclipsed? Or do the novels mystify the actuality of State power and State oppression by rendering it simply in terms of a disorder of the spirit? Individual judgements and individual answers will, of course, differ, according to the historical, or cultural, or political viewpoints of individual questioners, but whatever judgements and answers such questioners reach – if they are to be convincing – will need to be based upon the multiplicity of historical and literary evidence which contextual readings produce.

In the first part of this essay, I have suggested that, if we are to understand D. H. Lawrence's *The Rainbow* and *Women in Love* accurately, we need to place them in the context not only of English but of

European literature, and in the context, not of the fiction of the nine-teenth century but of the fiction of the early twentieth century. It is an assertion which almost inescapably involves the following questions. If this is the case, why has a quite contrary interpretation of Lawrence, dating from F. R. Leavis's *D. H. Lawrence: Novelist* (1955) been estab-lished and accepted within the English critical tradition, even by recent critics, such as Raymond Williams and Terry Eagleton, who rebut the form, if not the content, of Leavis's reading of Lawrence?[46] By what process of critical revision has the individualist and anti-nationalist perspective which I have described been transformed into the epic, quintessentially English one of F. R. Leavis's study?

Again, the contextual method, conscious that criticism, like litera-ture, and reading, like writing, has to be placed in its cultural, social and political context, helps us to find an answer. For Leavis, as he makes his case for Lawrence, does so by rejecting the specific charges made against Lawrence in the most influential literary journalism of the 1920s and the 1930s. Against Wyndham Lewis, who had argued in *Paleface* (1929) that Lawrence advocated capitulation to mindless instinct, Leavis argued that Lawrence made plain that 'without proper use of intelligence there can be no solution of the problems of mental, emotional and spiritual health' (p. 310). Against John Middleton Murry, who had suggested in *Son of Woman* (1931) that Lawrence's fiction was the record of his sexual failure and of his deep hatred of women, Leavis asserted its health and normality. In *The Rainbow*, the pieties of life at Marsh Farm, Leavis suggested, were clearly feminine and matri-archal: Lawrence celebrated throughout the novel the moral and creative vitality of women. Against Murry's assertion that Lawrence used his fiction after *The Rainbow* as a vehicle for his 'thought-adventures', Leavis defended the artistry of *Women in Love*. Against T. S. Eliot, who had suggested in *After Strange Gods* (1934) that Lawrence was an ignoramus who had come from an intellectual and spiritual tradition in decay, Leavis argued that Lawrence's non-conformist background was one of rich and sustaining intellectual life. He alerted Eliot to the 'extraordinarily active intellectual life enjoyed by that group of young people of which Lawrence was the centre' (p. 306). It was just such a rich and central tradition which Lawrence celebrated in *The Rainbow*, and as he did so, he celebrated an essential strand of English history. For the Congregationalism of Lawrence's youth had played an important part in English civilisation, as Eliot would see if he read Élie Halévy. The English non-conformist tradition was one from which the major works of nineteenth-century English fiction, from George Eliot to Thomas Hardy, had come. This tradition, and the fiction which it inspired, was not, as Eliot suggested, eccentric, but stood at the heart of English cultural, political and moral life.

Yet, in asserting Lawrence's normality, his love for and rootedness within English values and traditions, Leavis was engaged in defending Lawrence against a persistent and unusually grave charge, which underlies the criticism of Lewis, Murry and Eliot, that Lawrence had been no less than a traitor to his country during the First World War, and had continued to be so after the War with his support for Bolshevism. The allegation was seriously stated, and its truth widely accepted. It is a measure of Leavis's success in cultural rehabilitation that this central aspect of the immediate critical reception of Lawrence had been forgotten.

In the first two years of the First World War, Lawrence's public opposition to the War brought charges of treachery and of lack of patriotism, and the publication of *The Rainbow* in 1915, with its criticism of the nation-state, seemed to confirm them. Certainly, the banning of *The Rainbow* on the grounds of obscenity was widely, and correctly, thought to be a political act.[47] The morbid sexual content of *The Rainbow*, J. C. Squire argued in the *New Statesman*, revealing the prevailing association of Lawrence with the German cause, was suspiciously Hunnish. The book 'broods gloomily over the physical reactions of sex in a way so persistent that one wonders whether the author is under the spell of German psychologists.'[48] It was, however, with *Women in Love* in 1921 that the full case against Lawrence was made explicit. His most influential accuser was John Middleton Murry. 'It is part of our creed,' Murry wrote in the *Nation and Athenaeum*, 'that the writer must be responsible; but it is part of [Lawrence's] creed that he is not.'[49] His lofty and semi-official tone, passing considered judgement in the public interest, came from his recent, war-time role as censor at the War Office, but it came also from the new function which he, the most noted editor of the period, assumed for English criticism after the War. The English writer and critic should now, he believed, speak in the name of and in the defence of the special wisdom of the English race, which had been achieved through its Christian and its Protestant history. That should be his creed, for the English writer and critic was heir to a strain of heretical individualism, an instinct for freedom. This was English culture's unique contribution, politically and culturally, to world society. Even so, the impulse to freedom should never be anarchic; the individual should come freely to accept the loyalties and the allegiances which bound him, as an Englishman, to his people and to its unique heritage.

From this perspective, Lawrence, whose passionate individualism made him the 'most interesting figure' in English letters, had to be censured. 'We stand by the consciousness and the civilisation of which the literature we know is the finest flower,' Murry insisted, but

Lawrence was in rebellion against both:

> If we try him before our court he contemptuously rejects the juris-
> diction. The things we prize are the things he would destroy; what
> is triumph to him is catastrophe to us. He is the outlaw of modern
> English literature; and he is the most interesting figure in it. But he
> must be shown no mercy.

Murry's forensic language was not accidental. Lawrence, who had left
England for America in 1918 via the Pacific route, was being tried *in
absentia*. He, 'the outlaw of modern English literature', had repudiated
his ties with and his allegiances to England and to English culture.
His rejection of the decencies of English life, his opposition to the
Allied cause in the War – which alone could explain his relish in por-
traying the collapse of English society in *Women in Love* and his own
abandonment of England for foreign lands – these formed the implicit
basis of Murry's public indictment.

Lawrence, Murry insisted, wanted above all to destroy that level of
consciousness upon which European civilisation was founded.
Through Birkin, who had 'a negroid as well as an Egyptian avatar',
Lawrence advocated, Murry wrote, quoting *Women in Love*, 'sensual
mindless mysteries to be achieved through an awful African process.'
This process was, for Murry, a literal degradation, a falling back to the
'sub-human and bestial, a thing that our forefathers had rejected when
they began to rise from the slime.' Lawrence, quite simply, delighted
in imagining the overthrow of England by the forces of darkness and
of barbarism. The qualities of Lawrence's genius, 'no longer delight
us', Murry had announced at the beginning of his review: 'They have
been pressed into the service of another power, they walk in bondage
and in livery.' Murry's language is vague and shrill, but its import
would be clear to a contemporary audience. Lawrence had rejoiced
during the War to think of England defeated by the Prussians whom
he served, just as he rejoiced after the War, to think of his native
country overthrown by his new masters, the Bolshevists.

When Murry returned to Lawrence in his major study of
Lawrence's novels, *Son of Woman* (1931), he made use of the new languages of psychoanalysis and of sociology, but his charge of treachery
against Lawrence remained the same. Lawrence was, Murry argued, a
dangerous demagogue, for the novel had become a vehicle for his
'thought-adventures', his aim as a writer 'to discover authority, not to
create art' (p. 173).[50] He had gone to America as a second Moses, as a
Law-giver who 'should bring its soul to consciousness'. If the
Mahatma Gandhi could convulse and revivify a whole Empire, he
suggested, 'there was no reason why Lawrence should not give laws
to a people' (pp. 169–70). Lawrence's intention in America had been

to bring about, through the disintegration of traditional, white consciousness, the end of Western civilisation. By comparing Lawrence's teaching with that of Gandhi, by suggesting their common revolt against the West, Murry indicated the revolutionary threat Lawrence's teachings were thought to pose.

But why should Lawrence do this? Murry found a ready psychological and sociological explanation in Lawrence's upbringing. Although born into the working class, with its warmth of human contact, Lawrence had been dominated in childhood by his mother. Having aspirations to middle-class gentility, she caused Lawrence to repress his sexual vitality as gross and vulgar. Accordingly, he grew up a guilt-ridden sexual weakling, 'a sex-crucified man' (p. 21), and remained 'a child of the woman' (p. 73), with deep resentment at his inadequacy and limitations. In his dreams, he was 'a wild, untamed, dominant male' (p. 73), yet he wanted also to be a child, with the happiness and oblivion of childhood.

*Sons and Lovers*, Murry suggested, had been an assertive fantasy of social and sexual independence. *The Rainbow*, which concentrated throughout on unsatisfactory relationships, first of Anna and Will, then of Ursula and Anton, reflected the failure of his marriage to Frieda. It was 'radically, the history of Lawrence's final sexual failure' (p. 88). Thereafter, he took his revenge upon the social order itself, which the mother and wife enshrined, in fantasies of destruction and of extravagant sexual assertion. *Women in Love*, in which Birkin-Lawrence demanded of Ursula a kind of sexual or sensual homage, was the first of a series of aggressive fantasies in which the female, insatiably demanding satisfaction, was annihilated by the man who could not satisfy her (p. 118). The woman was humiliated, and the man formed, in the place of marriage, emotional alliances with other men. Love was turned into hate, loyalty into betrayal and the quest for life became the unconscious veneration of chaos and of death. In *Women in Love*, Lawrence envisaged a whole culture within a death-miasma in order to 'feed his sense of doom and death and corruption; to fulfil his own injunction that "we must disintegrate while we live"' (p. 330). In his American writings, Lawrence exulted in the destruction of England and of Europe, and hoped for his own, vengeful resurrection by absorbing the dark blood-consciousness of America's primitive races. Yet for Murry, these writings, with their fantasies of leadership, with their celebration of primitive communism, merely expressed Lawrence's power-fantasies and his craving for death (p. 333). It was clear that the Bolshevist Lawrence, embittered by his sexual perversity and by his proletarian origins, wished, in the spirit of revenge, to destroy the normal and wholesome world of culture, refinement and adult relationship, from which he had been excluded.

Murry was not the only critic to find in Lawrence's work the example of a resentful or treacherous Bolshevist temperament. Wyndham
Lewis, whose writings of the 1920s and 1930s were concerned to
identify those writers who, in his opinion, were working towards the
overthrow of the West by what he termed 'Oriental Bolshevism',
found Lawrence to be the most prominent and the most dangerous foe
of the West: 'In contrast to the White Overlord of this world in which
we live, Mr Lawrence shows us a more primitive type of "consciousness", which has been physically defeated by the White "consciousness,"
and assures us that the defeated "consciousness" is the better of the
two' (*Paleface*, 1929, p. 193).[51] Lawrence was, Lewis suggested, 'a natural
communist' because he was unmanly, preferring the mindless and
feminine merging of Oriental Bolshevism to the masculine separateness of the Greco-Christian West:

> With *Sons and Lovers* . . . he was at once hot-foot upon the fashion-
> able trail of incest; the book is an eloquent wallowing mass of
> Mother-love and Sex-idolatry. His *Women in Love* is again the same
> thick, sentimental, luscious stew. The 'Homo'-motive, how could
> that be absent from such a compendium, as is the nature of Mr
> Lawrence, of all that has passed for 'revolutionary,' reposing mainly
> for its popular effectiveness upon the meaty, succulent levers of sex
> and supersex, to bait those politically-innocent, romantic, Anglo-
> Saxon simpletons, dreaming their 'Anglo-Saxon dreams,' whether
> in America or the native country of Mr Lawrence? (pp. 180–1).

Lewis suggested that Lawrence advocated Communism and homosexuality in order to encourage young Anglo-Saxons to repudiate the
masculine dreams of Empire which had inspired their fathers, in
favour of the feminine and homosexual fantasy of subjugation beneath
an Oriental Bolshevist despotism. Lawrence was the most sinister and
the most subtle propagandist against the West.

T. S. Eliot, similarly, saw Lawrence's ideas and writing to be the
principal challenge to traditional values and ideals in England and
America. What made the task of maintaining these values and ideals
in the modern period particularly difficult, Eliot stated in *After Strange
Gods* (1934), was the undermining of intellectual and religious orthodoxy by Protestant heresies. The chief clue to the immense influence
of Lawrence's work was to be found in the decay of Protestantism in
England and America, and in the rise of a semi-educated public
unable to grasp the intellectual definitions by which orthodoxy in
thought and in religion had been maintained. In Eliot's view,
D. H. Lawrence was the foremost example of heresy in modern Anglo-
Saxon literature. Influenced by the degenerate Protestantism of his
infancy, with its 'vague, hymn-singing pieties' (p. 39), educated on a

fare of English literature notable, in Eliot's judgement, only for its eccentric and individualist morality, Lawrence lacked 'the critical faculties which education should give' (p. 58).[52] Lawrence started life 'wholly free from any restriction of tradition or institution'. He had 'no guidance except the Inner Light, the most untrustworthy and deceitful guide that ever offered itself to wandering humanity' (p. 59). It is hardly surprising, therefore, that Lawrence should come to see himself as a second Messiah, or that he should win a large following among 'the sick and debile and confused', appealing not 'to what remains of health in them, but to their sickness' (p. 61). It was, nevertheless, the influence of Lawrence's supposedly ill-educated and perverse ideas upon the young with which Eliot concerned himself, for, following Murry and Lewis, he saw Lawrence as the instrument of sinister and demonic forces, which threatened to destroy the Christian West. 'His acute sensibility, his violent prejudices and passions and lack of social and intellectual training,' Eliot argued, made Lawrence 'admirably fitted to be an instrument for forces of good or of evil' (p. 59). It seems, for a moment, that Eliot will withhold final judgement, but his censure is all the more effectively made by being delayed. Not trained, he continued, as had been the mind of James Joyce, Lawrence's mind was not 'always aware of the master it is serving' (p. 59).

A review of Lawrence's early critical reception reveals how much Leavis's championship of Lawrence involved an essentially liberal recovery of his work from the often hysterical and inflexibly reactionary misreadings to which it had been subject. Yet the cost of such a rehabilitation, as we have seen, was considerable, for as Leavis tried to counter the effect of previous readings, to cancel what he considered to be a distortion of Lawrence, he not only removed Lawrence from the literary and historical context in which he had written, but also made his work acceptable by ignoring its original political intentions. If we wish to read and understand *The Rainbow* and *Women in Love* accurately, we have, I believe, to restore them to their original contexts. This essay is an attempt to sketch one way out of many in which this can be done, and to show how much the past criticism of Lawrence's *The Rainbow* and *Women in Love* has proceeded by falsifying or repressing those original contexts. Of course, to readers long instructed in the contextual method, my account of it may seem to refer to the prehistory of modern criticism, and is, therefore, the procedure of an archaeologist rather than that of an innovator. Even so, the archaeologist can usefully remind his or her readers of the difficulty of reconstructing the past accurately and warn them that our tools of excavation, if too crudely used, can obliterate altogether the object under examination.[53]

Alistair Davies's essay offers a fitting conclusion to a book essentially concerned with the passage of Lawrence's work through eight decades of critical activity and discourse. In this final extract we are taken back to the original reception of the novels, and, from there, encouraged to re-read the works for our own age. Davies's examination of the critical-literary, social and political parameters within which the novels were written and published leaves us with some sense of the possibilities open to the student of the 'postmodern Lawrence'. For the vast majority of readers, who have been schooled (literally so) in a view of Lawrence commanded by Leavis's liberal reading, any revaluation of the context in which the novels were written is immensely useful. Set against Graham Holderness and Mark Kinkead-Weekes's interestingly opposed accounts of the novels, Alistair Davies's essay also serves to draw us back to the forces that helped shape and drive Lawrence as an artist, and to the critical arena in which he and his writings first received attention. We are left with several new vantage points from which to view the novels, and of course, we are also left with a more thoroughly developed sense of the profound interplay existing between works and their time – not only through the direct forces on art and artist, but through the cultural and political templates applied to each age by later generations.

The writers of all the essays and extracts in this volume ask us, in one way or another, to reconsider Lawrence's art – such is the function of criticism. From the early reviews of *The Rainbow* and *Women in Love* to the essays of this final chapter, however, we find an increasingly persistent and persuasive call to become conscious critics, aware of the working critical process and its ramifications. We are made to engage with our role as readers more directly, placing the developing body of critical material, and the activity of criticism itself, nearer the centre of our picture of Lawrence and his works. There is thus a suitably cyclical and phoenix-like quality in all of the regenerative and re-evaluative readings that make up the closing chapters of this book: our understanding of Lawrence's ideas, his novels, and the critical practices which have shaped and illuminated them, is richer for the attention to the critical process itself. It is hoped that this volume will help its readers to consider and develop their own critical practice and to arrive at a more fulfilling and meaningful understanding of Lawrence's great novels at the same time.

# BIBLIOGRAPHY

W. T. Andrews (ed.), *Critics on D. H. Lawrence* (London: George Allen & Unwin, 1971)

Simone de Beauvoir, *The Second Sex*, trans. H. M. Parshley (London: Jonathan Cape, 1953)

Anthony Burgess, *Flame into Being* (London: Sphere Books, 1986)

David Cavitch, *D. H. Lawrence and the New World* (London: Oxford University Press, 1969)

Jessie Chambers, *D. H. Lawrence: A Personal Record* (London: Jonathan Cape, 1935; Cambridge: Cambridge University Press, 1980)

Colin Clarke, *River of Dissolution: D. H. Lawrence and English Romanticism* (London: Routledge & Kegan Paul, 1969)

Colin Clarke (ed.), *D. H. Lawrence: The Rainbow and Women in Love* (London: Macmillan Casebook Series, 1969)

James C. Cowan, *D. H. Lawrence: An Annotated Bibliography of Writings About Him*, 2 vols. (De Kalb: Northern Illinois University Press, 1985)

Herman M. Daleski, *The Forked Flame: A Study of D. H. Lawrence* (Evanston: Northwestern University Press, 1965)

Emile Devalenay, *D. H. Lawrence: The Man and His Work. The Formative Years, 1885–1919* (London: Heinemann, 1972)

Carol Dix, *D. H. Lawrence and Women* (London: Macmillan, 1980)

R. P. Draper, *D. H. Lawrence: The Critical Heritage* (London: Routledge & Kegan Paul, 1970)

Terry Eagleton, *Myths of Power* (London: Macmillan, 1975)

Terry Eagleton, *Criticism and Ideology* (London: Verso, 1976)

T. S. Eliot, *After Strange Gods: A Primer in Modern Heresy* (London: Jonathan Cape, 1933; New York: Harcourt & Brace, 1934)

Frank Gloversmith (ed.), *The Theory of Reading* (Brighton: Harvester Press, 1984; New Jersey: Barnes & Noble Books, 1984)

Leo Hamalian (ed.), *D. H. Lawrence: A Collection of Criticism* (New York: McGraw-Hill, 1973)

Christopher Heywood, *D. H. Lawrence: New Studies* (London: Macmillan, 1987)

Graham Holderness, *D. H. Lawrence: History, Ideology and Fiction* (Dublin: Gill & Macmillan, 1982)

Aldous Huxley (ed.), *The Letters of D. H. Lawrence* (London: Heinemann, 1932)

A. A. H. Inglis, (ed.), *A Selection from Phoenix* (Harmondsworth: Penguin, 1971)

Dennis & Fleda Brown Jackson (eds.), *Critical Essays on D. H. Lawrence* (Boston: G. K. Hall, 1988)

Frank Kermode, *Lawrence* (London: Fontana, 1973, revised 1985)

Mark Kinkead-Weekes, 'The Marble and the Statue: The Exploratory Imagination of D. H. Lawrence', from Maynard Mack & Ian Gregor (eds.), *Imagined Worlds: Essays on Some English Novels and Novelists in Honour of John Butt*, (London: Methuen, 1968)

Mark Kinkead-Weekes (ed.), *Twentieth Century Interpretations of The Rainbow* (New Jersey: Prentice-Hall, Twentieth Century Views Series, 1971)

Frieda Lawrence, *The Memoirs and Correspondence*, ed. E. W. Tedlock (New York: Knopf, 1964)

F. R. Leavis, *D. H. Lawrence: Novelist* (London: Chatto & Windus, 1955; Harmondsworth: Penguin, 1985)

Edward D. McDonald (ed.), *Phoenix: The Posthumous Papers of D. H. Lawrence* (London: Heinemann, 1936)

Jeffrey Meyers, *D. H. Lawrence , A Biography* (London: Macmillan, 1990)

Henry Miller, *The World of D. H. Lawrence: A Passionate Appreciation* (London: Calder Press, 1985)

Kate Millett, *Sexual Politics* (New York: Avon, 1970; reprinted London: Rupert Hart-Davis, 1971, Virago Press, 1977)

Harry T. Moore, *The Life and Works of D. H. Lawrence* (New York: Twayne, 1951)

Harry T. Moore (ed.), *A D. H. Lawrence Miscellany* (Carbondale: Southern Illinois University Press, 1959)

Harry T. Moore, *The Intelligent Heart: The Story of D. H. Lawrence* (New York: Farrar, Straus & Young, 1954); reprinted and enlarged as *The Priest of Love: A Life of D. H. Lawrence* (London: Heinemann, 1974)

John Middleton Murry, *Son of Woman* (London: Jonathan Cape, 1931)

Edward Nehls (ed.), *D. H. Lawrence: A Composite Biography*, vols. I–III (Madison: University of Wisconsin Press, 1957–59)

Alistair Niven, *D. H. Lawrence: The Novels* (Cambridge: Cambridge University Press, 1978)

Tony Pinkney, *D. H. Lawrence* (Hemel Hempstead: Harvester New Readings Series, 1990)

Vivian de Sola Pinto & Warren Roberts (eds.), *D. H. Lawrence: The Complete Poems* (Harmondsworth: Penguin, 1977)

Peter Preston & Peter Hoare (eds.), *D. H. Lawrence in the Modern World* (London: Macmillan, 1989)

Warren Roberts, *A Bibliography of D. H. Lawrence*, 2nd edition (Cambridge: Cambridge University Press, 1982)

Keith Sagar, *The Art of D. H. Lawrence* (Cambridge: Cambridge University Press, 1966)

Keith Sagar, *D. H. Lawrence: Life into Art* (Harmondsworth: Penguin, 1985)

Gamini Salgado & G. K. Das (eds.), *The Spirit of D. H. Lawrence: Centenary Studies* (London: Macmillan, 1988)

Gamini Salgado, *A Preface to Lawrence* (Harlow: Longman, 1982)

Carol Siegel, *Lawrence Among the Women: Wavering Boundaries in Women's Literary Traditions* (Charlottesville: The University Press of Virginia, 1991)

Hilary Simpson, *D. H. Lawrence and Feminism* (Beckenham, Kent: Croom Helm, 1982)

Anne Smith (ed.), *Lawrence and Women* (London: Vision Press, 1978)

Mark Spilka, *The Love Ethic of D. H. Lawrence* (Bloomington: Indiana University Press, 1955)

Mark Spilka (ed.), *D. H. Lawrence: A Collection of Critical Essays* (New Jersey: Prentice-Hall, Twentieth Century Views Series, 1963)

Eliseo Vivas, *D. H. Lawrence: The Failure and the Triumph of Art* (Evanston: Northwestern University Press, 1960; London: Allen & Unwin, 1961)

Peter Widdowson (ed.), *D. H. Lawrence* (London: Longman, 1992)

Raymond Williams, *The English Novel from Dickens to Lawrence* (London: Chatto & Windus, 1970)

Raymond Williams, *Culture and Society 1780–1950* (London: Faber & Faber, 1958)

John Worthen, *D. H. Lawrence and the Idea of the Novel* (London: Macmillan, 1979)

D. H. Lawrence, *Study of Thomas Hardy and Other Essays*, ed. Bruce Steele (Cambridge: Cambridge University Press, 1985)

D. H. Lawrence, *Fantasia of the Unconscious; Psychoanalysis and the Unconscious* (Harmondsworth: Penguin, 1960)

D. H. Lawrence, *Mr Noon* (Cambridge: Cambridge University Press, 1984)

D. H. Lawrence, *Aaron's Rod* (Harmondsworth: Penguin, 1977)

D. H. Lawrence, *Kangaroo* (Harmondsworth: Penguin, 1950)

D. H. Lawrence, *The White Peacock* (Cambridge: Cambridge University Press, 1984)

D. H. Lawrence, *The Plumed Serpent* (Harmondsworth: Penguin, 1983)

D. H. Lawrence, *Sons and Lovers* (Harmondsworth: Penguin, 1962)

D. H. Lawrence, *Lady Chatterley's Lover* (Harmondsworth: Penguin, 1974)

D. H. Lawrence, *Phoenix II: Uncollected, Unpublished and Other Prose Works*, eds. Warren Roberts & Harry T. Moore (Harmondsworth: Penguin, 1978)

D. H. Lawrence, *Women in Love* (Harmondsworth: Penguin, 1982)

D. H. Lawrence, *The Rainbow* (Harmondsworth: Penguin, 1981)

D. H. Lawrence, *The Lost Girl* (Cambridge: Cambridge University Press, 1981)

# NOTES

## NOTES TO INTRODUCTION

1 'The Novel', *Reflections on the Death of a Porcupine* (1925). Reprinted in Inglis (ed.), *A Selection from Phoenix* (Harmondsworth: Penguin, 1971), p. 161.

2 Ibid., pp. 161–2.

3 Anthony Burgess, *Flame into Being* (London: Sphere Books, 1986), p. 202. [My italics.]

4 Quoted in Jeffrey Meyers, *D. H. Lawrence, A Biography* (London: Macmillan, 1990), p. 60.

5 Unsigned review in *The Standard*, 30 May 1913, 5.

6 Unsigned review in *The Westminster Gazette*, 14 June 1913, xli, 17.

7 Letter to Edward Garnett, 5 June 1914. Aldous Huxley (ed.), *The Letters of D. H. Lawrence* (London: Heinemann, 1932), p. 197.

8 Ibid., pp. 198–9.

9 Ibid., p. 295.

10 See Chapter 5 for a discussion of these writers.

11 Philip Larkin, 'Annus Mirabilis', *High Windows* (London: Faber & Faber, 1974).

12 For a fuller account of the progress of Lawrence's novel, see *D. H. Lawrence's "Lady": A New Look at "Lady Chatterley's Lover"*, Michael Squires & Dennis Jackson eds., (Athens: University of Georgia Press, 1985), p. 238.

13 Dennis & Fleda Brown Jackson (eds.), 'D. H. Lawrence's Critical Reception: An Overview', *Critical Essays on D. H. Lawrence* (Boston: G. K. Hall, 1988), pp. 11–12.

14 See, for a more recent example, Peter Widdowson (ed.), in his Introduction to *D. H. Lawrence* (London: Longman, 1992), pp. 7–9.

15 Eliseo Vivas, *D. H. Lawrence: The Failure and the Triumph of Art* (London: Allen & Unwin, 1961), pp. vii–viii.

16 James C. Cowan, *D. H. Lawrence: An Annotated Bibliography of Writings About Him*, 2 vols. (De Kalb: Northern Illinois University Press, 1985).

17 *The D. H. Lawrence Review*, founded by James C. Cowan, carries regular bibliographical updates.

18 D. H. Lawrence, Foreword to *Women in Love* (American edition, 1920). Reprinted as Appendix 1, Cambridge edition of *Women in Love* (Cambridge: Cambridge University Press, 1987), p. 483.

## NOTES TO CHAPTER ONE

1 Review by James Douglas, in *The Star*, 22 October 1915, 4. Douglas was the literary critic of *The Star* before becoming editor of the publication. He was an influential reviewer and journalist who rose to become the editor of *The Sunday Express*.

2 For a much more detailed commentary on the anti-nationalist elements of *The Rainbow*, see Alistair Davies's essay on pp. 158–74.

3 We can observe an interesting – and pleasing – reversal of this situation in the trial against Lawrence's other banned novel *Lady Chatterley's Lover* in October–November 1960, when the testimonies of numerous 'expert witnesses' from the literary world were instrumental in having the case against Penguin dismissed.

4 Quoted from a report of the trial: Jeffrey Meyers, *D. H. Lawrence: A Biography* (London: Macmillan, 1990), p. 189.

5 Unattributed review, the *Athenaeum*, No. 4594, 13 November 1915.

6 The *Athenaeum* was edited by John Middleton Murry. For Murry's review of *Women in Love* see the last review in this chapter. For Murry's comments on the novels in *Son of Woman*, see pp. 36–43.

7 For further discussion of *The Rainbow* as a 'great English family-chronicle novel', see Marvin Mudrick's essay on pp. 73–89.

8 The other, unsigned, was printed in *The Standard*, 1 October 1915, 3.

9 Catherine Carswell in *The Glasgow Herald*, 4 November 1915, 4.

10 When the novel was printed commercially by Seltzer in America, the print-run of 15,000 copies nearly suffered the same fate as *The Rainbow*. In July 1922, The New York Society for the Suppression of Vice attempted to have *Women in Love* banned. Seltzer defended both his company and Lawrence against charges of obscenity, and had the case dismissed in September – since when the novel has enjoyed healthy sales.

11 Unsigned review in the *Saturday Westminster Gazette*, LVIII (2 July 1921), 14–15.

12 Letter to Edward Garnett, 5 June 1914. Aldous Huxley (ed.), *The Letters of D. H. Lawrence* (London: Heinemann, 1932), pp. 197–99.

13 For extracts from Leavis's work, and an assessment of his part in initiating 'The Lawrence Revival', see Chapter 3.

14 F. R. Leavis, *D. H. Lawrence: Novelist* (Harmondsworth: Penguin, 1985), p. 176.

15 Ibid., p. 177.

16 John Middleton Murry in *Nation and Athenaeum*, XXIX (13 August 1921), pp. 713–14.

## NOTES TO CHAPTER TWO

1 James C. Cowan, *D. H. Lawrence: An Annotated Bibliography of Writings About Him* (De Kalb: Northern Illinois University Press, 1982–85).

2 Dennis Jackson, '"The Stormy Petrel of Literature is Dead": World Press Reports of D. H. Lawrence's Death', *D. H. Lawrence Review* 14 (Spring 1981), pp. 33–72.

3 Paul Rosenfield, *New Republic*, LXII (26 March 1930), pp. 155–56.

4 See Introduction, pp. 9–10.

5 E. M. Forster, *Nation and Athenaeum*, XLVI (29 March 1930), p. 888.

6 F. R. Leavis, *Cambridge Review*, LI (13 June 1930), pp. 493–95. Also, a revised version of the same article in *D. H. Lawrence* (Cambridge: Gordon Fraser, Minority Pamphlet No. 6, 1930).

7 Lionel Trilling, 'D. H. Lawrence: A Neglected Aspect', *Symposium*, I (July 1930), pp. 361–70.

8 Colin Clarke (ed.), Introduction to *D. H. Lawrence: The Rainbow and Women in Love* (London: Macmillan, 1969).

9 Vivian de Sola Pinto & Warren Roberts (eds.), *D. H. Lawrence: The Complete Poems* (Harmondsworth: Penguin, 1977), p. 28.

10 'The Novel', first published in *Reflections on the Death of a Porcupine*, 1925. Reprinted in Inglis, (ed.), *A Selection from Phoenix* (Harmondsworth: Penguin, 1971), p. 161.

11 For a more positive account of the novel, see '"Reading Out" a "New Novel": Lawrence's Experiments with Story and Discourse in *Mr Noon*' in Jackson & Jackson (eds.), *Critical Essays on D. H. Lawrence* (Boston: G. K. Hall, 1988), pp. 110–17.

12 Murry, *Son of Woman* (London: Jonathan Cape, 1931), p. 75.

13 Ibid., p. 88

14 Ibid., p. 112. For clarification of Murry's confusion about Ursula's knowledge of Hermione and Birkin's affair, we may look to the cancelled 'Prologue' to the novel, first published in *The Texas Quarterly*, VI, 1963. This volume includes George Ford's Introductory Note to the Prologue, an essay which explores the value of the chapter and its effect on the novel, had it been included in the published version.

15 Ibid., pp. 117–18.

16 See David Cavitch, *D. H. Lawrence and the New World* (London: Oxford University Press, 1969).

17 John Middleton Murry, 'Women in Love' from *Son of Woman* (London: Jonathan Cape, 1931), pp. 106–38.

18 Herbert J. Seligman's *D. H. Lawrence: An American Interpretation* (New York: Thomas Seltzer, 1924); Edward D. McDonald's *A Bibliography of The Writings of D. H. Lawrence* (Philadelphia: Centaur Book Shop, 1925 – with a Supplement, 1931); Richard Aldington's *D. H. Lawrence: An Indiscretion* (Seattle: University of Washington Bookstore, 1927); Stephen Potter's *D. H. Lawrence: A First Study* (London: Jonathan Cape, 1930). In addition, there had been more than 670 articles, reviews and essays written on Lawrence by this time.

19 Aldous Huxley (ed.), *The Letters of D. H. Lawrence* (London: Heinemann, 1932), pp. x–xxiii.

20 T. S. Eliot, *After Strange Gods: A Primer in Modern Heresy* (London: Jonathan Cape, 1933; New York: Harcourt & Brace, 1934).

21 Wyndham Lewis, 'Paleface; or, "Love? What ho! Smelling Strangeness"', in *Enemy*, II (September 1927), pp. 3–112. The essay was revised and significantly enlarged, to be reprinted as *Paleface: The Philosophy of the "Melting Pot"* (London: Chatto & Windus, 1929).

22 F. R. Leavis did respond to Eliot's book, and noted that the alliance with Lewis did little to enhance its arguments – rather, such attacks had the effect of presenting Lawrence as the more enlightened and truly cultured artist: 'Mr. Eliot, Mr.

Wyndham Lewis and Lawrence', *Scrutiny*, III (September 1934), pp. 184–91.

23 Jacques Debu-Bridel, 'Lettres Etrangères', *La Nouvelle Revue Française*, XLVI (Jan–June 1936), pp. 606–8.

24 Ernest Seillière, *David Herbert Lawrence et les Récentes Idéologies Allemandes* (Paris: Boivin et Cie, 1936).

25 Edward D. McDonald (ed.), *Phoenix: The Posthumous Papers of D. H. Lawrence* (London: Heinemann, 1936).

26 Granville Hicks, 'D. H. Lawrence as Messiah', *New Republic*, LXXXVIII (28 October 1936), pp. 358–59; Harry T. Wells, 'A Disagreement with Mr. Hicks', *New Republic*, LXXXIX (18 November 1936), p. 77; Arvin Newton, 'D. H. Lawrence and Fascism', *New Republic*, LXXXIX (16 December 1937), p. 219; T. K. Whipple, 'Literature in the Doldrums', *New Republic*, XC (21 April 1937), pp. 311–14; Harry T. Wells, 'D. H. Lawrence and Fascism', *New Republic*, XCI (16 June 1936), p. 161.

27 Diana Trilling (ed.), *The Portable D. H. Lawrence* (New York: Viking Press, 1947); *The Indispensable D. H. Lawrence* (New York: International Book Society, 1950).

## NOTES TO CHAPTER THREE

1 Dennis & Fleda Brown Jackson (eds.), *Critical Essays on D. H. Lawrence* (Boston: C. K. Hall, 1988), p. 7.

2 Harry T. Moore, *The Life and Works of D. H. Lawrence* (New York: Twayne, 1951); Harry T. Moore, *The Intelligent Heart: The Story of D. H. Lawrence* (New York: Farrar, Straus & Young, 1954); reprinted and enlarged as *The Priest of Love: A Life of D. H. Lawrence* (London: Heinemann, 1974).

3 F. R. Leavis, *D. H. Lawrence: Novelist* (London: Chatto & Windus, 1955), p. 23.

4 *Letters*, p. 272.

5 A point made by Lawrence in an article reprinted in *Phoenix*, 'The Novel and the Feelings'.

6 e.g. '. . . he never succeeded in making a work of art'. *The Criterion*, Vol. X, p. 769. *The Criterion* was a literary periodical for critical essays and reviews founded by T. S. Eliot in 1922. He edited it until its last issue in 1939.

7 Eliot, *After Strange Gods*, p. 58.

8 *La Nouvelle Revue Française*, Mai 1927 (Vol. 28, p. 671).

9 Eliot, in his Foreword to Father William Tiverton's *D. H. Lawrence and Human Existence* (1951).

10 *Phoenix*, p. 308.

11 *La Nouvelle Revue Française*, Mai 1927 (Vol. 28, p. 671).

12 And yet Eliot could talk about Lawrence's 'emotional disease' (review of Murry's *Son of Woman* in *The Criterion*, July 1931).

13 *Phoenix*, p. 308.

14 The point is made more fully in the closing pages of Leavis's chapter on *The Rainbow*, pp. 169–71.

15 Mark Spilka, *The Love Ethic of D. H. Lawrence* (Bloomington: Indiana University Press, 1955).

16 Ibid., pp. 3–4.

17 As André Gide points out, Dostoievsky is another writer who poses rather than resolves some of the more difficult problems which confront him.

18 Witness his handling of Ursula's lesbian affair in *The Rainbow*, and of Loerke's implied affairs in *Women in Love*. His objections to such unions were based, I think, on two distinct beliefs: 1) that men and women must be singled out into pure malehood and pure femalehood; and 2) that homosexual love, like Oedipal love, is mechanistic and obsessive – an imposition from without, and therefore a sin against spontaneous life.

19 Harry T. Moore points out (not quite correctly) that 'none of these scenes suggests any form of sexual gratification'. He also shows that John Middleton Murry, the chief source for Gerald Crich, did not accuse Lawrence of 'what is generally understood by the word homosexuality', and that other critics and biographers, friendly or hostile, generally concur on this point (*Life and Works*, pp. 165–66). Several of these critics have argued, however, that Lawrence proffers another and more innocent brand of homosexuality, which seems to correspond with 'the bisexuality of our own infant pasts' (e.g., Diana Trilling, *The Portable D. H. Lawrence*, p. 22). I believe there is one genuine example of this sort of experience in Lawrence's first novel, *The White Peacock*, as George Saxton gives Cyril Beardsall a rubdown after a short swim:

'He saw that I had forgotten to continue my rubbing, and laughing he took hold of me and began to rub me briskly, as if I were a child, or rather, a woman he loved and did not fear. I left myself quite limply in his hands, and, to get a better grip of me, he put his arm round me and pressed me against him, and the sweetness of the touch of our naked bodies one against the other was superb. It satisfied in some measure the vague, indecipherable yearning of my soul; and it was the same with him. When he had rubbed me all warm, he let me go, and we looked at each other with eyes of still laughter, and our love was perfect for a moment, more perfect than any love I have known since, either for man or woman.' (p. 248) But after *The White Peacock*, Lawrence seems to understand the direction of such contacts, and he rejects them. In *The Rainbow*, for example, the affair between Ursula Brangwen and Winifred Inger begins with a kind of innocent voluptuousness, but gradually proves nauseous and degrading. Significantly enough, it also centres around a series of swimming scenes – which makes the change in Lawrence's thought seem all the more conscious and obvious.

20 For a further example of the 'healing powers' of touch, take the completely impersonal scene in *The Lost Girl*, when Arthur Witham hurts his leg while working in the organ loft.

21 There is, however, an element of 'sexual sympathy' in all these forms of love. The men in Lawrence's world are drawn together, for example, by a certain amount of fellow-feeling over their common mistreatment at the hands of women. As Lawrence explains it in one of the late essays: '. . . this silent sympathy is utterly different from desire or anything rampant or lurid . . . it is just a form of warmheartedness and compassionateness, the most natural life-flow in the world . . . And it is this that I want to restore into life: just the natural warm flow of common sympathy between man and man, man and woman . . . It is the most important thing just now, this gentle physical awareness. It keeps us tender and alive at a moment when the great danger is to go brittle, hard, and in

some way dead. Accept the sexual, physical being of yourself, and of every other creature. Don't be afraid of it.' (*Sex, Literature, and Censorship*, pp. 66–7.)

22 Mark Spilka, *The Love Ethic of D. H. Lawrence* (Bloomington: Indiana University Press, 1955). Extracted from Chapter 7, 'No Man's Land', pp. 148–64.

23 Marvin Mudrick, 'The Originality of *The Rainbow*', *Spectrum*, III (Winter, 1959), pp. 3–28. The essay also appeared in Harry T. Moore (ed.), *A D. H. Lawrence Miscellany* (Carbondale: Southern Illinois University Press, 1959).

24 Edward Nehls (ed.), *D. H. Lawrence: A Composite Biography*, vols. I–III (Madison: University of Wisconsin Press, 1957–59).

## NOTES ON CHAPTER FOUR

1 Eliseo Vivas, *D. H. Lawrence: The Failure and the Triumph of Art* (Evanston: Northwestern University Press, 1960; London: Allen & Unwin, 1961), p. xi.

2 Ibid., p. 17.

3 Eliseo Vivas, *D. H. Lawrence: The Failure and the Triumph of Art* (Evanston: Northwestern University Press, 1960; London: Allen & Unwin, 1961). This extract is an expanded and revised version of an essay that appeared in *The Sewanee Review* under the title, 'The Substance of *Women in Love*' (LXVI, 4: Autumn, 1958).

4 George H. Ford, 'Introductory Note to D. H. Lawrence's Prologue to *Women in Love*', *Texas Quarterly*, VI (Spring 1963).

5 *Study of Thomas Hardy*, originally published in Edward D. McDonald (ed.), *Phoenix: The Posthumous Papers of D. H. Lawrence* (London: Heinemann, 1936).

6 Herman M. Daleski, *The Forked Flame: A Study of D. H. Lawrence* (Evanston: Northwestern University Press, 1965).

7 Mark Kinkead-Weekes, 'The Marble and the Statue: The Exploratory Imagination of D. H. Lawrence', in Maynard Mack & Ian Gregor (eds.), *Imagined Worlds: Essays on Some English Novels and Novelists in Honour of John Butt* (London: Methuen, 1968), pp. 371–412.

8 *The Crown* was originally published in three parts in the journal *Signature* (founded by Lawrence, Middleton Murry and Katherine Mansfield) on 4, 18 October and

4 November 1915.

9 Mark Kinkead-Weekes, Ibid., p. 396.

10 Frank Kermode, *Lawrence* (London: Fontana, 1973, revised 1985).

11 Ibid., pp. 38–42.

12 Ibid., pp. 50–53.

13 Colin Clarke, *River of Dissolution: D. H. Lawrence and English Romanticism* (London: Routledge & Kegan Paul, 1969), pp. xi–xii.

14 Ibid., p. xiv.

15 *D. H. Lawrence: Novelist*, p. 176.

16 Colin Clarke, *River Of Dissolution*, pp. 70–87.

**NOTES TO CHAPTER FIVE**

1 *Fantasia of the Unconscious*, (London: Heinemann, 1961), p. 279.

2 Ibid.

3 Ibid., p. 280.

4 Simone de Beauvoir, *The Second Sex*, trans. H. M. Parshley (London: Jonathan Cape, 1953), pp. 248–9.

5 Kate Millett, *Sexual Politics* (New York: Avon, 1970; reprinted London: Rupert Hart Davis, 1971, Virago Press, 1977).

6 Quoted by Keith Sagar, *The Art of D. H. Lawrence* (Cambridge: Cambridge University Press, 1966), p. 19.

7 Norman Mailer, 'The Prisoner of Sex', *Harper's Magazine*, March 1971, pp. 70, 78.

8 Cf. Harry T. Moore, *The Intelligent Heart* (1954), pp. 131–2, 165.

9 Standard Edition of *Complete Psychological Works of Sigmund Freud*, J. Strachey & A. Freud (eds.), (London: Hogarth Press, 1955), Vol. XXII, p. 135.

10 Moore, op. cit., pp. 41–61.

11 Standard Edition, Vol. X

12 Standard Edition, Vol. XXI, p. 122.

13 Standard Edition, Vol. XXII, p. 209.

14 *D. H. Lawrence: Novelist* (1956), p. 179.

15 *Son of Woman* (1931), pp. 95, 28, 71.

16 Standard Edition, Vol. XVII, p. 215.

17 Philippa Tristram, 'Eros and Death (Lawrence, Freud and Women)', in Anne Smith (ed.), *Lawrence and Women* (London: Vision Press, 1978), pp. 136–55.

18 Carol Siegel, *Lawrence Among the Women: Wavering Boundaries in Women's Literary Traditions* (Charlottesville: The University Press of Virginia, 1991), p. 1.

19 D. H. Lawrence, *Study of Thomas Hardy*, in *Phoenix: The Posthumous Papers of D. H. Lawrence*, ed. Edward D. McDonald, 1936 (reprinted Harmondsworth: Penguin, 1978), p. 479. All further references to this work, designated *Study*, are incorporated in the text.

20 D. H. Lawrence, *The Symbolic Meaning: The Uncollected Versions of Studies in Classic American Literature*, ed. Armin Arnold (New York: Viking, 1964), p. 18.

21 D. H. Lawrence, *Studies in Classic American Literature*, 1923 (reprinted New York: Viking, 1964), p. 2.

22 Frank Kermode, *Lawrence* (New York: Viking; London: Fontana, 1973), pp. 15, 63.

23 Wayne C. Booth, *The Company We Keep: An Ethics of Fiction* (Berkeley & Los Angeles: University of California Press, 1988), p. 446. Booth is more sceptical than I am about whether any of these voices actually represents the author.

24 Ibid., pp. 445–7; Dale Bauer, *Feminist Dialogics: A Theory of Failed Community* (Albany: State University of New York Press, 1988), p. xiii.

25 D. H. Lawrence, *Women in Love*, 1920 (reprinted New York: Viking, 1960), p. 473.

26 E. M. Forster, *Aspects of the Novel*, 1927 (reprinted New York: Harcourt & Brace, 1954), p. 141.

27 Hilary Simpson, *D. H. Lawrence and Feminism* (De Kalb: Northern Illinois University Press, 1982), p. 160.

28 Kermode, *Lawrence*, p. 117.

29 F. R. Leavis, *D. H. Lawrence: Novelist* (New York: Knopf, 1956), pp. 30–31, 50, 41.

30 Booth, *The Company We Keep*, p. 446.

31 Carol Siegel, *Lawrence Among the Women*, pp. 7–10.

**NOTES TO CHAPTER SIX**

1 For the construction of this chapter, I owe a major debt to Peter Widdowson, for his selection and discussion of Graham Holderness and Alistair Davies's essays in Widdowson (ed.), *D. H. Lawrence* (London: Longman Critical Heritage Series, 1996). His collection of essays and extracts and his fine introductory essay will offer much satisfaction to readers who wish to pursue the 'postmodern Lawrence' further.

2 Graham Holderness, *D. H. Lawrence: History, Ideology and Fiction* (Dublin: Gill &

Macmillan, 1982), p. 1.

3 Ibid., p. 186.

4 Terry Eagleton, *Criticism and Ideology* (London: Verso, 1976), p. 160.

5 F. R. Leavis, *D. H. Lawrence: Novelist* (1955), p. 151.

6 Marvin Mudrick, 'The Originality of *The Rainbow*', in Harry T. Moore (ed.), *A D. H. Lawrence Miscellany* (1959), p. 62.

7 See Georg Lukács, 'The Ideal of the Harmonious Man in Bourgeois Aesthetics' in *Writer and Critic*, ed. and trans. Arthur Kahn (London: Merlin Press, 1970).

8 Terry Eagleton, *Myths of Power* (London: Macmillan, 1975), p. 98.

9 Graham Holderness, *D. H. Lawrence: History, Ideology and Fiction*, pp. 174–89.

10 Peter Preston & Peter Hoare (eds.), *D. H. Lawrence in the Modern World* (London: Macmillan, 1989), pp. 121–39.

11 Graham Holderness ('its evolving generational structure has no realist or historical content') and John Worthen ('the historical conflicts of the nineteenth century are alien to the progression of the novel') seem to me to mar a good case on the first generation by generalising to the novel as a whole. Both point out, rightly, that Lawrence is not very interested in the work of the Marsh Farm – though we do get glimpses, and would have seen more had Lawrence not cut a fine ploughing scene from the manuscript. However, in Chapter 5 of his *Study of Thomas Hardy*, Lawrence had argued that the real significance of work is not socio-economic but to do with the evolutionary development of consciousness and selfhood. So it is not surprising that work, too, should figure more in the second generation (though it will be Will's carving that is important rather than the lace factory), and most in the third generation, when it moves centre-stage in 'The Man's World'. See G. Holderness, *D. H. Lawrence: History, Ideology and Fiction* (Dublin: Gill & Macmillan, 1982), p. 186; D. H. Lawrence, *The Rainbow*, ed. J. Worthen (Harmondsworth: Penguin, 1981), p. 31. All page references will be given to the latter, cited as *The Rainbow* (Penguin, ed. Worthen).

12 Day and month are given in Lawrence, *The Rainbow* (Penguin, ed. Worthen), p. 167; the year is arrived at from the ages of all concerned; but it turns out that 23 December was indeed a Saturday that year.

13 James T. Boulton (ed.), *Lawrence in Love: Letters to Louie Burrows* (Nottingham: University of Nottingham Press, 1968) p. x.

14 C. N. Wright (ed.), *Directory of Nottingham and Twelve Miles Round*, 15th edn. (Nottingham: J. Bell, 1891), p. 488, though the credit is given to a Mr. Brand, who turns out to have been the clergyman.

15 D. Wardle, *Education and Society in Nineteenth-Century Nottingham* (Cambridge: Cambridge University Press, 1971), p. 95.

16 Manuscript, p. 449, 'called a taxi-cab'; first edition, p. 284, line 10, 'had a motor-car'; so also Penguin edition, Worthen, p. 350, line 16.

17 'Nottinghamshire Register of Motor Cars and Motor Cycles, 1903', ed. P. A. Kennedy, in *A Nottinghamshire Miscellany*, ed. J. H. Hodson et al. (Thoroton Society Record Series, xxi, 1962), pp. 65–79.

18 *Letters*, i, pp. 287–8.

19 Lawrence has Dorothy belong to the Women's Social and Political Union a year before it was founded; and Will could not have gone to the Empire Music Hall before 1897 – but these are rare examples, and not very significant.

20 He was the author of a history of Greasley, *Griseleia in Snotinghscire* (Nottingham: Murray, 1901), which contains a portrait of him; cf. *The Rainbow*, Chapter 7. He claimed to have escaped the Russians by swimming the Vistula.

21 Edwin Trueman, *History of Ilkeston* (Ilkeston: John F. Walker, 1880), p. 98; cf. Lawrence, *The Rainbow* (Penguin, ed. Worthen), p. 72.

22 Perhaps the most spectacular illustration of this point, for me, was to be told by Louie Burrows's youngest sister that the flood at the Marsh Farm had actually occurred, when her mother was alone in the house with young children. There could hardly be a more striking example of the fission of the biblical/symbolic with the historical.

23 'Nottinghamshire Register of Motor Cars, 1903.'

24 The foundation stone is dated 16 February 1864.

25 On the A6096 Ilkeston to Eastwood road, just on the Ilkeston side of the turning to Cossall. The canal is choked and its old narrow-arched aqueduct has been replaced by an ugly new one; the colliery has gone; but the situation described in the novel is easily re-imagined from the canal bank.

26 Charles Hadfield, *The Canals of the East Midlands* (London, 1966), p. 55.

27 R. Leleux, *Regional History of the Railways of Great Britain*, vol. ix: *The East Midlands* (Newton Abbot: David & Charles, 1984), p. 143; E. G. Barnes, *The Rise of the Midland Railway* (London: George Allen & Unwin, 1966) Chapter 1.

28 Alan R. Griffin, *Mining in the East Midlands* (London: Frank Cass, 1971), p. 53.

29 Frank Grafton Cook, *Some Notes on Cossall and its Past* (privately printed, 1971), pp. 4–5; cf. Greenwood's *Map of the County of Nottingham*, surveyed 1824–5, pub. 1826. But Ellis's map, also 1824–5, pub. 1825, portrays the existing situation, so the facts remain rather obscure. Trueman's *History of Ilkeston*, p. 99, records the bursting of 'the embankment close to this aqueduct' in 1823, so there was already an aqueduct of some sort by then.

30 Harry T. Moore, *The Intelligent Heart* (Harmondsworth: Penguin, 1960), p. 25.

31 D. H. Lawrence, *Study of Thomas Hardy and Other Essays*, ed. Bruce Steele (Cambridge: Cambridge University Press, 1985), pp. 36–7.

32 Wardle, *Education and Society*, p. 145; Geoffrey Trease, *Nottingham: A Biography* (London: Macmillan, 1970), pp. 202–3.

33 Wardle, *Education and Society*, pp. 100–1; Lawrence, *The Rainbow* (Penguin, ed. Worthen), p. 281.

34 W. H. G. Armytage, *Four Hundred Years of English Education* (Cambridge: Cambridge University Press, 1965), p. 186; and Wardle, *Education and Society*, p. 88. Those not allowed to leave lingered in Standard V, Ursula's class, hence its difficulties.

35 *Letters*, ii, p. 165.

36 Lawrence, *The Rainbow* (Penguin, ed. Worthen), p. 441.

37 *Letters*, ii, p. 165.

38 Lawrence, *The Rainbow* (Penguin, ed. Worthen), p. 487.

39 Lawrence, *The Rainbow* (Penguin, ed. Worthen), p. 541.

40 Ibid., p. 540.

41 Ibid., p. 543.

42 Ibid., p. 547.

43 Cf. 'I would wish the time to remain unfixed', in unpublished 'Foreword to *Women in Love*'; see the Random House Modern Library edition and *Phoenix* ii, p. 275.

44 Mark Kinkead-Weekes, 'The Sense of History in *The Rainbow*', in Peter Preston & Peter Hoare (eds.), *D. H. Lawrence in the Modern World* (London: Macmillan, 1989), pp. 121–39.

45 F. R. Leavis, *D. H. Lawrence: Novelist* (London: Chatto & Windus, 1955).

46 See Raymond Williams, *The English Novel from Dickens to Lawrence* (London: Chatto & Windus, 1970), pp. 177–9; Terry Eagleton, *Exiles and Emigrés* (London: Chatto & Windus, 1970), pp. 202–4; Terry Eagleton, *Criticism and Ideology* (London: New Left Books, 1976), pp. 157–61.

47 See Emile Devalenay, *D. H. Lawrence: The Man and His Work. The Formative Years, 1885–1919* (London: Heinemann, 1972), pp. 235–48.

48 See R. P. Draper, *D. H. Lawrence: The Critical Heritage* (London: Routledge & Kegan Paul, 1970), p. 106.

49 See Colin Clarke (ed.), *D. H. Lawrence*, op. cit., pp. 67–72.

50 John Middleton Murry, *Son of Woman* (London: Jonathan Cape, 1931).

51 Wyndham Lewis, *Paleface* (London: Chatto & Windus, 1929).

52 T. S. Eliot, *After Strange Gods: A Primer in Modern Heresy* (London: Faber & Faber, 1934).

53 Alistair Davies, 'Contexts of Reading: The Reception of D. H. Lawrence's *The Rainbow* and *Women in Love*', in Frank Gloversmith (ed.), *The Theory of Reading* (Brighton: Harvester Press, 1984; New Jersey: Barnes & Noble Books, 1984), pp. 199–221.

# ACKNOWLEDGEMENTS

The editor and publishers wish to thank the following for their permission to reprint copyright material: Associated Newspapers (reviews from *The Star* and *Saturday Westminster Gazette*); *The New Statesman* (reviews from the *Athenaeum* and *Nation and Athenaeum*); *The Glasgow Herald* (review in *The Glasgow Herald*); the Society of Authors (for material from *Son of Woman*); Random House (for material from *The Letters of D. H. Lawrence*); Chatto & Windus (for material from *D. H. Lawrence: Novelist*); Indiana University Press (for material from *The Love Ethic of D. H. Lawrence*); Jeanne Mudrick (for 'The Originality of *The Rainbow*'); Routledge & Kegan Paul (for material from *D. H. Lawrence: The Failure and Triumph of Art*); HarperCollins (for material from *Lawrence*); Barnes & Noble Books (for material from *Lawrence and Women*); University of Virginia Press (for material from *Lawrence Among the Women*); Gill & Macmillan (for material from *D. H. Lawrence: History, Ideology and Fiction*); Macmillan (for material from *D. H. Lawrence in the Modern World*); Frank Gloversmith (for material from *The Theory of Reading*).

Every effort has been made to contact the holders of any copyrights applying to the material quoted in this book. The publishers would be grateful if any such copyright holders whom they have not been able to contact, would write to them.

Richard Beynon graduated from The University of Kent, and holds higher degrees from The Open University and The University of London. He has taught in further, adult and higher education for more than twelve years, and is currently Teaching and Learning Officer at the University of Sussex. He lives in Brighton with his wife, two cats and a word-processor.

# INDEX